TECHNOLOGY AND INDUSTRIAL DEVELOPMENT IN PRE-WAR JAPAN

THE NISSAN INSTITUTE/ROUTLEDGE JAPANESE STUDIES SERIES

Other titles in the series:

The Myth of Japanese Uniqueness, Peter Dale
The Emperor's Adviser: Saionji Kinmochi and pre-war Japanese Politics, Lesley Connors
Understanding Japanese Society, Joy Hendry
Japanese Religions, Brian Bocking
Japan in World Politics, Reinhard Drifte
A History of Japanese Economic Thought, Tessa Morris-Suzuki
The Establishment of Constitutional Government in Japan, Junji Banno, translated by J. A. A. Stockwin
Japan's First Parliaments 1890–1910, R. H. P. Mason, Andrew Fraser and Philip Mitchell
Industrial Relations in Japan: the peripheral workforce, Norma Chalmers
Banking Policy in Japan: American attempts at reform during the occupation, William Minoru Tsutsui
Educational Reform in Contemporary Japan, Leonard Schoppa
How the Japanese Learn to Work, Ronald Dore and Mari Sako
Militarization in Contemporary Japan, Glenn D. Hook
Japanese Economic Development: theory and practice, Penelope Francks
Japan and Protection, Syed Javed Maswood
Japan's Nuclear Development, Michael Donnelly
The Soil, by Nagatsuka Takashi: a portrait of rural life in Meiji Japan, translated and with an introduction by Ann Waswo
Biotechnology in Japan, Malcolm Brock
Britain's Educational Reform: a comparison with Japan, Michael Howarth
Language and the Modern State: the reform of written Japanese, Nanette Twine
Industrial Harmony in Modern Japan: the invention of a tradition, W. Dean Kinzley
Japanese Science Fiction: a view of a changing society, Robert Matthew
The Japanese Numbers Game: the use and understanding of numbers in modern Japan, Thomas Crump
Ideology and Practice in Modern Japan, Roger Goodman and Kirsten Refsing

TECHNOLOGY AND INDUSTRIAL DEVELOPMENT IN PRE-WAR JAPAN

Mitsubishi Nagasaki Shipyard 1884–1934

Yukiko Fukasaku

London and New York

First published 1992
by Routledge
11 New Fetter Lane, London EC4P 4EE

Simultaneously published in the USA and Canada
by Routledge
a division of Routledge, Chapman and Hall, Inc.
29 West 35th Street, New York, NY 10001

© 1992 Yukiko Fukasaku

Typeset in Palatino by
J&L Composition Ltd, Filey, North Yorkshire
Printed and bound in Great Britain by
Mackays of Chatham PLC, Chatham, Kent

British Library Cataloguing in Publication Data
A catalogue record for this book is available from the British Library.

Library of Congress Cataloging-in-Publication Data

Fukasaku, Yukiko, 1950–
Technology and industrial development in pre-war Japan:
Mitsubishi Nagasaki shipyard, 1884–1934 / Yukiko Fukasaku.
p.   cm.
Includes bibliographical references and index.
ISBN 0–415–06552–6
1. Mitsubishi Zōsen Kabushiki Kaisha. Nagasaki Zōsenjo—History.
2. Shipbuilding industry—Japan—Nagasaki-shi—History—
20th century.   3. Japan—Industries—History—20th century.
4. Technology transfer—Japan—History—20th century.
I. Title.
VM301.M5F85   1992
338.4′762383′0952244—dc20
91–46065
CIP

CONTENTS

Figures and tables   viii
Foreword   xi
General Editor's preface   xiii
Preface   xv
List of abbreviations   xvii

1 TECHNOLOGY AND INDUSTRIAL
   DEVELOPMENT – AN INTRODUCTION   1
   International technology transfer and technological change –
   changing perspectives   1
   Technology transfer and technological learning in pre-war
   Japan – need for more research   9
   Mitsubishi Nagasaki Shipyard – a case study   12

2 SETTING THE STAGE –
   INDUSTRIALIZATION, SHIPBUILDING
   INDUSTRY AND THE MITSUBISHI
   NAGASAKI SHIPYARD   17
   Foundations for a modern industrial state   17
      The transition   17
      Government enterprises and early industrial policies   19
   Growth, structural change and industrial policies, 1884–1934 22
      Industrial growth and structural change   22
      Industrial policies   25
   Development of the shipbuilding industry   27
      Early developments   27
      Growth and technological development   29
      The role of the navy   33
   Development of the Mitsubishi Nagasaki Shipyard   34

Early developments and the Mitsubishi firm   34
The Nagasaki Shipyard under Mitsubishi   36

3 TECHNOLOGY IMPORTS AT MITSUBISHI
NAGASAKI SHIPYARD   43
Early national strategies in technology imports   43
Employment of foreigners   43
Overseas missions   44
Other modes of technology imports   46
Technology imports at Nagasaki Shipyard   47
Employment of foreigners   47
Overseas missions   51
Imports of machinery and materials   55
Purchases of manufacturing and sales licences   57
Journals, books and professional societies   60

4 EDUCATION AND TRAINING AT
MITSUBISHI NAGASAKI SHIPYARD   62
The development of formal education   62
The diffusion of education   62
Formal educational programmes in naval architecture
and marine engineering   65
*Within-enterprise training programmes for workers and
technicians at the Nagasaki Shipyard*   67
On-the-job training of workers   67
Mitsubishi Kogyo Gakko and the training of
shugyosei   70
Mitsubishi Shokko Gakko   74
Training engineers and short-term training programmes   77
Recruiting and training engineers   77
Short-term training programmes   82

5 RESEARCH AND INVENTIVE ACTIVITIES
AT MITSUBISHI NAGASAKI SHIPYARD   85
National efforts in industrial research   85
The role of in-house research bodies   96
Jikkenba, the laboratory at Nagasaki and the
Experimental Tank   96
Mitsubishi Shipbuilding Company Research Institute   102
Management of research and inventive activities   104
Policy towards inventive activities   104
Technological research committees   106

Mitsubishi Technological Research Meeting and
links with universities, research institutes and
professional societies 108

6 INDIGENOUS TECHNOLOGICAL
DEVELOPMENTS AT MITSUBISHI
NAGASAKI SHIPYARD 112
Steam turbine engines 112
Importing the technology and the development of
design capability 112
Research on blade material and rotor balancing 119
Impulse turbines 121
Electric welding 123
Importing and the diffusion of the technology 123
Research and the training programme for electric
welders 127
Diesel engines 133
Vickers' diesel engines 133
Sulzer's diesel engines 136
MS diesel engine 138

7 TECHNOLOGICAL LEARNING AND
INDUSTRIAL DEVELOPMENT –
CONCLUSIONS AND POLICY
IMPLICATIONS 146
*Technological learning and technological strategies at
Mitsubishi Nagsaki Shipyard – conclusions* 146
Some policy implications of the Japanese experience 150

*Appendix: Overseas missions from Mitsubishi Nagasaki
Shipyard 1896–1935* 153

Notes 162
Bibliography 177
Index 185

FIGURES AND TABLES

FIGURES

3.1	Foreign employees at Nagasaki Shipyard	48
6.1	Average tensile strength of test pieces made by electric welders at Nagasaki Shipyard	129
6.2	Number of welders and the consumption of electrodes at Nagasaki Shipyard	130

TABLES

2.1	Commercial ships constructed in Japan	29
2.2	Tonnage launched in 1,000Gt – international comparison	32
2.3	Vessels of IJN	33
2.4	Employees at Nagasaki Shipyard	37
2.5	Tonnage built at Nagasaki	38
2.6	Investments in physical facilities in 1,000 yen	39
2.7	Technological milestones at Mitsubishi Nagasaki Shipyard	40
3.1	Missions abroad 1896–1935	52
3.2	Purchases of machines and materials at Nagasaki Shipyard in 1,000 yen	56
3.3	Manufacturing licences purchased by Mitsubishi Nagasaki Shipyard	58
4.1	Rate of mobility of workers at Nagasaki Shipyard	69
4.2	Careers of MKG graduates	73
4.3	MKG graduates working at Nagasaki Shipyard	74
4.4	Apprentice (graduate) workers in the yard (as of 10.1924)	77

4.5	Study and training missions within Japan	80
5.1	Government research institutes founded before 1900	86
5.2	Government research institutes founded during 1900–35	88
5.3	Government funding of research and inventive activities	91
5.4 (a)	Gakushin research grants in yen (%)	92
5.4 (b)	Break-up of individual research grants according to field in %	93
5.4 (c)	Break-up of cooperative research grants according to field in %	93
5.5	Number of research bodies founded by industrial enterprises	94
5.6	R&D efforts in engineering	95
5.7	Number of laboratory employees and reports	98
5.8	Lectures at Mitsubishi Technological Research Meetings	109
6.1	Marine turbines for mercantile ships built at Nagasaki	115
6.2	Steam turbines for naval vessels built at Nagasaki	116
6.3	Turbo-generators built at Nagasaki	117
6.4	Marine diesel engines built at Nagasaki	142

FOREWORD

Japan's extraordinary economic success has spawned many books, papers and pronouncements about its underlying causes. Nearly all recognize the high priority given to training and technology. Many speculate as to how this was done. But relatively few empirical studies by Japanese scholars have emerged that describe and evaluate the policies, procedures and institutions that enabled Japan to catch up with the world's best practice technology and, in many cases, to improve upon it.

Yukiko Fukasaku's study of technology and training in the Mitsubishi Nagasaki Shipyard throws considerable light on the subject. Using original archival material she sets out to explore how a deliberate policy for technological development was put in place and carried out. Her conclusions are important for those interested in the modern history of Japan, in science and technology policy and in the determinants of industrial modernization.

Among other things, she confirms the very important fact that the effective assimilation of foreign technology is not costless, but requires the establishment of indigenous training, design and R&D activities that are part of a web of international linkages and exchanges. The conventional (and misleading) dichotomy between indigenous technological development, on the one hand, and the purchase of foreign technology, on the other, breaks down since both are essential and complementary parts of the process of technological learning.

Dr Fukasaku's research also confirms that competitive advantage is created and not God given. Japan's shipbuilders assimilated, and in some cases surpassed, foreign best-practice technology, and became a major world force in the industry.

But this process of technological accumulation took time and involved industrial firms, and academic and financial institutions, as well as government policies. It was very different from the assumptions of strategic trade theory, that governments can create a competitive advantage by giving firms a quick pre-emptive nudge down the learning curve.

Finally, Dr Fukasaku's research shows that Japan's considerable technological achievements in shipbuilding go back well beyond the second world war and did not emerge only in the 1950s and 1960s. In these and related subjects, this book makes an important contribution.

C. Freeman and K. Pavitt

GENERAL EDITOR'S PREFACE

With growing speed, as we move into the 1990s, Japan in her many aspects is becoming a subject of interest and concern. The successes of the Japanese economy and the resourcefulness of her people have long been appreciated abroad. What is new is an awareness of her increasing impact on the outside world. This tends to produce painful adjustment and uncomfortable reactions. It also often leads to stereotypes based on outdated or ill-informed ideas.

The Nissan Institute/Routledge Japanese Studies Series seeks to foster an informed and balanced – but not uncritical – understanding of Japan. One aim of the series is to show the depth and variety of Japanese institutions, practices and ideas. Another is, by using comparison, to see what lessons, positive and negative, can be drawn for other countries. There are many aspects of Japan which are little known outside that country but which deserve to be better understood.

In the latter half of the nineteenth century Japan was an 'underdeveloped' country in the true sense of the term. Ahead of her lay the incredibly arduous task of importing, adapting, developing and dispersing the technologies needed for the creation of an industrialized society. Much technological experience had already been accumulated by the time of the second world war, and it was this solid base upon which the post-war economic 'miracle' was able to be built.

This book examines in detail the ways in which technological innovation and training were developed at the Mitsubishi Shipyard in Nagasaki between 1884 and 1934. The author demonstrates that there was an impressive accumulation of technological capabilities within the firm and at national level at quite early stages of industrialization, and that this was a cumulative process. She is sceptical of theories identifying cultural uniqueness as the secret of Japan's industrial success, and the book implies that Japan's early industrializing experiences are indeed of real relevance to the developing world today.

J. A. A. Stockwin

PREFACE

This book is a revision of the doctoral thesis that was submitted to the University of Sussex in 1988. I would like to thank Professor Keith Pavitt, Professor Christopher Freeman and Dr Norman Clark of Science Policy Research Unit, University of Sussex, for supervising the research for the thesis and for reading and commenting on the drafts. Special thanks are due to Professors Freeman and Pavitt for kindly writing a foreword to the present book.

The case study on technological development at Mitsubishi Nagasaki Shipyard constitutes the core substance of the book, and this would not have been possible without the availability of historical materials on the shipyard. In starting the research for the book I had doubts as to the existence of relevant materials, and even if they did exist, whether they would be available for consultation. It turned out that there were some very interesting materials, and the members of Mitsubishi Heavy Industries Ltd were very generous in helping me consult these materials, for which I am most grateful. They are Mr H. Takahashi, Mr T. Matsumoto, Mr Y. Kubo and Mr K. Murata at the Nagasaki Shipyard; Mr M. Hirato, Mr M. Hashimoto, Mr S. Imagawa, Mr T. Shimao and Ms Iguchi at the Tokyo headquarters. I would also like to thank the following persons who have recounted to me their experiences at the Nagasaki Shipyard in the pre-war period: Mr N. Kitaoka, Mr T. Kato, Dr H. Fujita, Dr M. Kanamori and Mr K. Noguchi. Some of them also provided me with access to some valuable materials.

Thanks are due to Ms H. Yamamoto and Ms Omura of Mitsubishi Economic Research Institute, Mr T. Miyagawa,

Mr O. Ozeki, Ms N. Hama and Ms Horie of Mitsubishi Research Institute and Mr K. Tomonari of Ryoju Kabushiki Kaisha for providing and facilitating access to Mitsubishi materials kept at these places. Mr S. Higashi, formerly of Japan Ship Center, London, Mr T. Iwata of the Japan Society of Naval Architects, Mr I. Takahashi of the Japan Society of Engineers and Mr Y. Nakamura of Shiryo Chosakai Kaigun Bunko also assisted me in consulting related materials for the case study, for which I am grateful. I would also like to thank Professor Y. Torii for letting me have access to the library at Keio University. Mr M. Moss and Mr H. Scrope have aided me in consulting archives at the universities of Glasgow and Cambridge, for which I am grateful.

A part of the research for the book was funded by a research grant from the Esso Petroleum Company of Tokyo. I would like to thank the company for this support. Finally, I am grateful to Ms Debbie Barker for helping me put the manuscript in diskettes, to Marie-Christine Horie and Mme K. Doghri for having taken care of my children during my busy hours, and to Kiichiro, Kotaro and Yuji for letting me be preoccupied with something other than the family during the preparation of the book.

LIST OF ABBREVIATIONS

ICERC Internal Combustion Engine Research Committee
IJN   Imperial Japanese Navy
MKG   Mitsubishi Kogyo Gakko (Industrial School)
MSCRI Mitsubishi Shipbuilding Company Research Institute
MSG   Mitsubishi Shokko Gakko (Workers' School)
MZKK Mitsubishi Zosen Kabushiki Kaisha (Shipbuilding Company)
NYK   Nippon Yusen Kaisha (Japan Post Ship Company)
OSK   Osaka Shosen Kaisha (Osaka Commercial Ship Company)
TKK   Toyo Kisen Kaisha (Oriental Steam Ship Company)

AUTHOR'S NOTE

Japanese names are written with the family name preceding the given name.

1

TECHNOLOGY AND INDUSTRIAL DEVELOPMENT – AN INTRODUCTION

This book examines how technological capabilities were developed in the industrialization of Japan before the second world war. Industrialization in Japan in the pre-war period was based upon fairly complex processes centring around absorbing and improving imported technologies which had significant implications for the so-called Japanese 'miracle' of rapid economic growth in the post-war years. More importantly, the examination of these processes sheds light on the currently much discussed issue of the role of technological capabilities and technological change in the international transfer of technology and industrial development.

INTERNATIONAL TECHNOLOGY TRANSFER AND TECHNOLOGICAL CHANGE – CHANGING PERSPECTIVES

Although the benefit of importing technology for industrializing countries has long been recognized and stressed, it is only relatively recently that the nature of the processes involved in the acquisition and development of technology has become clear. For long it was taken for granted that latecomers to industrialization had a definite advantage presented by the opportunity to utilize technology already developed by the early industrializers.[1] Helped by the conventional assumption in economic thinking that technological knowledge is a free-flowing public good, the international diffusion of industrial technology was considered to be a relatively easy process. However, the actual experiences of transfer of technology often did not testify to this. A major obstacle was the absence of capabilities to utilize imported technology effectively. Despite the awareness of the central importance of this problem, earlier studies on the transfer of technology failed to come to grips with the question, but rather focused on issues such as costs and appropriateness of imported technology (Vaitsos 1974, Stewart 1973, Cooper 1973). This stems from the view of technology as 'static' and 'given'; so that the problems boil down to choosing suitable technologies and purchasing them at reasonable prices. High cost, inappropriateness of imported technology and the lack of capabilities to utilize them effectively were largely attributed to the 'mechanism' of technology transfers (Cooper and Sercovitch 1971), in which firms supplying technology controlled the transfer processes for reasons of their own commercial interests. Because of such supplier dominance, transferred technologies were often very costly, and inappropriate in view of factor endowments and development goals of the recipient country, and the transfer of the necessary technological capabilities was neglected. Thus, the problems associated with transfers of technology were seen to reside with the suppliers, while the recipient firms and countries remained their passive victims.

It should be noted that some forms of the so-called 'technological dependency' view went as far as to argue that technological development could not take place in 'structurally dependent' economies because 'quasi-monopolistic' control by supplier firms of transfers of technology 'marginalized' indigenous technological developments, perpetuating the state of 'technological dependence'.[2] This view naturally tended to advocate the policy of restraining technology imports in favour of supplying all needed technologies indigenously, as a way out of the degenerating 'structural dependence'. Reality, however, has not supported this argument. Some of the newly industrializing countries are supposedly 'dependent', but their industrial sectors are showing promising signs of growth. Also, many NICs (to say nothing of Japan) happen to be avid importers of technology, which implies that technology imports and indigenous technological development are not substitutes but interrelate in a complementary manner. The crucial problem is to stimulate the development of capabilities to absorb, adapt and improve imported technology, so that, eventually, needed technologies can be supplied indigenously.

As pointed out by Bell (1982), the radical technological dependency view rested on little empirical evidence. In fact, research efforts since the second half of the 1970s started to show that indigenous technological developments were actually taking place in many 'dependent' economies. Such evidence suggested that problems do not lie so much on the supplying mechanism as on the ability on the part of the recipient to generate capabilities to assimilate and change imported technology. In recent years, there has been a growing amount of research on the process of technological learning, i.e. the development of indigenous technological capabilities in industrializing countries.

This shift in research interest converged with, and was at the same time a result of, the evolution in perspective on the nature of technology and the role of technological change[3] in economic growth that emerged from the studies of these processes in industrialized countries. Despite the importance that classical economists attached to technological change as a dynamic force in economic development, and Schumpeter's preoccupation with innovation as an agent of change, the mainstream economic tradition of this century viewed technological change as 'exogenous' to the economic system and largely neglected its analysis. It was as a result of the recognition of the large and important role of the 'residual' (a substantial part of which was attributed to technological change) relative to labour and capital inputs in economic growth (Abramovitz 1956, Solow 1957) that technological change attracted the attention of economists as a factor in need of analysis.

In the neoclassical formulation, technological change is defined as a shift in production function affecting a whole range of production techniques, and, as such, only major innovative breakthroughs in the Schumpeterian sense were considered to have significant economic consequences. There has, however, been an increasing realization that this view does not correctly reflect reality. As pointed out by Rosenberg (1976), it is unlikely that an entire range of techniques as represented by a production function actually exists, but what is available is very limited. This implied that technological changes are also 'localized' (Atkinson and Stiglitz 1969) and are often minor and incremental in nature. Such changes, however, are no less economically significant, since it is this type of technological change that 'perfects' a major innovation, rendering it more competitive, or makes a certain technology adapt to a different resource environment. Rosenberg (1982) cites the work of Gilfillan (1935a, 1935b) and Usher (1954) to say that the process of technological innovation itself consists of 'innumerable minor improvements and modifications', the cumulative effect of which is nonetheless important. The economic significance of minor changes was demonstrated, for example, by studies of Hollander (1965) and Enos (1962). The former's study of Du Pont rayon plant found that the cumulative minor technological changes were more instrumental in cost reduction than major technological changes, while the latter's study of petroleum refining processes showed that more cost reduction was seen in the improvement phase than by the introduction of major refining processes.

These works demonstrated also that technological changes, although minor, are largely generated within productive processes. The notion of the 'endogenous' nature of technological change was formalized in the 'learning by doing' model of Arrow (1962) which was an attempt to explain the importance of the 'residual' in economic growth. The model proposed that productivity rises without having to make new investments, because learning takes place as a by-product of accumulating experience in production. Studies of some industries showed that productivity indeed increased with fixed resources, demonstrating that 'learning by doing' was actually taking place (Alchian 1963, David 1975).

This was how 'technological learning' was originally conceptualized. The model was significant in that it viewed learning as a process leading to technological change; however, it was limited in that it defined learning as a function of experience only, and as such, it was conceptualized as a largely unconscious and passive process. Also, the effects of learning were seen only in terms of productivity rise, i.e. unit cost reduction. Learning, however, could be enhanced by such inputs as education and research (as Arrow himself realized); hence it can be a conscious and active process for which investments are required. Effects other than unit cost reduction could be induced, such as adaptation or improvement of the production technology and/or the product and the substitution of local materials for imported ones. This would involve physical

4

changes in the production process which in the 'learning by doing' model was fixed.

It is the active and conscious forms of learning entailing minor, incremental technological changes that have been demonstrated as playing key roles in a number of case studies on transfer of technology. The studies of Argentine rayon and steel plant (Katz *et al.* 1977, Maxwell 1977) and a Brazilian steel mill (Dahlman and Fonseca 1978)[4] show that R&D investments by these enterprises brought about minor, incremental technological changes which in turn led to better exploitation of the capacity of existing plant, diversification and quality improvement of products and substitution of locally available raw materials and parts for imported ones. Investments in training were also important in accumulating knowledge and skills to substitute for foreign technical assistance (Dahlman and Fonseca 1978, Seoul National University 1980). Technology importing firms had 'technological strategies' to bring about desirable technological changes. These strategies responded not only to problems in the technology itself, but also to such economic variables as the degree of competition, cost and availability of raw materials, relative factor prices and exchange rate (Katz 1978). The domestic technological learning efforts also resulted in a flow of technology exports to other developing countries, which suggests that these technologies have successfully been adapted by the original importer to suit prevailing conditions in developing countries (Katz and Ablin 1978, Lall 1980).

In developing countries, 'learning by doing' seems to take place less easily than in developed countries. A study by Bell *et al.* (1982) of galvanized steel sheet plant in Thailand shows a case in which neither 'learning by doing' nor any technological change of whatever form took place. The authors attribute this failure to the neglect on the part of the technology importing firms to invest in training and R&D to develop capabilities beyond what was needed for basic operation of the plant. This implies that 'learning by doing' depends not only on experience in a particular production process but also on the ability to relate that experience to knowledge and skills acquired elsewhere. This ability may be taken for granted in industrialized countries but not in developing countries; hence the importance of investing in R&D and training to generate those skills and knowledge.

In the above study, the authors argue that the failure to invest in the acquisition of technological capabilities was precipitated by the protectionist policy of the government. While Westphal (1981) and Lall (1980) point to the positive role of protection in enhancing learning in infant industries, the extent of that effect seems to be limited. Based on a study of machinery industry in Hong Kong, Fransman (1982) argues that free trade enhances technological learning by providing access to cheap, high-quality inputs and relevant information. He makes a reservation, though, that free trade 'may also have precluded the attainment of more sophisticated technological capabilities'. Protectionist measures are effective only to the extent that the industrial sector is given a chance to launch the accumulation of those capabilities which otherwise it would not have under free trade. This would be justified only if the development of such capabilities were necessary in view of national industrial development goals. Technological learning itself is stimulated rather than suppressed by technology imports. Lall (1985) adds an important qualification to his earlier argument in support of protectionism to foster technological capabilities by saying that carrying protectionist policies too far and long results in technological stagnation manifesting itself in inefficiency, obsolescence and non-competitiveness of the protected industry in the international market and concludes that 'injections of fresh foreign technologies' are needed to sustain continuous development of technological capabilities.[5]

In the stream of recent research on international transfer of technology discussed so far, technology is viewed as something that has to be adapted and changed to make it viable in the recipient country. Given that, as Rosenberg (1976) concludes from a study on the transfer of steam engine and metallurgy technologies to America in the last century, the selection, adaptation and modification of technologies are 'activities which typically require a very high degree of technological sophistication'. This technological sophistication is a product of the accumulation of necessary knowledge and capabilities by the technology importing firm or country. This means that, contrary to conventional assumptions, knowledge can be acquired only with costly efforts. Therefore, rather than being explicit knowledge, which can be embodied in machines and codified in blueprints and manuals, an important part of technological knowledge is 'tacit' (Nelson 1978, 1981), hence 'uncodified', and can be acquired only by trial and error experiences, involving problem solving and trouble shooting activities to 'make imported technology work'. The emerging knowledge and capabilities are, therefore, specific to the firm which is 'a locus where the progressive accumulation of technical knowledge takes place, with production processes tending to display many specific and idiosyncratic components' (Rosenberg and Frischtak 1985: vii). The specific and cumulative nature of technology points to the importance of the examination of the behaviour of the firm in understanding technological diffusion and productive performance. This diverges from the neoclassical view of the firm as a profit maximizing entity which operates production by choosing from a given set of available technologies.

The important role of firm-level accumulation of technological capabilities in technology transfer and the firm-specific nature of technology imply that the problems associated with technology transfer from developed to developing countries and the diffusion of technology among developed countries are, in essence, very similar. Among the OECD countries it is pointed out that 'the independent technological capabilities of the countries importing technology have probably been the most important factors in determining the rate and direction of technology transfer', and that the successful assimilation of technology depends upon firm-level efforts in R&D and production engineering (Pavitt 1985). It may be noted here that the convergence of issues surrounding technology transfer, whether from developed to developing countries or among the former group of countries, points to the validity of the neo-Schumpeterian and evolutionist views of technology[6] in understanding technological diffusion, since these attach central importance to the behaviour of the firm and its innovative activities and the resulting technological dynamism in explaining economic change.

The preoccupation with 'technological learning' and the 'accumulation of technological capabilities'[7] which has dominated much of the literature on international transfers of technology over the last decade has not only produced an increasing flow of evidence demonstrating the importance of these processes in the successful assimilation of imported technologies, but also this line of research has identified the existence of different types of learning processes and technological capabilities. Lall (1980) has described a three-stage (elementary, intermediate and advanced) classification with two substages in each by which the learning process increases in degree of sophistication from simple 'learning by doing' through adapting and improving stages to the final 'learning by innovation' stage where in-house R&D 'extends into basic research and development and is able to offer new processes or new products'. Bell (1982) stresses the active nature of the necessary learning processes as opposed to the passiveness associated with the 'learning by doing' concept, by pointing to the importance of such activities as learning by operating, changing, learning through training, by hiring and by searching. Rosenberg (1982) points out the importance of 'learning by using' in which productivity-improving technological changes may be induced by information feedback from users in high technology industries such as aircrafts. Dore (1984) distinguishes between 'ITLC (independent technology learning capacity)' which corresponds to the capability to assimilate foreign technology and 'ITCC (independent technology creating capacity)' which corresponds to the capability to adapt and change, to explain the mediocre technological performance of India, whose policy as well as social sentiment stressed the latter, while neglecting the former. This distinction is similar to Lall's (1985) 'know how' and 'know why' capabilities in which the former refers to the ability to operate imported production processes, while the latter corresponds to the ability to change product or process technology.

The presence of the varied forms of learning process and the different types of technological capabilities reflects the extremely complex nature of learning and capability accumulating processes. While the identification of the varied categories is useful in understanding the behaviour of different industries or countries at different industrial development stages, the importance of continuity among them should also be stressed. The different categories constitute an integrated process, and, in the long run, all components have roles to play at one time or another to make the industrial sector, and eventually the economy as a whole, innovative and dynamic.

The discussion so far has concentrated on the process of

learning and the accumulation of technological capability within industrial firms; however, it is evident that these processes can be enhanced if they are complemented by external training and R&D activities. While scientific infrastructures in developing countries often failed to contribute effectively to the technological efforts of industrial enterprises (Cooper 1973, Herrera 1973, Crane 1977), if they are judiciously interrelated with firm-level efforts, there is little doubt that the learning process would be accelerated. Nelson (1986) gives evidence that external institutions do play relevant roles in enhancing innovation in private firms in the USA. Scientific and educational infrastructures could, therefore, effectively complement firm-level efforts.

The conceptualization of the process of international transfer of technology and technological change has thus undergone a drastic change. This suggests that the re-examination of the industrialization process in Japan according to the emerging conceptual framework may lead to findings that so far have been overlooked. This book is an attempt to do this.

TECHNOLOGY TRANSFER AND TECHNOLOGICAL LEARNING IN PRE-WAR JAPAN – NEED FOR MORE RESEARCH

The changing conceptualization of the process of international transfer of technology discussed in the foregoing section strongly suggests the following hypothesis. In a late industrializing country like Japan whose industrialization was based on effective utilization of imported technology, substantial accumulation of technological capabilities must have taken place within industrial enterprises from the early stages of industrialization through training and research. Despite the voluminous amount of literature that has appeared recently that attempts to explain the Japanese 'miracle' of rapid economic growth in the post-war period, relatively little attention has been paid to the analysis of the role of technology.

What has attracted more interest have been factors such as 'cultural traits' (e.g. the pervasive Confucian ethos of loyalty as discussed by Morishima 1982); or institutions unique to Japan, especially labour management practices which include the oft-cited components of life-time employment, a seniority wage system and enterprise unions; or the benefits of 'free-riding' on the alliance with the United States which saved defence expenditures and provided easy access to necessary foreign technologies and to export markets for Japanese industrial products.[8] These types of analysis simply see industrial and technological development as a result of the characteristics they point to, without examining it. However, as discussed so far, technological development is a complex process which requires proper analysis. Some of the 'unique institutions' view argues that, because Japan was a 'late developer', her institutions related to industrial development turned out to be different from those of the early developers.[9] Dore (1973) argues this in reference to the Japanese employment system. Johnson (1982) and Yamauchi (1983) see it in industrial policy. Although this provides an explanation of why the institutions are different, it cannot explain why Japan was able to generate institutions that benefited and were well adapted to its 'late development' while so many other countries failed. 'Late development' can serve only as a motive. Between that and the creation and operation of effective institutions lies the question of how suitable capabilities were accumulated, which is not addressed by the above works nor by Gershenkron's (1952) original latecomer hypothesis.

The works that have focused on the role of technological innovation and technology transfer in post-war Japan (Oshima 1973, Ozawa 1974, 1984, Peck and Tamura 1976, Peck and Goto 1981) have revealed some important characteristics of her technological development. For one thing, there is a high correlation between the growth of R&D expenditures, technology imports and economic growth, indicating that technology was indeed an important component in economic growth, and that in this process, R&D and technology imports were complementary activities. More importantly, a major part of the R&D effort, especially in the 1950s and 1960s, was directed at 'adaptive' research or, more appropriately, 'improvement engineering' (Rosovsky 1970, Peck and Tamura 1976) which aimed at upgrading product quality and cost reduction, in short, making industrial products produced by originally imported technology more competitive. These works as well as others, most notably Johnson 1982, have stressed the importance of MITI (Ministry of International Trade and Industry) in controlling the flow of technology imports and in guiding the overall technological effort in post-war Japan. Freeman (1987) has suggested the existence in Japan of a distinctive type of 'national system of innovation', i.e. the institutional framework that organically interrelated industrial policies, research and innovation, education and training (both industrial and formal), management practices and industrial structure. He argues that this has successfully led Japan not only to close the technology gap she faced at the end of the second world war, but also to open a new one with herself as the leader, based on the incorporation of information technology in the industrial system.

If, as these works have demonstrated, technology was an important component in post-war economic growth, it must also have played a similar role in the earlier industrialization of Japan, since technology is cumulative. Inquiry into this is significant for the following reasons. First, because of similarities in the level of economic growth, pre-war Japanese experiences are more relevant than those of the post-war period for the contemporary developing countries. Second, as Ohkawa and Rosovsky (1965) have pointed out, the Japanese economy shows an accelerated growth or what they term 'trend acceleration', characterized by the rapid increase in productivity and investment in the modern sector, starting in the first decade of this century. Significant growth had thus already started in the pre-war period, and this warrants investigation with respect to the role of technology. Third, despite the material devastation of the second world war and the radical reforms imposed during the Occupation, knowledge and experiences accumulated before the war survived, and there were important continuities, especially with regard to human resources and institutions. Although reorganized, most pre-war educational and research institutions survived. Also, despite such measures as dissolution of large concerns, the major industrial firms kept their engineers who eventually contributed to post-war innovations, and the practices that were established before the war were largely preserved.

It is only recently that pre-war technological development in Japan has caught the attention of scholars as a subject in need of socio-economic analysis. Minami (1976) has examined the economic consequences of the diffusion of electric power generation in pre-war Japan. Odaka (1984) has studied productivity rises and some aspects of technological change in the

11

shipbuilding industry in relation to his study of the dual structure in the industrial sector in pre-war Japan. Minami and Kiyokawa (1987) have collected case studies on technological change and industrial growth in pre-war Japan which focus upon economic analysis of choice of techniques in various industries.[10]

Studies on the development of industrial training (Levine and Kawada 1980, Sumiya 1971, Hyodo 1971) have been illuminating in providing evidence of the existence of extensive within-enterprise training activities in pre-war industrial enterprises. An interesting work by the science historian Hiroshige (1973), who has taken a social history approach in tracing the development of scientific infrastructure in pre-war Japan, argues that because of the national goal of rapid industrialization, research institutions and funding for R&D as well as government legislation were designed to promote and facilitate industrial research, rather than basic research. By so doing, the government successfully 'integrated science and technology into the national system'.

All of these works suggest that technology played an important role in pre-war industrial development in Japan. This book attempts to go further by focusing on the process of technological learning.

MITSUBISHI NAGASAKI SHIPYARD – A CASE STUDY

In order to study the technological learning process in pre-war Japan, this book examines in detail technology imports, training and research activities in relation to the development of technological capabilities at Mitsubishi Nagasaki Shipyard during the period 1884–1934. The shipbuilding industry in pre-war Japan exhibited several features which are significant from the viewpoint of this book. It was one of the earliest modern industries to develop in Japan. Haphazard attempts started well before 1868, and the Nagasaki Shipyard was already set up as a government enterprise by 1857. This preoccupation with shipbuilding from early days is explained by the strategic and commercial importance of the industry resulting from the geographical features of Japan. It was in the national interest to form a strong navy and an efficient merchant fleet. Modern shipbuilding was also one of the earliest heavy industries to develop in the private sector. The relatively early start of industry in the course of industrialization makes possible the observation of the effects of traditional factors in the economy, which has implications for the contemporary developing countries. Its strategic importance resulted in interactions with the navy. The industry benefited from the diffusion of technology and manpower from the navy; also, by the first decade of the century, the industry had become an important complement to the country's naval construction capacity. The development of the industry was brought about by importing foreign technology through various channels, and the assimilation and improvement of those imported technologies.

The most characteristic feature of the industry was that, compared to an early industrializing country like Britain, where the shipbuilding industry grew in a context of well-developed machinery- and material-supplying industries, the industry in Japan developed without them. This meant that the shipbuilding industry had to assume the role of the supplier for itself. Consequently, the industry was also a machinery industry. It made not only engines and other machinery needed for ships, but also machinery for other industries, such as mining and electrical power generation. The importance of the capital goods industry for industrialization in providing a source of technological change and a medium of technological diffusion has already been well argued (Rosenberg 1976). In the case of Mitsubishi, specialized producers of electrical machinery, internal combustion engines (including aircraft) and optical instruments branched out from its shipbuilding enterprise. The shipbuilding industry was, therefore, a diversified and complex industry, which fostered other machinery industries.

Mitsubishi Nagasaki Shipyard occupied a position of importance in relation to technology within the pre-war shipbuilding industry. It was not only the earliest shipyard to develop as a private enterprise, but also the largest shipyard in Japan, and Mitsubishi's shipbuilding enterprise, which included two other shipyards at Kobe and Hikoshima, was the largest in the industry. Only one other firm came anywhere close in scale, the Kawasaki Shipbuilding Company, and the competition between the two served as a stimulant in their development. Being the leading firm in the industry meant that Mitsubishi aimed at (and was also expected to) competing with foreign shipbuilders in the market for large and sophisticated ships which the growing Japanese shipping industry required. This in turn implied the imperative to attain the level of world's 'best practice' technology by importing the most advanced technologies, and the survival of the firm depended on its ability to absorb and improve them. Such a firm is appropriate for examining technology transfer and learning processes.

The mid 1880s marked the start of modern economic growth in Japan. During the next half century, the Japanese economy not only grew in per capita production, but also underwent a structural shift from an agricultural to an industrial economy. It experienced wars and the resulting booms and recessions, until its economy became overtly war-oriented and controlled by the second half of the 1930s. The first fifty years of the development of Nagasaki Shipyard under Mitsubishi correspond to the above period. In 1884 the Nagasaki Shipyard was leased out to Mitsubishi. In 1934 Mitsubishi Shipbuilding Company merged with Mitsubishi Aircrafts Company to become an even larger and more complex strategic industry. During this period the Nagasaki Shipyard evolved from a state of complete dependence on foreign technical assistance for its operations to a level of technological capability at which the shipyard could design and build commercial and naval vessels and engines of competitive quality.

Information for the case study was drawn mostly from the written records and materials of the Mitsubishi firm. Although available materials were limited and dispersed in several places within and outside the firm (the Nagasaki Shipyard, the Tokyo head office of Mitsubishi Heavy Industries Ltd, Ryoju Kabushiki Kaisha, Mitsubishi Economic Research Institute and Mitsubishi Research Institute), the research was facilitated by the existence of several sets of core materials. These are:

1 *Mitsubishi Shashi* (referred to as *Shashi* in text): a compilation of a selection of official documents of the original Mitsubishi firm since 1870 and the shareholding company of the Mitsubishi concern, Mitsubishi Goshi Kaisha. This contains some of the firm rules, personnel movements, and managerial decisions and actions relating to Nagasaki Shipyard up to 1917.

2 *Shashi Shiryo*, compiled by Mitsubishi Heavy Industries Ltd, is a similar set of materials for the period from 1917. This set has two supplementary volumes containing memoirs of staff and workers written during the 1940s and 1950s (*Kaikyuroku 1 and 2*).

3 *Shiryo Iho*, a series of reports on various topics compiled by the information department of Mitsubishi Goshi Kaisha, and the department's annual report, *Shiryoka Nenpo*.

4 Annual reports of Nagasaki Shipyard (referred to as *Nenpo* in text), compiled for the years 1898 to 1925, record all the ships and other products manufactured at the shipyard, additions to machines and facilities, personnel and worker movements, including dispatches on missions, and welfare activities.

5 Reports of the laboratory (*Jikkenba*) at Nagasaki Shipyard since 1921; also a list of their titles (Kubo 1972).

6 A series of monographs (Yano 1966) describing the activities and personnel movements of the laboratory at Nagasaki.

These core materials were supplemented by pieces of archival materials found at Nagasaki Shipyard and Mitsubishi Research Institute, published firm histories, published and unpublished memoirs and notes. Some valuable information was obtained from interviews with the following persons, all of whom worked at the Nagasaki Shipyard in the pre-war period. In alphabetical order, they are: Dr Fujita Hideo, a member of the diesel engine design team at Nagasaki from 1929, who at the time of the interview was an adviser to the Technical Head-quarters of Mitsubishi Heavy Industries Ltd; Dr Kanamori Masao, who started his career as a researcher on electric welding at the Nagasaki Shipyard laboratory in 1935, who at the time of the interview was the chairman of the board of directors of Mitsubishi Heavy Industries Ltd; Mr Kato Tomoo, recruited to Nagasaki in 1925 as an engineer in hull design, whose father was one of the earliest university trained engineer recruits to Nagasaki; Mr Kitaoka Nobuo, a 1923 Mitsubishi Industrial School graduate who spent his career as a worker, technician and engineer in hull design at Nagasaki; and Mr Noguchi Ken-ichi, who started his career as an engineer in turbine design section at Nagasaki in 1937. Finally, some interesting information about technology imports was obtained from the archives of some of the British firms which exported them to

Mitsubishi. They were consulted at the universities of Glasgow and Cambridge.

The chapters are structured as follows. After reviewing the historical setting of the case study in the next chapter, chapters 3 to 5 examine technology imports, training and research activities respectively. The first section of these chapters reviews the overall national effort on each aspect during the period, and the remaining sections examine the activities at the Nagasaki Shipyard. This juxtaposing approach has been taken so that the interrelationship between national and firm-level efforts can be seen easily. Chapter 6 traces the development of three technologies at Nagasaki Shipyard, namely, turbine engine, electric welding and diesel engine. These 'case studies within a case study' were done in order to examine exactly how firm-level efforts in technology imports, training and research facilitated the development of specific technologies. These three were among the major innovations that had a profound impact upon the development of shipbuilding technology during the first few decades of this century. The final chapter of the book draws conclusions by relating the major findings to the conceptual issues raised in this chapter and discusses their implications for policy making.

2

SETTING THE STAGE – INDUSTRIALIZATION, SHIPBUILDING INDUSTRY AND THE MITSUBISHI NAGASAKI SHIPYARD

FOUNDATIONS FOR A MODERN INDUSTRIAL STATE

The transition

The modern era in Japan is normally considered as beginning in 1868, the year the feudal regime was overthrown. From the viewpoint of economic and industrial development, however, significant growth started only in the mid-1880s. This was preceded by a period of transition during which the foundations of modern industrial development were laid.

By the mid-nineteenth century, the supposedly static and isolated agrarian society under the Tokugawa *bakufu* (shogunate)–*han* (feudal fiefs) political order had undergone significant transformations. A quarter of a millennium of peace had given rise to a lively money economy which undermined the rigid feudal class structure by making the lower merchant class rich and causing impoverishment and dissatisfaction of the aristocratic warrior class. Politically, the Tokugawa regime's Confucian ideological foundations were being undermined by the rise of schools of intellectual inquiry critical of it. *Kogugaku* (national scholarship) was arriving at the conclusion that the long-neglected emperor should be the real active sovereign of the state. *Rangaku* (Dutch scholarship) was deeply critical of the static Tokugawa order which was depriving the country of the modern technological progress taking place in the West. Economically, *bakufu's* mismanagement of public finances made the lot of the warrior and peasant classes deteriorate even more

17

rapidly, and the *bakufu* was bankrupt by the mid-nineteenth century. On top of these internal changes, mounting foreign pressures to open Japan for trade gave a definitive blow. The commercial treaties of 1857 and 1858 with Britain, the USA, France, Holland and Russia, imposing a very low scale of tariffs and granting extraterritorial rights to foreigners, not only brought enormous economic pressures, but also raised violent political opposition among the dissatisfied lower rank warriors of some *han*, culminating in the *coup d'état* and the establishment of the Meiji government in 1868.

Until the 1880s, the new government effected reforms which created socio-economic institutions congenial to modern industrial development, the most important goal of the new government. In the eyes of the new leaders, the failure to have the 'unequal' commercial treaties of 1857 and 1858 revised left modern industrialization as the only means to counteract foreign commercial competition which was fatally damaging the economy. Moreover, there was a realization that industrial power was the basis of military strength to which the new nation aspired.

One line of reform effected was the liquidation of feudal institutions. The semi-independent *han* were replaced by prefectures in 1871. Restrictions on land proprietorship, cropping, freedom of mobility, internal trade and the right to enter new occupations were removed. Feudal classes were abolished, enforced most radically by the conscription law of 1871, which made national defence a shared responsibility of all, not a privilege of one class. A pension scheme was introduced to the now jobless ex-warrior class, later commuted to government bonds. Land tax, formerly paid in rice as a fixed percentage of harvest, was revised to be paid in money as a fixed rate on the assessed valuation of taxable land. Another line of reform directly conducive to industrialization was also pursued. Government administration was systematized, legal reforms were instituted, the police, the army and the navy were created. A cabinet system was set up, and a modern constitution was drawn up by which a bicameral parliamentary legislative system was established. The government revised fiscal systems, created banks, a postal system and a telegraph network. Schools were founded and primary education became compulsory.

These reforms were effected very rapidly. The new government could do so because Japan was already a well-developed
society at the end of the Tokugawa era. As pointed out by Dore
(1965), the literacy rate was very high by the mid-nineteenth
century. Japan's socio-political institutions were highly sophisticated. More importantly, traditional industries were growing
steadily. These facilitated the transformation of the country into
a modern industrial state.

GOVERNMENT ENTERPRISES AND EARLY
INDUSTRIAL POLICIES

The Meiji government itself undertook numerous modern
industrial enterprises. Some of these were precursors of enterprises which later became major private undertakings. Practices
adopted by these enterprises served as models for private
enterprises like Mitsubishi. Some Meiji government enterprises
had their origins as strategically oriented enterprises of *bakufu*
and *han* such as gunpowder and ordnance manufacturing,
iron smelting and naval construction. These early enterprises
drew upon knowledge acquired through *rangaku*.[1] Machines
and facilities were actually built by translating Dutch books.
Soon, more direct methods of importing modern western technology were adopted: purchasing machines, employing foreign
engineers and workers, sending overseas missions. The *bakufu*
naval construction enterprise at Nagasaki, originally called
Nagasaki Iron Works, which later became Mitsubishi Nagasaki
Shipyard, started in 1857 by importing machines and employing
a team of Dutch engineers. *Bakufu* sent officials and workers in
1862 to Holland to study shipbuilding. Within-enterprise
training saw its origins in the *bakufu* naval yard and iron
foundry at Yokosuka which had formal training programmes for
engineers, technicians and workers.

The enterprises of the Meiji government were far bigger in
scale and wider in range than those of *bakufu* and *han*. Lighthouses, railroads, model manufacturing factories were built, a
telegraph network was laid, mines were modernized and agricultural experimental stations were set up. This does not mean
that the Meiji government was financially well prepared for
such an ambitious scale of industrial undertakings, for the
liquidation of feudal order consumed a large part of government

income. Despite this the government devoted a significant part of its expenditure on industrial enterprises.[2] The government administrative machinery accommodated the requirements of modern industrialization by creating Kobusho (Ministry of Engineering and Public Works) in 1870. Lighthouses, telegraph lines, railroads, mines, shipyards (including the Nagasaki Shipyard), iron and steel mills, and model factories for manufacturing machines, glass, cement and bricks were run by this ministry.

This selection of enterprises reflects the early Meiji government policy to hastily transplant heavy industries. This, however, came under the criticism of the ranks of officials who held the view that improvement and modernization of agriculture-oriented traditional industries deserved priority, for the purpose of export promotion. They thought this a more effective way to achieve economic stability under the terms of the 'unequal' treaties.[3] This policy was implemented by Naimusho (Ministry of Internal Affairs) which set up agricultural experimental stations and textile mills. The Meiji industrial policy until the 1880s was the simultaneous pursuit of these two different policy objectives.

As with *bakufu* and *han* enterprises, Meiji industrial undertakings relied on foreign technical assistance. During the 1870s, the number of foreigners in the government's employ frequently exceeded 500 (Umetani 1965). The largest number was found in railroad construction, the biggest and the most expensive enterprise of Kobusho. The practice of within-enterprise training was also adopted. There were both on-the-job type training and the establishment of schools within the enterprises. In each case the purpose was to train Japanese engineers and workers to replace foreign employees, and they were in fact mostly replaced by the end of the 1870s.

The visible achievements of the government enterprises remained rather modest. Barely adequate numbers of lighthouses were built so that coastal navigation became relatively safe, major urban centres were connected by telegraph lines, about 100 kilometres of rail tracks were laid, and a few small steamships built. Some enterprises were far from a technical success and many more were managerial and financial failures due to bureaucratic inefficiency and inexperience.[4] Despite this, the major significance of government enterprises lies in the fact that experiences in modern industrial entrepreneurship had been gained, and certain practices in going about it, e.g. employing foreigners and within-enterprise training, were established.

As pointed out by Smith (1955), it was not the intention of the government to undertake so much; however, despite attempts to induce investment, private capital was still too weak, the technical and managerial difficulties too great and the potential investors at this stage were still too conservative to respond to government inducement. The government did make some attempts to encourage private industrial undertakings. In cotton spinning, for example, the government imported spinning machines and sold them on easy terms together with government loans to potential entrepreneurs. The industry that the government did most to encourage was shipping, for it was the foreign shippers who were profiting from the growth of trade since the opening of the country by dominating coastal shipping. The government wanted to see the growth of strong domestic competitors. The 1869 decree permitting private possession of western ships had failed to produce an adequate response, and the shipping enterprise of Iwasaki Yataro set up in 1870, which later became the Mitsubishi firm, was about the only noticeable undertaking. The government turned to direct subsidies in the form of giving up government-owned ships, grants for navigation and training for officers. The government was generous on this, being in need of shipping because of warrior rebellions and the Taiwan Expedition of 1874. As the largest shipping firm, Mitsubishi benefited well from the subsidies and the firm succeeded in competing out foreign shippers from Japanese coasts.

In the 1880s, many of the government enterprises were sold to private entrepreneurs. The major reason for the sale was to relieve the worsening financial state of the government under the deflationary policy adopted in 1881. Also by this time, buyers could be found. The government was also anxious to let private initiative take over, and the enterprises were sold for much less than the government had originally invested. It was at this time that Nagasaki Shipyard was sold to Mitsubishi. The sales marked the beginning of industrialization under private initiative which coincided with the start of substantial industrial growth.

GROWTH, STRUCTURAL CHANGE AND INDUSTRIAL POLICIES, 1884–1934

Industrial growth and structural change

Statistics indicate that from the 1880s modern economic growth as defined by Kuznets (1966) started in Japan. Per capita product showed sustained growth and population increased; also, rapid shifts in industrial structure took place. During the period 1889 to 1938, per capita gross national expenditure grew at an average rate of 2 per cent and the population at 1 per cent. The structure of production shifted from a predominantly agricultural one to one in which the share of manufacturing exceeded agriculture, which was reflected also in the shift in percentage share of gainfully occupied population. In 1885, 80 per cent was in the primary sector and 7 per cent in the secondary; by 1935, the respective percentages were 47 per cent and 20 per cent. Fastest growth took place in the secondary sector. Between 1889 and 1938, the average growth of the primary sector was 1.3 per cent, whereas the secondary sector grew at 6.3 per cent (mining and manufacturing: 6.25 per cent, construction: 5.36 per cent, facilitating industry: 7.8 per cent) and the tertiary sector at 2.6 per cent (Minami 1981, Ohkawa 1957).

Within the secondary sector, facilitating industry's (transportation, communication, public utilities) growth was the largest at an average of 7.8 per cent. This was due to the rapid growth of railroads, electric power and shipping during the period. Railroads extended from a mere 29 kilometres in 1872 to 6,480 km in 1900 and 27,289 km in 1940. Electric power generation grew rapidly after the first hydraulic power station was built in 1892; from 25,000 kW in 1903 to 7,881,000 kW in 1940 (Arisawa 1959, Minami 1981).[5] Total tonnage of ships owned by shippers in Japan increased by more than fifty times between 1884 and 1934. With the rise in tonnage, domestic shipping companies increasingly took over the handling of foreign trade. In 1890, they carried only 10 per cent of imports and exports; by 1925, the percentage had risen to 70 per cent. This increase was considerable, for during the same period exports increased nearly fifty times and imports thirty (Ando 1975).

Less in growth rate, but in terms of relative contribution to real GDP growth, the growth of mining and manufacturing was larger, and the contribution of this subsector alone was larger than that of the primary or tertiary sector.[6] During the half century from the mid-1880s, there was a structural shift from the dominance of light industries to that of heavy and chemical industries. In terms of the relative contribution of each industry to overall growth of the manufacturing sector, light industries accounted for 75 per cent of the growth in the period up to 1990. After 1920, heavy industries accounted for 60 per cent (Minami 1981). Therefore, it was in the light industries that rapid growth first occurred, especially in textiles, as in the case of England.

Helped by the diffusion of mechanization in the 1870s, silk grew steadily as an export product. In cotton spinning, mechanization diffused less easily,[7] but the industry started to grow rapidly after relatively large cotton mills were set up with government loans in the 1880s. The introduction of all-night operations made possible by the newly adopted facility of electric lighting spurred its growth.[8] In 1891 domestic production exceeded imports, and in 1897 exports overtook imports. During the first thirty years of this century, textiles accounted for over half of Japan's commodity exports (*Oriental Economist* 1934).

In contrast to light industries, heavy industries took time to take off, mainly because of the lack of capital and technological expertise. Take, for example, the case of iron and steel. The Meiji government enterprise in operating a blast furnace at Kamaishi with the aid of British engineers and machines was both a technological and managerial failure resulting in the closure of the works in 1883.[9] The sudden rise in demand for iron and steel after the Sino-Japanese War again prompted the government to set up a mill. In 1896, the Imperial Diet adopted legislation for the construction of the government-owned Yawata Mill. This mill, which started operation in 1901, imported machinery from abroad and employed foreign engineers, mainly from Germany. Again technical difficulties arose and it was Noro Kageyoshi, engineering professor at Tokyo University, and his team of Japanese engineers who solved them,[10] and by the time of the Russo-Japanese War, the mill was operating well. Several private mills were also set up during the first decade of the century. Iron and steel production started to grow slowly but steadily.

The machinery industry developed even more slowly. For a long time government ordnance factories and naval yards and the few large private shipyards such as Mitsubishi Nagasaki were about the only significant machinery manufacturers. They, too, were mostly dependent on imports, but did make some necessary machines and machine tools. In addition, large shipyards built machines for other industries such as mining machines and rail steam engines. Even the production of those machines that had a rapidly growing demand, such as textile machinery, did not develop easily. The situation was worse with machine tool industry, for which the government did little to induce development. The cutting of imports during the first world war finally gave a stimulus to the industry and numerous machine tool makers sprang up. They eventually supplied half of the domestic demand.

The first world war had a tremendous impact on heavy industrial development in Japan. Not only machinery but also other industries, thus far dependent on imports, suddenly expanded. Also the severed access to foreign technology brought about the awareness of the importance of research for industrial application, and research institutes were founded. Adoption of industrial standards started. As a consequence, although production stagnated after the war, technological advances continued, especially in mechanical engineering (Nippon Kagagushi Gakkai 1966). The effect of post-war recession during the 1920s was equally serious. Japan was again inundated with imports. The government tried to implement measures to promote domestic production, but with limited success, and many large manufacturing firms underwent drastic rationalization during the decade. However, in the attempt to survive in the severe competitive environment, considerable technological improvements were seen. Also, despite recession, certain industries experienced rapid expansion, notably the electrical and chemical industries, owing to the diffusion of hydro-electric power generation. The country attempted to recover from recession in the first half of the 1930s by abandoning the gold standard and increasing government expenditure and exports, which for a while increased production, employment and investment in the manufacturing sector. When the creation of the bloc economy system lessened the effects of these measures, direct economic controls were instituted in the second half of the decade. By this time heavy and chemical industries accounted for over 50 per cent of manufacturing production.

The modern economic growth and industrial development in Japan during the half century in question could not have taken place without the simultaneous growth of agriculture and traditional industries which provided sources of capital and labour, since there were no significant capital imports. Agricultural production grew rapidly in the second half of the nineteenth century due to increased use of fertilizers and improvements in irrigation methods. The surplus was channelled into developing modern industries through the Meiji land tax system. Traditional industries such as tea and silk which grew rapidly as export industries provided a source of foreign exchange needed for necessary imports of the modern industries. Accelerated growth of the traditional sector continued until the first decade of this century. By this time modern industries had developed well enough to grow rapidly in turn (Ohkawa and Rosovsky 1965).

Industrial policies

Conscious policy making played an important role in bringing about the growth and structural change that took place after the 1880s. As a result of the sale of government enterprises in the first half of the 1880s, administrative machinery was shuffled by extracting those responsibilities relating to agriculture, commerce, mining and manufacturing in the existing ministries to create Noshomusho (Ministry of Agriculture and Commerce) which effectively became the policy making body for industrialization.[11] Although the overall goals of import substitution and export promotion were still pursued, in the first comprehensive policy statement, the voluminous *Kogyo Iken* (*Opinion on the Promotion of Industries*) of 1884, Noshomusho placed a definite priority on the development of agriculture, traditional manufacturing and light industries, in effect following the policy line adopted by Naimusho (Ministry of Interior) in the 1870s. Legislation on industrial property, industrial standards, factory regulation and worker protection; the establishment of industrial testing (research) institutes and agricultural experimental stations; and the holding of industrial exhibitions and competitions were also recommended (Maeda 1884).

These policies took shape in the recommendations made by the industrial and economic conferences, research councils and committees of Noshomusho from 1896. The first one (1896–98), while identifying industrialization and expansion of trade as major goals, stressed the importance of improving traditional manufacturing by creating experimental stations and promoting tea and silk exports. Although heavy and chemical industries were not stressed, included was the recommendation to incorporate foreign capital. This was a significant shift from the former policy of shutting out foreign capital investments, and had the effect of stimulating some sectors of heavy and chemical industries. The second one, Productivity Research Council (1910–13), clearly stressed the encouragement of heavy and chemical industries, promoting industrial education and taking legislative measures for improving factory environments. The two subsequent ones held during and immediately after the first world war turned their attention to the immediate and direct stimulation of heavy and chemical industries along with the promotion of industrial research and legislation on industrial standards. The three conferences and committees held during the 1920s recommended import substitution of heavy and chemical products by subsidies, tariff protection and other tax measures, as well as emphasizing the importance of industrial research and innovation which tended to stagnate during the years of recession (Tsushosangyosho 1979). Thus, in terms of basic policy line there occurred a definite shift from the encouragement of traditional and light industries to that of heavy and chemical industries after the Sino-Japanese War. In terms of trade, this implied a shift in emphasis from export promotion of traditional and light industrial products to the import substitution of heavy and chemical industrial products, a trend facilitated by the regaining of tariff autonomy in 1911 and spurred by import cuts during the first world war.

The recommendations of Noshomusho councils were enacted by the Imperial Diet. Until the end of the Sino-Japanese War, the government concentrated its efforts on creating experimental stations for improving agriculture and sericulture. For the rapidly growing cotton industry, the policy responses were the abolishment of excise tax on cotton yarn exports in 1894 and tariffs on raw cotton imports in 1896. The heavy industries first subject to government policy were iron and steel, and shipbuilding. The legislation for the establishment of the government-run Yawata Steel Mill was passed in 1896; in the same year, laws for the encouragement of shipping and shipbuilding by subsidizing the purchase or construction of large size vessels were passed. For iron and steel, the government extended protection to private enterprises by tax reductions during the first world war. Rationalization and raising of tariffs were implemented during the recession in the 1920s. The shipbuilding encouragement law was abolished in 1917 because of the war boom, but during the 1920s, the government adopted other measures to aid the industry in recession.

In spite of the policy shift to encourage heavy and chemical industries, some industries were not subject to direct stimulation policy for a long time, such as machinery. Although the Productivity Research Council of 1910–13 did explicitly make a recommendation for the encouragement of the machinery industry, no measure was taken during the demand boost caused by the first world war. The machinery industry, especially machine tools, consequently grew only slowly. The first significant attention given by the government was Noshomusho's exhibition of machine tools in 1921, which among other things made clear the basic problem of the lack of uniform standards. In cooperation with the Japan Society of Mechanical Engineering, the government proceeded to study and establish industrial standards. The legislative measure for the direct promotion of machine tools was only taken in 1938.

Long-range indirect measures also played an important role in industrial development. These included measures for importing technology, diffusion of education, encouragement of innovation and internal diffusion of technology, adoption of industrial standards and promoting research activities. These are discussed in the chapters to follow.

DEVELOPMENT OF THE SHIPBUILDING INDUSTRY

Early developments

Under the Tokugawa isolationist policy, the construction of ocean-going ships was banned until 1853. Because of this the traditional shipbuilding technology was suitable only for building small wooden sailing-boats for coastal navigation. Therefore, building large ships required adopting western shipbuilding technology. The absorption process was difficult and slow because of the great difference in the nature of the technology;

however, because the traditional shipbuilding technology was fairly sophisticated, the traditional artisans could play an active role in assimilating new and different techniques. The very early attempts at modern shipbuilding in the 1850s were haphazard trials based on 'sight' and 'book' learning through *rangaku*. A few wooden barques were built from 'seeing' western ships or by translating Dutch books, but with less than satisfactory results. The first opportunity for more direct and systematic learning was provided when, in 1854, a visiting Russian frigate was shipwrecked, and the Russians asked to have a replacement built. *Bakufu* eagerly seized the opportunity to send officials, carpenters and blacksmiths to assist and learn modern shipbuilding technology. The value of direct learning from foreigners was experienced. *Bakufu* eventually built ten other boats of the type built for the Russians.

Direct learning of shipbuilding technology was a part of the *bakufu*'s naval training programme at Nagasaki which operated from 1855 to 1859 with Dutch instructors. Using the facilities of Nagasaki Iron Works, a small steamer was successfully built in 1857 under their supervision. The fruit of 'learning' through *bakufu* programmes was the building without foreign assistance of the steam gunboat *Chiyoda-gata*, successfully completed in 1866 under the supervision of those trained at Nagasaki Naval School and those who took part in the building of a Russian frigate (Teratani 1979). Confidence gained from this project led *bakufu* to build a large shipyard and iron works at Yokosuka with the aid of French naval engineers. Part of its operation started in 1867, including a training school for engineers, technicians and workers. Thus, the significance of the experiences in modern shipbuilding between 1853 and 1868 is not in what was actually accomplished, but rather in the adoption of methods of importing and assimilating foreign technology: employing foreigners, sending students abroad and establishing within-enterprise training programmes.

The Meiji government took over *bakufu* and *han* facilities at Nagasaki, Hyogo, Yokosuka and Ishikawajima as government enterprises. Yokosuka became a naval yard under the Ministry of the Navy in 1872. Nagasaki came under Kobusho which attempted to start construction of iron ships with iron expected to be produced at the Kamaishi furnace. The failure of the latter cut short this ambition, and the yard occupied itself with mastering the building of wooden steamers. The enterprise proved to be a managerial failure, and the shipyard was leased out to Mitsubishi in 1884, and subsequently sold to it in 1887. Hyogo and Ishikawajima were likewise sold.

Growth and technological development

During the half century from the 1880s, the shipbuilding industry grew as indicated in the increase in the tonnage of ships constructed (Table 2.1). This growth was neither steady nor easy, for the industry was sensitive to economic ups and downs since the shipping industry was easily affected by it. Moreover, large shipbuilding firms faced severe foreign competition in terms of quality and cost. They had to catch up and keep up with foreign technological advances to construct ships of similar performance, which implied having to invest heavily in imports of technology. The shipbuilders also had to import or supply internally most materials and machinery which resulted in higher costs of capital inputs. This situation lasted for a long time because of the slow growth of iron and steel and machinery industries. Until 1931, because of this and despite lower wage levels, the cost of new ships was always higher in Japan than in Britain (Kaneko 1964). Given these odds, in order to survive it was imperative that shipyards raised their productive efficiency

Table 2.1 Commercial ships constructed in Japan

	Number	*Tonnage (Gt)*
1870–74	20	346
1875–79	82	2,833
1880–84	147	11,916
1885–89	105	9,062
1890–94	154	16,896
1895–99	249	48,835
1900–4	370	124,577
1905–9	417	214,003
1910–14	575	236,270
1915–19	1,201	1,678,734
1920–24	744	992,348
1925–29	522	344,456
1930–34	524	557,940

1870–1930: all steamships
1934: all steel ships
Source: Bank of Japan 1966

and filled the technological gap in every way possible. They also had to diversify their activities, e.g. do repair works, and build machinery and structures other than ships, because building new ships was neither a very profitable nor a stable business. This resulted in the complexity and versatility that characterized the large shipyards in pre-war Japan.

For a decade after the sale of major government yards, shipbuilding as an industry stagnated; however, technologically, these major yards turned from wooden shipbuilding to iron, then to steel during this short period. In the meantime, the shipping industry kept expanding with ships purchased abroad due to the growing amount of trade. In addition to Nippon Yusen Kaisha (NYK), founded in 1885, Osaka Shosen Kaisha (OSK) and Toyo Kisen Kaisha (TKK) along with numerous small shippers were set up by 1896. In response to this expansion of shipping, which was given added stimulus by the Sino-Japanese War (1894–95), the government took action to promote the domestic shipbuilding industry by adopting the shipbuilding encouragement law in 1896 to subsidize the construction of iron or steel ships of over 700Gt and their engines.[12] This law made possible the construction of large ships which thus far had been impossible.[13] By 1910 more than 30 per cent of ships of more than 1,000Gt in the possession of Japanese shippers were built in Japan. This figure rose to more than 90 per cent during the first world war, and the law was then abolished (Kaneko 1964, Bank of Japan 1966). However, not all the shipyards benefited from this law. Although there were more than 150 shipyards by the turn of the century, only twelve constructed ships that actually received subsidies under this law. Three of these, Mitsubishi, Kawasaki and Osaka Iron Works, accounted for nearly 90 per cent of the total tonnage subsidized, and Mitsubishi alone accounted for nearly 40 per cent (Zosen Kyokai 1973b). Therefore, the government policy in effect selectively protected a few large firms which in turn were responsible for both quantitative and qualitative development of the industry.

The evolution from wooden to iron to steel shipbuilding having already taken place by the mid-1890s,[14] now the technological challenge was to build increasingly larger vessels and more powerful engines. The largest commercial ship built by the start of the Russo-Japanese War in 1904 was 7,460Gt, the greatest power 6,700hp and the speed 17 knots. Size and speed continued to increase. Marine engineering technology advanced by importing foreign technology through licensing agreements. Turbines, auxiliary machinery and boilers could now be manufactured. These 'best practice' technologies underwent further improvements in Japanese shipyards.

In the first decade of the century, the industry experienced a boom and a depression resulting from the Russo-Japanese War. The government tried to ease the effects of recession by having large shipyards undertake an increasing amount of naval construction. Far more serious was the effect of the first world war and its post-war recession. The industry underwent a drastic expansion and a contraction in less than a decade.[15] The war caused a sudden boost in demand for ships because of the elimination of foreign competition in both shipping and shipbuilding. The renewed competition after the war in the face of greatly expanded capacity put the industry in a crisis. This was aggravated by the reduction of naval orders following the Washington arms reduction agreement of 1922. The recession dragged well into the 1930s, with only a slight improvement in the late 1920s. Shipyards responded by contracting over-expanded capacity by rationalizing and by devoting a major part of their operations to manufacturing land machinery. Also, an effort was made to further technological improvements.

It is worth noting that recession stimulated rather than depressed technological developments. There was now an incentive to construct ships and engines of better performance at lower cost. The increase in the size of vessels had already reached a limit before the war, but the performance of engines kept improving. Reciprocated engines could produce power exceeding 10,000hp by the mid-1920s. Turbines improved in fuel economy, and power was increased by the adoption of gears and combined impulse-reaction turbines. All-impulse turbines also started to be built, especially as generators. In the 1920s diesel engines for the reason of fuel economy came to be increasingly adopted, and improvements were effected on imported diesel engine technologies. The use of electric welding was given a spur by the need to reduce the weight of naval vessels following the Washington treaty. Model tests came to be more widely used to reduce resistance and increase speed. Rationalization improved construction procedures, reduced the number of workers and lowered production costs. Domestic manufacturing of auxiliary machinery and parts, which had started during the war, continued to be encouraged.

The government effected measures to aid the industry during this period. Production of steel for shipbuilding started to be subsidized from 1921. The imposition of tariffs was lifted from steel materials for ships, certain fittings and parts of engines and auxiliary machinery that had to be imported. The government also took measures to aid the shipping industry which indirectly aided shipbuilding. In 1925 the government decided to give subsidies to replace ships in service on certain long-distance commercial lines. Ships for service to North and South America and Europe of NYK and OSK were ordered to be built at large shipyards. The shipping companies decided to adopt diesel engines for these new vessels, which in turn stimulated the development of diesel engine manufacturing capability. In 1932 the government launched a two-year project to subsidize the scrapping of 400,000Gt of old ships and replace them with 200,000Gt of new ones with domestically produced materials and parts. Model tests were made obligatory. This project aided the construction of diesel cargo ships of more than 6,000Gt, with speeds of 14 to 18 knots. Finally, in 1933, imports of ships became subject to permission of the Minister of Communications, which curbed imports considerably. Through these measures Japan became a major shipbuilding nation by the mid-1930s, as seen in Table 2.2.

Table 2.2 Tonnage launched in 1,000Gt – international comparison

	UK	Germany	USA	Japan	Holland	France
1912–13	3,670	840	422	122	203	286
.	.	.	.	.	.	.
.	.	.	.	.	.	.
1921–23	2,914	1,379	1,197	383	461	491
1924–27	4,389	1,105	408	173	355	320
1928–31	4,949	974	602	503	626	367
1932–35	1,279	423	211	426	156	182

Source: Kaneko 1964
Original source: Lloyd's Register 1912–35
(Lloyd's statistics not available or incomplete for 1914–20)

32

The role of the navy

The Japanese navy (IJN) played a significant role in the development of large shipyards like Mitsubishi Nagasaki. Up to the mid-1880s the Meiji government devoted a substantially larger part of its resources to enlarge and elaborate the facilities of the Yokosuka naval yard than its other shipyards. Since the civilian yards did not develop on a notable scale until the shipbuilding encouragement law of 1896, the Yokosuka naval yard was the only yard that could build and repair large ships. In fact, large commercial ships were also built there until they could be built at civilian shipyards. IJN now, in turn, started to place orders for naval construction with private yards which gave them the opportunity to learn from the more technologically sophisticated naval construction.

Table 2.3 Vessels of IJN

	Imports			*Built at IJN yards*			*Built at private yards*		
	Number	Tonnage (Dt)	(%)	Number	Tonnage (Dt)	(%)	Number	Tonnage (Dt)	(%)
1868–83	13	16,446	(75.0)	9	5,495	(25.0)	–	–	–
1884–1903	81	216,049	(87.6)	38	30,035	(12.2)	1	614	(0.2)
1904–21	11	100,593	(13.4)	85	455,326	(61.0)	54	189,569	(25.6)
1922–28	4	22,050	(9.6)	11	58,125	(25.4)	40	118,292	(65.0)

Does not include submarines, transport vessels and miscellaneous small boats.
Source: Zosen Kyokai 1973b

Table 2.3 shows that civilian shipyards accounted for an increasing share of naval construction. When the post Russo-Japanese War recession hit large shipyards, the government adopted the policy of placing naval orders with private yards as a means of aiding them. As a part of this, Mitsubishi and Kawasaki received orders in 1911 to construct sister vessels of the large cruiser *Kongo*, built at Vickers in Barrow-in-Furness. For this the two shipyards were able to send a number of their engineers to Vickers to study as naval inspectors for *Kongo*. During the first world war, IJN requested some yards to build submarines and their engines, and for this purpose the private yards purchased foreign licences. This did much to develop the diesel engine manufacturing capability of the shipyards. Under the naval expansion programme drawn up immediately after the first world war, large orders were given to private yards easing the effects of post-war recession. But most of these were cancelled in 1922 because of the Washington arms reduction agreement. During the 1920s the government adhered to the policy of placing as many naval orders as possible with private yards. In fact, as Table 2.3 indicates, between 1922 and 1928 private yards undertook more naval construction than naval yards. Also, the need to reduce the weight of naval vessels at this time had the effect of furthering electric welding technology. In this manner IJN aided private yards, especially during periods of recession. It should be noted that the naval demand was selective, i.e. as with the shipbuilding encouragement law it benefited a handful of large shipyards. Mitsubishi and Kawasaki accounted for nearly 80 per cent of naval construction in terms of tonnage up to 1928 (Zosen Kyokai 1973a,b).

The within-enterprise training of engineers and workers that started in 1867 in the Yokosuka naval yard served as a model for within-enterprise training programmes of private yards. The practice of sending overseas missions, including workers, to learn new technology, which the navy had adopted from the very beginning, was also adopted by private firms as a channel of technology imports. The navy also served as a source of managerial, engineering and skilled manpower for private shipyards. Many engineer officers went to work for private yards after a career in the navy. There was a migration of workers trained in the naval yards to private yards. With the manpower flow, naval technology diffused to private firms.

DEVELOPMENT OF THE MITSUBISHI NAGASAKI SHIPYARD

Early developments and the Mitsubishi firm

The Mitsubishi shipbuilding enterprise occupied a special place in the industry as one of the few private enterprises responsible for the growth and technological advancement of the Japanese shipbuilding industry in the pre-war period. For these firms the role of government policy was important, but equally significant were the efforts of the firms in raising productive efficiency and making technological advances. The complementarity between the two brought about the development of the large shipyards like the Mitsubishi Nagasaki Shipyard.

Nagasaki Shipyard was the oldest of the *bakufu* shipyards that survived. From its founding to its leasing to Mitsubishi in 1884, the yard was more of a machinery factory for repairing ships than a yard for their building. The original works built by Dutch engineers in 1857 consisted of a foundry shop, a blacksmith shop and a machinery shop. It worked closely with the *bakufu* naval school at Nagasaki. The naval students guided by Dutch teachers did repair works on *bakufu* warships and built small wooden sail cutters as part of naval training. The notable achievement in machinery making was the 60hp engine for *Chiyoda-gata*. The shipyard also made guns, cannons and even agricultural tools at this time.

The Meiji government set out to make Nagasaki a real shipyard when it took over the enterprise from *bakufu*. British and French engineers and workers were employed to assist the operations of the yard and to build a dockyard. The factory facilities were expanded, and the yard built sixteen ships, mostly wooden steamers of 100–300Gt, their steam engines, boilers and propellers. The most notable achievement was the construction of the first wooden steamer of more than 1,000 gross tons in Japan, the 1,416Gt *Kosuga* completed in 1883. Technologically a significant accomplishment, but managerially a disaster, it took more than six years to build and cost double its original budget (Nakanishi 1983). As with many other Kobusho enterprises, the Nagasaki yard suffered from bureaucratic inefficiency and managerial inexperience. The 1881 deflationary policy of the government aggravated the situation, resulting in the decision of its sale.[16]

The Mitsubishi firm originated as a shipping enterprise which Iwasaki Yataro, an ex-official of Tosa *han*, set up in 1870. During the decade the business expanded steadily with the aid of subsidies which the government gave out in order to promote the domestic shipping industry for the purpose of ousting foreign shippers from Japanese coasts. In the early 1880s, some opinions in the government turned critical of its generosity toward Mitsubishi, and a semi-government shipping enterprise was set up to compete with Mitsubishi. The resulting competition became so fierce that the government had to resolve the situation by amalgamating the two to form Nippon Yusen Kaisha (NYK) in 1885. At this time Mitsubishi gave up its interests in shipping entirely to turn to shipbuilding, mining and banking. Mitsubishi already had some experience in ship-building in its repair yard in Yokohama which had been set up jointly with the Boyd firm of Shanghai in 1875.[17] Here, small steamers of several tons were built in addition to repair works. When Mitsubishi gave up its shipping business in 1885, the firm transferred most of the machinery and staff to Nagasaki.

The Nagasaki Shipyard under Mitsubishi

In 1884, Mitsubishi Nagasaki Shipyard was undoubtedly the largest private shipyard and its facilities were second only to the naval yard at Yokosuka.[18] This position was to be maintained for the next half century. Growth and development, however, did not come easily. Being the largest shipyard destined to build large ocean-going vessels made the situation more difficult, since its competitors were the advanced foreign shipbuilders.

The description of business and the figures given for *sagyodaka*, the productive activities and the account balance found in *Nenpo*, the annual report of the shipyard, show that the business was unstable for most of the period under study. The production increased fairly steadily until the post Russo-Japanese war depression which cut the production level for 1910 to less than half that for 1908. Production picked up again from 1911 due to the increase in naval construction as seen in Table 2.5. During the first world war boom, production showed an explosive increase, as well as a drastic decrease during the first half of the 1920s. Notable is the large share that repair works occupied up to 1902 which was as much as 25 to 35 per cent. Building new ships before this time accounted for only about 50 per cent on average. Machinery production accounted for about 10 per cent of the production. The account balance often plunged into the red until 1909 which shows that the shipyard was far from being a stable enterprise until this time. The changes in the number of staff and workers in the yard (Table 2.4) between 1884 and 1934 also indicates the ups and downs of the enterprise.

Up to 1910, the shipbuilding encouragement law of 1896 did not have the effect of increasing the share of building new ships in the total productive activities at the Nagasaki Yard. The amount of subsidies provided by the law was not enough even to cover the cost of transportation and tariffs on the materials

Table 2.4 Employees at Nagasaki Shipyard

	Staff	Workers		Staff	Workers
1884	42	766	1910	619	5,752
1885	?	780	1911	696	7,264
1886	?	781	1912	761	8,017
1887	?	799	1913	827	9,448
1888	?	1,104	1914	902	10,445
1889	?	1,173	1915	937	9,788
1890	?	1,254	1916	1,027	12,685
1891	?	1,576	1917	1,113	14,543
1892	?	1,468	1918	1,294	14,337
1893	?	1,212	1919	1,474	16,798
1894	69	1,450	1920	1,737	16,847
1895	103	1,749	1921	1,829	*18,008
1896	124	2,607	1922	1,690	9,250
1897	136	2,948	1923	1,534	9,250
1898	148	3,517	1924	1,090	*8,954
1899	173	3,232	1925	1,044	6,672
1900	199	4,074	1926	1,215	6,850
1901	234	4,992	1927	1,200	*7,131
1902	269	5,245	1928	1,251	8,516
1903	293	5,416	1929	1,200	8,705
1904	316	5,243	1930	1,207	8,032
1905	348	7,003	1931	1,000	5,197
1906	395	8,946	1932	950	5,177
1907	446	9,695	1933	950	7,038
1908	759	8,081	1934	1,000	9,565
1909	592	5,579	1935	1,100	9,295

Number as of end December of respective years except until 1898 when the figures are of end June of each year.
* Number as of end June of the year.
Source: Nishinippon Jukogyo Kabushiki Kaisha 1951

that had to be imported for the construction of large commercial vessels (Nishinarita 1978). The law, however, had the effect of increasing significantly the tonnage built at Nagasaki, as shown in Table 2.5. Note the tenfold increase between the 1890–94 and 1895–99 periods. The commercial tonnage built continued to increase through the second half of the first decade of the century, but then decreased during the next five-year period. This decrease, however, was well compensated by the increase in naval construction during 1910–15. The government policy of placing more naval orders with civilian yards at times of recession played a significant role for the Nagasaki Yard in protecting it from unfavourable fluctuations in the economy. As the table

Table 2.5 Tonnage built at Nagasaki

| | (1) Commercial vessels (over 100Gt) | | (2) Naval vessels | (3) Naval tonnage converted to commercial | (4) (1) + (3) (%) |
	Number	Tonnage (Gt)	Number	Tonnage (Dt)	equivalent*	
1885–89	2	406	–	–	–	–
1890–94	4	2,184	–	–	–	–
1895–99	10	21,073	2	164	820	3.7
1900–4	23	54,473	1	120	600	1.1
1905–9	19	94,234	6	3,255	16,275	14.7
1910–14	18	91,133	3	6,936	34,680	27.6
1915–19	38	185,124	7	62,657	313,285	62.9
1920–24	22	124,829	13	48,720	243,600	66.1
1925–29	15	87,465	3	24,200	121,000	58.0
1930–34	31	197,820	1	10,000	50,000	19.4

* This is obtained by multiplying by a factor of five.
Source: Nishinippon Jukogyo Kabushiki Kaisha 1951

shows, naval orders also eased the effect of post-first world war depression during the 1920s. Naval construction at this time exceeded commercial construction in terms of tonnage.

The instability of the shipyard as an enterprise until around 1910 was in part caused by the necessity to expand facilities for the building of increasingly larger and more technologically sophisticated ships. Extensive additions and improvements to facilities were carried out for the building of the first steel ship (*Chikugogawa*, completed in 1891), the first super 5,000Gt liner subsidized under the shipbuilding encouragement law (*Hitachi*, completed in 1898), the first super 10,000Gt turbine vessel (*Tenyo*, completed in 1908) and the first heavy cruiser for IJN (*Kirishima*, completed in 1915). The annual sum spent on expanding and improving facilities shown in Table 2.6 reflects this. The large investments for the years 1906–7 and 1912 were for the building of *Tenyo* and *Kirishima* respectively. An unusually large sum was also invested in 1921 when the warship *Tosa* was being built as part of the post-first world war naval expansion programme. However, because of the Washington arms reduction agreement, the warship was destroyed before completion. The table indicates that investments in machines and tools accounted for a very large part of the total sum spent. This was in part because most machinery had to be imported.

Table 2.6 Investments in physical facilities in 1,000 yen

	Docks, berths slipways	Machines, tools	Railroads, cranes buoys	Buildings	Land, roads	Vessels	Others	Total
1887	325	54	–	64	16	–	–	459*
1887–98	226	681	–	339	156	18	8	1,420
1899	–	54	–	16	8	1	9	88
1900	–	149	–	100	264	–	49	562
1901	9	363	–	101	90	1	12	576
1902	1	633	–	256	24	198	45	1,157
1903	–	349	6	163	12	12	34	576
1904	–	349	5	132	27	19	3	533
1905	235	339	4	19	165	–	26	788
1906	956	170	3	130	7	48	11	1,325
1907	63	834	19	442	195	5	14	1,572
1908	26	644	2	368	64	–	47	1,151
1909	–	90	1	77	19	–	12	199
1910	–	58	286	5	–	–	2	351
1911	–	535	0	97	84	–	3	719
1912	54	865	508	500	417	27	10	2,381
1913	66	448	197	70	264	0	9	1,054
1914	59	720	8	88	86	0	9	970
1915	22	238	42	36	101	78	10	527
1916	53	484	–	334	128	–	8	1,007
1917	–	633	–	196	102	98	12	1,041
1918	26	1,567	24	574	673	174	48	3,086
1919	–	1,744	157	171	60	10	16	2,158
1920	–	2,116	34	738	–	177	8	3,073
1921	143	4,280	73	1,625	258	10	0	6,389
1922	–	1,242	458	515	30	78	7	2,330
1923	–	421	–	203	69	–	0	693
1924	1	244	5	136	42	–	14	442
1925	3	164	1	52	44	6	29	299

* This was the sale price of the shipyard.
Source: Nenpo 1898–1925

Also, large sums had to be devoted to expanding the machinery factory. Of the two major factories of the shipyard, machinery and hull, the former claimed a much larger share of the sum used for expansion and improvement (Nishinarita 1978). The need to import or make most machines within the shipyard required a high cost of capital investment.

Having to keep up with the advancing shipbuilding technology also implied the need to invest significantly in adding and improving facilities. Since the major cause of the cost disadvantage of the large vessels built at Nagasaki lay in the inability to supply materials and machines domestically, it was imperative that the ships built be qualitatively competitive. As vessels became larger and more sophisticated, docks, berths and slipways had to be enlarged to accommodate them. Quality considerations implied the necessity not only of improving the physical facilities, but also of choosing, importing and absorbing new technologies in as efficient a manner as possible. Nagasaki Shipyard imported technology through various channels suited to the current technological level of the yard. By so doing, the shipyard filled the technological gap and kept up with foreign technological advances.

As the largest private shipyard in Japan, Nagasaki was often the technological pioneer in the industry. The major technological events are summarized in Table 2.7. The building of *Hitachi*, the first large vessel built under the 1896 encouragement law, was such an extremely difficult challenge that the experience is a famous episode in the history of the shipyard. Despite subsidies, expenses for building (including the improvement of facilities, importing of materials and working plans and the employment of a British consultant naval architect) far exceeded the sale revenue. In the end the shipyard had

Table 2.7 Technological milestones at Mitsubishi Nagasaki Shipyard

1891	Chikugogawa	610Gt, first steel ship built in Japan
1898	Hitachi	6,172Gt, first ship of over 5,000Gt
1908	Tenyo	13,454Gt, first turbine ship built in Japan
1909	Sakura	3,205Gt, with first Mitsubishi-built turbines
1913	Anyo	9,534Gt, first geared turbine ship in Japan
1915	Kirishima	27,500Dt, first large naval vessel built
1920	Suwa	421Dt, first all-welded ship in Japan
	Sawakaze	1,345Gt, with first Mitsubishi impulse-reaction turbines
1922	Hakone	10,423Gt, first double reduction geared turbine ship
1924	Tsugaru	3,432Gt, with first Mitsubishi all-impulse turbines
1925	Santos	7,267Gt, first diesel ship fitted with Sulzer-made diesels
1926	Montevideo	7,267Gt, with first Mitsubishi-made Sulzer diesels
1929	Ural	6,377Gt, with first Mitsubishi-built Zölly turbines
1933	Nankai	8,416Gt, with first MS diesels
1934	Engines for Kano	first Mitsubishi-built Sulzer double acting diesels
1936	Akagi	7387Gt, with first MSD (double acting) diesels

Source: Mitsubishi Nagasaki Zosensho 1957

to bring a surveyor at its own expense from Britain because the Lloyd's surveyor stationed in Japan did not approve of the riveting even after a second trial. Ten years later, the building of *Tenyo*, double the tonnage of *Hitachi*, is not recounted as being such a difficult experience; hence, a considerable accumulation of technological capabilities must have taken place through the building of *Hitachi*. Nagasaki also kept up well with advances in shipbuilding and marine engineering through technology imports. Technology for various types of marine and land turbines, diesel engines, boilers, stabilizer and auxiliary machinery as well as electric welding was imported very soon after these technologies had been commercialized.

Improvement of productive efficiency was important in compensating for the high cost of building new vessels. Until about 1910, firm policy stressed quality considerations rather than efficiency,[19] but gradually means were introduced to raise efficiency. In 1908, the cost accounting system was adopted. This defined production procedures and the method of recording accounts which in turn clarified the cost of each step of production and made possible the elimination of unnecessary or undesirable costs. During the 1910s, factory operations were made more efficient by mechanization of such operations as drilling, riveting and caulking by the adoption of pneumatic compressors. Gas cutting and electric welding started to be used. Operational rationalization was pursued through the 1920s when, for instance, in the hull factory, more parts of the hull came to be assembled in the factory, and the transportation of materials in the factory was made easier and more rapid by the use of cranes and hoists (Mimura in *Kaikyuroku 2*). Similar improvements were effected in the machinery factory (Fukao 1979). According to Odaka (1984), between 1900 and 1930, the average labour productivity of the shipyard increased steadily. Between 1915 and 1920, this increase was especially rapid.[20]

The shipyard also instituted various programmes to train its workers, technicians and engineers.[21] Notable was the founding of Mitsubishi Kogyo Gakko, the industrial school, in 1899. The shipyard did not content itself with just importing new technologies, but always tried to improve them. In doing so, the research laboratory at Nagasaki played a significant role by making important contributions in improving turbine and diesel engine and electric welding technologies.

After 1917, when Mitsubishi Zosen Kabushiki Kaisha (MZKK, Mitsubishi Shipbuilding Company) was set up,[22] the firm became more technology conscious, in part because of the difficulty of importing technology during the first world war. The Mitsubishi Shipbuilding Research Institute was founded in 1918. Firm-level technological research committees on various topics started to be organized. Equipped with these, the firm continued to place importance on improving technology despite the recession of the 1920s and 1930s. Notable was the successful development of the MS diesel engine in 1932. The firm also diversified its productive activities to build more land machinery and other products especially turbine generators and even steel furniture. In 1934 the firm amalgamated with Mitsubishi Aircraft Company to become Mitsubishi Jukogyo Kabushiki Kaisha (Mitsubishi Heavy Industries Ltd).

3

TECHNOLOGY IMPORTS AT MITSUBISHI NAGASAKI SHIPYARD

EARLY NATIONAL STRATEGIES IN TECHNOLOGY IMPORTS

Employment of foreigners

The most frequently used mode of importing technology in the early stages of modernization was the employment of foreigners. In shipbuilding this has been adopted since the 1850s. The effectiveness of this method was demonstrated when *bakufu* officials and workers were able to learn a good deal about shipbuilding when helping Russians build a replacement for a shipwrecked frigate in 1854. On this occasion the Russians taught the basics of shipbuilding to the *bakufu* officials and workers and left behind all working plans and tools after a wooden sail schooner had been completed. This experience was behind the decision to employ a number of Dutch naval engineers and workers for the *bakufu* Nagasaki Naval School in 1855. Foreigners were also employed for building, training and operations at the Yokosuka naval yard. Here, a total of twenty-five French engineers and workers were employed from 1865 through to the 1870s.

By the time the Meiji government took over *bakufu* enterprises, employment of foreigners was a well-established practice. The new government utilized this mode of technology importing extensively, especially in the 1870s. The studies that have been done on the foreign employees of the Meiji government (Umetani 1965, Jones 1980) show that during the 1870s the total number employed in any one year was in the order of several hundred. The number starts to decrease drastically from 1880 and by 1900 fewer than 100 remained. The largest number

43

employed during the 1870s were engineers and workers for Kobusho enterprises. Those that remained until the turn of the century were those on the university teaching staff.

The fact that the largest number of employees were involved in Kobusho enterprises indicates that the Meiji government intended them as agents of technology transfer, as, indeed, they were. In every enterprise of Kobusho, foreign engineers planned, surveyed and directly took part in the construction of railroads, telegraph lines and lighthouses. They were also held responsible for training their Japanese counterparts, which was as important as the actual construction works. Training was done both on the job and in schools set up within the enterprises. Kobusho also ran a college for educating prospective engineers in civil, mechanical and electrical engineering as well as mining. This Kobu Daigakko, the Imperial College of Engineering, had an all-British specialist teaching staff. Some in this team later became prominent scientists and engineers in their fields.

It was in part due to the appearance of trained Japanese engineers and workers that the number of foreign employees rapidly decreased from the second half of the 1870s. The major reason, however, was the deflationary policy adopted in the beginning of the 1880s. Also, the high salaries of foreigners imposed a substantial financial burden of which the government was anxious to dispose.[1] The high salaries are indicative of the high expectations placed on foreign employees as agents of technology transfer.

Foreigners were also employed in the private sector, mostly as teachers and engineers. Their function here was also to bring about knowledge and technical expertise. In contrast to government employees, the number of privately employed teachers and engineers continued to increase until 1890. After this, the number levelled off rather than decreased (Umetani 1965). This indicates that for the private sector foreigners played an important role for a much longer period than for the government.

Overseas missions

Another mode of importing technology adopted from the early days of industrialization was the gathering of foreign

44

technological knowledge by sending missions abroad. In ship-building, *bakufu* sent naval officials who were formerly students of Nagasaki Naval School and workers specifically for the purpose of studying shipbuilding technology in 1862.[2] These men later played a major role in the establishment of the Japanese navy. *Bakufu* sent several missions to Europe and America in the 1860s. These were mainly for diplomatic negotia-tions to have the 'unequal' commercial treaties revised, but included in each mission were a few whose task was to survey western science, technology (mainly military), medicine or literary and social sciences. Some *han* also sent students abroad to study. The number of these missions increased after *bakufu* abolished the ban on overseas travel in 1866.

After 1868, the Meiji government started to send students and officials abroad more systematically and on a larger scale. The Ministry of Education launched a programme to sponsor academic studies abroad. Between 1875 and 1912, nearly 1,000 students were sent abroad under this programme, two-thirds of whom studied science, engineering or medicine (Watanabe 1977). They were obliged to work for the government upon their return, or repay expenses. Most of them took up university teaching or research posts. Other ministries also had indepen-dent programmes for sending their officials for academic studies. Naval officers were sent as students, mostly to Britain, to study naval science and engineering. Government officials were sent abroad to survey specific matters, e.g. postal systems, public health and other public service systems, laws and specific industries. Missions were always sent to the frequent interna-tional exhibitions held in Europe and America, which presented excellent opportunities to gather information on new techno-logical developments and to publicize industrial products Japan could export.[3] During the 1870s, more students were sent for academic studies than for official missions; from 1880 to 1895, more than ten times as many were sent on official missions than for academic studies. Both the employment of foreigners and sending students and officials abroad required substantial finan-cial commitments on the part of the Meiji government. Between 1868 and 1877, the government spent 4.3 per cent of its total expenditure on them and between 1878 and 1892, 1.4 per cent. There were also those who went abroad on private funds. Although statistics are not available, their number continued to increase after the number sent by the government started to decrease (Emi 1963).

Other modes of technology imports

Employment of foreigners and sending missions entailed imports of machinery. Foreign engineers and workers as well as those sent abroad brought with them machines and tools. Numerous machines were brought from Holland together with engineers and workers when the Nagasaki Iron Works was set up. Imports of machines became a standard practice in starting industrial enterprises in both the government and private sectors. This persisted even after the practice of employing foreigners had been largely discarded. Importing machinery itself had become an independent means of incorporating foreign technology. The main reason for this continued reliance was the slow growth of the domestic machinery industry. The industrial sector was for a long time heavily dependent on imports for the supply of machinery. Domestic machinery production could supply only less than 10 per cent of the demand until 1910. During the first world war, the percentage rose to about 45 per cent because of the difficulty of imports from Europe. The share again dropped to about 25 per cent during the 1920s, but finally rose to over 50 per cent after 1930 (Ohkawa and Shinohara 1979).

Learning through books and other printed information was also an important channel of importing technology. Foreign employees, especially teachers, brought and used foreign technical books to teach. Those sent abroad also brought back books and journals. Periodicals of professional societies devoted a substantial number of pages to abstracts of books and articles published abroad. Industrial engineers gathered quite a bit of information on new foreign technical developments from books and professional journals.

Because the Meiji government was reluctant to let foreign capital flow into Japan in the early stages of industrialization, modes of importing technology until around the turn of the century were limited to the indirect modes discussed so far. The government policy line, however, changed when the high conference of Noshomusho, held in 1898, recommended the inflow of foreign capital. The adoption of the gold standard in

1897, following the receipt of indemnity from China as a result of the Sino-Japanese War, facilitated this move. As part of this policy shift, the Japan Industrial Bank was founded in 1902. In the heavy industrial sector, joint stock enterprises with foreign firms were set up in electrical machinery and ordnance. Foreign technology accompanied capital in these enterprises. In some other industries, notably shipbuilding, foreign capital did not come in, but technology imports in the form of licensing agreements started at this time.

TECHNOLOGY IMPORTS AT NAGASAKI SHIPYARD

Employment of foreigners

As a government enterprise, operations of the Nagasaki Shipyard were entirely dependent on foreign engineers and workers. Mainly Dutch during the *bakufu* days, and British and French under the Meiji government, they have always been present since the founding of the shipyard. All of them, however, were discharged before the shipyard came under the Mitsubishi management in 1884. The new management still needed to employ foreigners. The Mitsubishi Engine Works in Yokohama had several foreigners in their employ. These five men, one American and four British, were transferred to the Nagasaki Yard in 1884. In addition, Mitsubishi had recruited six others by the time the yard was in the firm's ownership in 1887 (Figure 3.1).

The foreigners held key jobs in the shipyard. According to Shiota Taisuke,[4] who came to Nagasaki in 1890, although the manager of the yard was a Japanese, foreigners had the real power over technical affairs of the yard. There was a British manager in charge of shops and the dockyard, an American accountant in charge of purchases, a boiler maker, rigger, engineer, outside engineer and a moulder who were held responsible for all the work of their respective specialities. Japanese engineers, even those trained at polytechnics, were placed under these foreigners who had formerly been seamen or workers (Shiota 1938).

This arrangement, however, did not last long, for the firm soon adopted the policy of placing university trained Japanese engineers in responsible positions. Shiota Taisuke, a

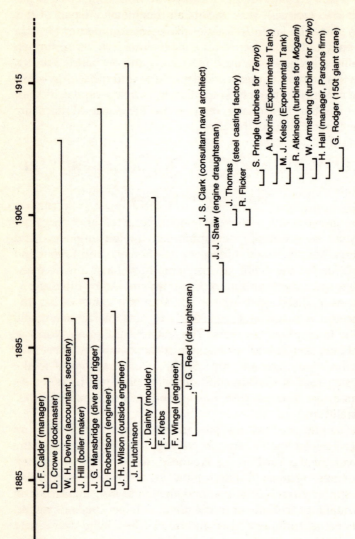

Figure 3.1 Foreign employees at Nagasaki Shipyard
Source: Mitsubishi Nagasaki Zosensho 1928

naval architecture graduate of Tokyo Imperial University, was recruited to replace J. Hutchinson, a draughtsman. Seven of the eleven foreigners recruited before 1887 left the shipyard by 1900. This policy of replacing foreigners was in line with that of Kobusho enterprises in the 1870s, and, as with Kobusho, the desire to achieve technological self-reliance and the high salaries of the foreign employees were the main motives. There was clearly another reason. According to Tadokoro Motoki, an engineer recruited in 1896, the foreigners were ungenerous in sharing their knowledge, and the essential construction works were done secretively (Tadokoro in *Kaikyuroku*). It was therefore difficult to expect an amicable, cooperative relationship between foreigners and the Japanese employees. Shiota always argued against employing foreigners or extending their contracts (Shiota 1938).

Despite the policy of replacing foreigners, the need for them did not disappear easily. They were still being recruited even after 1890, but the terms of their employment changed. They were now recruited for shorter periods and for specific purposes. J. Reed, recruited in 1888 as draughtsman for the first steel ships with the first triple expansion engines to be built in Japan, was employed for three years strictly for the above purpose. J. S. Clark, the consultant naval architect for *Hitachi*, was only reluctantly recruited, also for a three-year term, according to Shiota, to reassure NYK which was apprehensive about having Nagasaki build a large ship of which the shipyard thus far had no experience.[5]

The length and the purposes of employment of foreigners changed during the twenty-five years the shipyard was dependent on them. As seen clearly in Figure 3.1, the length of employment shortened drastically. The purpose of employing them shifted from fulfilling general needs of the shipyard, like boiler making, to doing very specific tasks, e.g. assembling the first Parsons' turbines to be imported or installing the Experimental Tank. An implication of this change is that the Japanese employees had, in the meantime, accumulated adequate capabilities to fill the jobs of the foreigners. In 1891, when the question of renewing Reed's contract came up, Shiota maintained that he and his colleagues could take over the job and Reed's contract was not renewed (Shiota 1938). From then on, foreigners were recruited for short periods to introduce new technologies.

Not much is known about the foreigners employed at Nagasaki. All except two who held non-technical positions were British, and most of the technical staff were formerly workers or sailors. Those who were transferred from the Mitsubishi Engine Works in Yokohama were probably recruited by Boyd, Mitsubishi's partner between 1875 and 1879 in this works, since the agreement between Mitsubishi and Boyd stipulated that the latter was to engage all necessary employees of the works (*Shashi*). J. F. Calder, the manager of the factories, recruited from the Osaka Iron Works in 1884, was formerly with Lobnitz, a dredger builder near Glasgow. Two others, F. Wingel and J. G. Reed, were also from Lobnitz, and were probably recruited by Calder (*Shashi*). After returning to Lobnitz, Reed became the chief draughtsman there.

J. S. Clark was formerly a manager of the shipyard at Barrow-in-Furness, which later became a part of Vickers Ltd. After returning to Britain, he was invited by the Spanish government to build warships (Shiota 1938). A. Morris, who came to install and operate the Experimental Tank, was a draughtsman with Wm Denny & Bros, a shipyard at Dumbarton on the Clyde.[6] Those who came to assemble turbines and other machines were sent by their employer firms from which Nagasaki had imported the machines.

The above information on the foreigners indicates that those recruited after 1887 were well trained in their specialities, but those employed before 1887 were not. Japanese employees who had had technical training were, in many cases, better informed. For example, Kamigo Denji, an engineer recruited in 1902, recollects an argument he had with Wilson, the outside engineer, over the metal material to be used in a part of *Nikko* (completed in 1903). Although the shipyard adopted Wilson's choice, this proved less favourable than the one chosen by Kamigo (Kamigo in *Kaikyuroku 1*). It is likely that there were similar incidents, and they probably influenced the shipyard's policy to replace them soon after 1890.

Another notable fact about foreigners employed at Nagasaki is the predominance of the British. Britain was the biggest ship-builder in the world at the time and also possessed the most advanced technology. This was of course well known among shipbuilders in Japan. Mitsubishi in fact had a British agent, the firm of A. R. Brown and MacFarlane,[7] which was given the task of purchasing machinery and negotiating licence agreements on behalf of Mitsubishi. J. S. Clark was recruited through this agent, and it is probable that some others were recruited via this route (Mitsubishi–Brown letters, Mitsubishi Research Institute). There is no doubt that Britain had the largest number of the most skilled workers and engineers who were able to bring the most advanced technology of the day. However, the most important point about the Nagasaki yard's policy towards foreigners was that the yard changed the nature of the role to be played by foreigners as the needs of the yard changed. It also adopted the policy of replacing the foreigners only several years after Mitsubishi took over Nagasaki. Long-term contracts were not given to those employed after 1887. An implication of the evolution of the role of foreigners is the complementary development of the technological capabilities of Japanese engineers and workers.

Overseas missions

This was another channel for importing technology which the shipyard adopted from 1896, at the time of the building of the first super 5,000Gt vessel, *Hitachi*. Table 3.1 summarizes the purpose and the number of the missions from the shipyard. A list of all the engineers and workers[8] sent and the purpose of their missions is found in the appendix. More than 150 people were sent up to 1935. The early missions were sent for the purpose of general inspection of the shipbuilding or machinery industries. From around 1905, missions started to be sent for more specific purposes: learning technologies imported under licence or to inspect or study certain technologies or industries. These two purposes accounted for more than half of the total number of missions. More than two-thirds of the missions were sent between 1905 and 1925. This was the period when importing technology was the most active. Also the fact that as many as fifteen were sent to Vickers in Barrow-in-Furness in 1912–13 as assistant naval inspectors for the construction of the IJN heavy cruiser, *Kongo*, whose sister vessel, *Kirishima*, was to be built at Nagasaki accounts for the high frequency of missions during this period.

The main function of overseas missions, therefore, was to import technology. A few engineers and workers were granted

Table 3.1 Missions abroad 1896–1935

Purpose	Number of persons sent				e: engineers w: workers	Total
	1896–1905	1906–15	1916–25	1926–35		
General inspection of shipbuilding and/or machinery industry	13e	1e	6e	1e		21e
Granted leave to be apprentices in foreign shipyards	3e, 2w	–	–	–		5 (3e, 2w)
Training in technologies imported under licence or negotiate licence contracts	1e, 1w	7e, 10w	17e, 4w	5e		45 (30e, 15w)
Inspection or study of specific technologies or industries	2e	6e	19e	17e		44e
Assistant naval inspectors for *Kongo*	–	15e	–	–		15e
Inspection of ships or machines ordered abroad, or inspection on voyage	–	9e	3e	7e		19e
Others	–	6e	–	1e		7e
Total	22	54	49	31		157 (140e, 17w)

Sources: Nenpo, Shashi, Shashi Shiryo, Mitsubishi Nagasaki Zosensho 1928

leave to be apprentices in foreign shipyards around 1900. As many as forty-five missions were sent in connection with licensing agreements. Whenever a licence contract was exchanged, a team of engineers and workers was sent to be trained in the new technology. Missions on which workers were sent were of this category. Overseas missions and licence contracts were complementary modes of importing technology. Although not directly connected with licensing agreements, as many as forty-four engineers were sent also to search for or study specific technologies such as the Experimental Tank, diesel and turbine engines and ship decorating works.

It is known that mission reports were written but were not

kept by the firm; therefore, it is difficult to know what exactly the engineers and workers learned in their missions. Two reports have, however, been found (Kato 1899, Yokoyama 1913), and partial accounts of missions are found in the memoirs of staff (*Kaikyuroku* and *Kaiso*), and from these it is possible to grasp to a certain extent what was accomplished in the missions. Shiota, in his autobiography, briefly touches upon his mission to Britain in 1897. He was one of those sent in preparation for the construction of *Hitachi*. Her sister ships were being built in Britain, and the main purpose was to inspect these works. Unfortunately, the autobiography does not recount any technological fruits of the mission; however, Shiota visited most of the major shipyards around Glasgow, Newcastle, Sunderland and London. He also visited a shipyard in Belgium before catching *Kawachi* (a sister ship of *Hitachi* built at Napier Shanks and Bell) on her maiden voyage to Japan.

The mission report of Kato Tomomichi, an engineer sent to Europe in 1898, has been found.[9] Like Shiota, he visited the major shipyards in Britain, France, Germany, Belgium and Holland. He gives details of the layout and the facilities of major yards and explains how certain operations like launching are conducted. What is interesting is that not only technical aspects but also managerial practices were inspected. He studied how workers were placed in the factories, determination of their wages and how they were paid. Also, the engineering estimate procedures and the system of cost accounting were studied.

Managerial practices, in this case the training of draughtsmen, were a major topic covered in the mission report of Yokoyama Kozo,[10] who was among those sent to Vickers as an assistant naval inspector for *Kongo* in 1912. His report also gives technical details of the machinery and parts used for *Kongo* and results of tests on them (Yokoyama 1913). We also know from his account of the development of turbine engines at Mitsubishi that, as a turbine expert, he also studied what he could about turbines during his stay (Yokoyama 1955).

Although not a mission report, Ito Kumezo[11] gave a lecture at a meeting of the Society of Mechanical Engineers on his four missions to Europe between 1911 and 1918. He inspected diesel engine manufacturers for the purpose of choosing the firm from which to import diesel engine technology. He visited all major manufacturers in Europe, and some of them more than once.

As with Kato and Yokoyama, Ito also examined other matters, in his case the organization of factories. He said he was impressed by how efficiently the factories were run, and he attributed the reason to the fact that the factory operations were well organized along the principle of the division of labour. He noted that machinery parts were made interchangeable by the use of a gauge jig which also contributed to better efficiency. He recommended adoption of these practices in Japan where productive efficiency was much worse than in Europe (Ito 1919).

These examples indicate that not only technology but also managerial and organizational practices were studied and imported through missions abroad. The most notable of the managerial practices imported was the system of cost accounting adopted by the shipyard under the initiative of the manager, Shoda Heigoro.[12] The engineers Hamada Hyo[13] and Mizutani Rokuro,[14] who were sent to Britain in 1898, brought back a book, *Commercial Organization of Factories*, written by Lewis in 1896. After reading the book, Shoda called a meeting of senior staff to discuss the adoption of cost accounting. A system of cost accounting adapted to the needs of the shipyard was formulated on the basis of the above book (Yadori 1932, Yamashita 1979, Matsumura in *Kaikyuroku 2*).

Even in missions in which learning a certain technology was the main purpose, engineers and workers were able to learn about a wider range of technological matters than just the specific subject of their missions. Matsumoto Koji,[15] sent to Vickers' Ipswich factory to study the building of submarines, adopted the method used at Vickers to build a wooden real-size model of the vessel under construction so that machine and apparatuses to be fitted could first be tried on the model. This greatly improved the efficiency of construction. (Ichikawa and Funakoshi in *Kaikyuroku 1*). Fukao Junji,[16] when he went to study the building of the turbo water feeding pump at the G. & J. Weir firm, noticed that there was nearly a tenfold difference in the time spent in making the pumps,[17] although the same machines were used. He observed that machines were arranged so as to save labour input. This, he said, was one of the most important fruits of his mission, and he tried to emulate this as much as possible (Fukao 1979). The engineers and workers sent to licenser firms were usually forbidden to use rulers and notebooks when inspecting factories, but this did not discourage them from trying to sketch the machines they saw from memory. Nagai Shonosuke, a foreman in the machinery factory sent to Parsons to study turbo-generators in 1914, saw that the blade-making machine in use there was much more efficient than the one at Nagasaki. He sketched the machine from memory and had one built when he returned to Nagasaki. This speeded up blade making twofold (Nagai in *Kaikyuroku* 2). Yokoyama Kozo, in his mission to Vickers, also sketched from memory a dynamic balancing machine for turbine engines (Yokoyama 1955).

Imports of machinery and materials

The Mitsubishi Nagasaki Shipyard was heavily dependent on imports of machinery and materials. Although it is not known how much was spent on imports, as compared to domestic materials, before 1915, the annual report of the shipyard for 1904 clearly states that materials used at the shipyard were mainly imported (*Nenpo*). Materials imported included materials for new ships (steel plates), stock materials (bolts and nuts, rivets, etc.), pig-iron, cokes and lumber. Between 1898 and 1914 over 90 per cent of imports were from Britain, and materials for new ships and machinery accounted for more than half the total amount of imports. The amount of imports, therefore, fluctuated according to the amount of work on new ships. Materials for new ships also included working plans. When the order for *Hitachi* was received, the shipyard requested D. & W. Henderson in Glasgow, which was constructing a sister ship, to supply all material and working plans (Mitsubishi Nagasaki Zosensho 1928).

There is no record of how much was spent on domestic materials and how much on imports before 1915, but it can well be imagined that the share of domestic supply was small. For one thing, tariff autonomy was regained only in 1911. For another, machinery and steel production in Japan was insignificant until the first world war. The machinery industry *per se* was practically non-existent. Shipyards were the major machinery makers; therefore, machinery used in the shipyards, aside from imports, was made there. Steel production in Japan was negligible until the Yawata Steel Mill started in 1901. Even with Yawata, domestic steel production could supply only

Table 3.2 Purchases of machines and materials at Nagasaki Shipyard in 1,000 yen

	Domestically supplied	Imports	Total	Domestically supplied (%)
1915	2,754	1,389	4,143	66.5
1916	5,122	2,626	7,748	66.1
1917	6,040	1,735	7,775	77.7
1918	12,302	1,218	13,520	91.0
1919	39,570	6,016	45,585	86.8
1920	19,717	4,173	23,890	82.5
1921	19,347	5,948	25,295	76.5
1922	12,566	2,373	14,939	84.1
1923	8,041	1,125	9,166	87.7
1924	7,216	1,535	8,751	82.5
1925	5,744	1,673	7,417	77.4

Source: *Nenpo* 1915–25

less than 20 per cent of domestic demand before 1909 (Tsushosangyosho 1979). In 1906 the Nagasaki Shipyard negotiated with Yawata for the purchase of steel material to build *Sakura*; however, because of the great difference in price, they were ordered in Glasgow (*Nenpo* 1906). The situation changed during the first world war when imports were severed and the necessary materials had to be supplied domestically. As seen in Table 3.2, by 1915, over 60 per cent of materials and machinery was domestically supplied, and the percentage rose to over 90 by 1918. After the war the percentage of domestic supply remained at around 80 per cent.

A few points should be made about imports of machinery. The purchase of licences was always accompanied by machinery imports. Adopting new technology entailed the buying of machinery required in the use of new techniques, e.g. machinery for electric welding. Also, it was the policy of the yard to purchase the first one or two products for which a licence agreement was made rather than manufacturing them. So the first Parsons' turbines for *Tenyo* in 1908 were imported. The Nagasaki Shipyard started to manufacture from the turbines for *Sakura* which was the third ship with Parsons' turbines to be built at Nagasaki. The first one, therefore, was obviously bought for the purpose of learning the assembling of the machinery to see how the parts fitted and functioned.

This became a strictly observed pattern of procedure for all machinery purchased under licence. Thus, machines were imported not only for use but also to study how they were made so that eventually the yard itself could make them. It is probable that quite a few machines, not necessarily those imported under licence, were subject to this kind of 'reverse engineering'. Imports of machinery were a means of learning technology.

The practice of assembling newly adopted machinery before manufacturing was a procedure adopted by IJN for the manufacture of torpedo boats from the 1890s. IJN imported various types of torpedo boats from Yarrow, Creusot and Sichau. For each type, IJN bought the first one intact, assembled the second one and started manufacturing from the third one (Zosen Kyokai 1973a). This may also have presented a model for practices adopted by private yards.

Machinery and materials were also brought back by engineers sent abroad. Ogata Masaya,[18] sent to the USA in 1917, was told that he could buy any machinery and materials that he wished under ¥1,500. Even those above that amount were permitted subject to authorization (Ogata in *Kaikyuroku 1*). This generosity may have been due to the war boom, but those sent on overseas missions were probably charged with buying machines and materials. Machines were imported through the agents of A. R. Brown in Glasgow and Stockton in London. According to Ichikawa Shigesaburo,[19] who was transferred to the Mitsubishi branch office in London in 1914 to be in charge of purchases for Nagasaki, orders from the machinery department of Nagasaki always specified choosing the 'best' one available. Cost considerations were secondary (Ichikawa in *Kaikyuroku 1*).

Purchases of manufacturing and sales licences

Relatively speaking, licensing agreements were the most recent form of importing technology adopted by the Nagasaki Shipyard. The first were the licences for Parsons' marine and land turbines purchased in 1904. As seen in Table 3.3, twenty-one licences were purchased between 1904 and 1934. Fourteen of these were purchased from British firms, thirteen of which were purchased before 1921. This indicates a heavy dependence on British technology up to this time. After 1920, however, only five licences were purchased and all but one were from German or Swiss firms.

Table 3.3 Manufacturing licences purchased by Mitsubishi Nagasaki Shipyard

Date of effect	Licenser	Item
1.1904	Parsons Marine Steam Turbine Co.	Marine steam turbine
1.1904	C. A. Parsons Co.	Land steam turbine
1.1904	Josiah Stone Co.	Stone's manganese bronze
1.1906	C. A. Parsons Co.	Continuous current dynamics and alternator
6.1907	Contraflo Condenser and Kinetic Air Pump Co.	Condenser
1909	Nesdrum Co.	Boiler
6.1910	Richardson & Westgars Co.	Stoker and superheater
10.1911	Contraflo Condenser and Kinetic Air Pump Co.	Auxiliary machines
2.1912	G. & J. Weir Co.	Auxiliary machines
2.1914	Elektriska Swetning Aktieboraget	Electric welding method
2.1914	Yarrow & Co.	Torpedo boat, boiler
9.1914	Joseph William Isherwood	Isherwood's method of hull construction
9.1917	Vickers	L-type submarine and diesel (Kobe)
10.1918	Sperry Gyroscope Co.	Sperry's gyroscope
2.1919	James Howden & Co.	Howden's forced draught
12.1920	Vickers	Vickers' mercantile diesel engine (Kobe)
7.1924	Sulzer Bros	Single acting marine diesel engine
6.1925	J. I. Thornycroft & Co.	Thornycroft's motor boat
11.1925	Durr Werke	Boiler
11.1925	Escher Wyss Engineering Works	Zölly's land and marine turbines
11.1931	Sulzer Bros	Double acting marine diesel engine

Source: Mitsubishi Jukogyo Kabushiki Kaisha 1956

By the 1920s, there was a clear preference for Germanic technology at the shipyard. When the shipyard surveyed available impulse turbine technology to import in the early 1920s, the choice was narrowed down to the Rateau turbine of Metropolitan Vickers and the Zölly of Escher Wyss. One reason for choosing the latter was the preference for more theoretical Germanic technology to the more empirically oriented British

(Yokoyama 1955). An engineer of the Kobe Shipyard who was sent to Europe in 1925 recounted that he felt that Germanic industrial technology was better than British (Niwa in *Kaikyuroku* 2). This was probably the view of many engineers by this time.

Not much record remains which explains exactly why the shipyard bought the licences it did. Some were obviously bought for the purpose of acquiring entirely new technology. The licence for Parsons' turbines, for example, was bought before any orders for it were received. The most probable motive for this was the acquisition of the 'best practice' technology. Turbines were indeed just starting to replace the reciprocated engine at this time. This motive is likely to have served as the reason for the purchase of other technologies which were imported at early stages of adoption in the more technologically advanced countries. Some other licences were bought to replace direct imports. This was the case with the forced draught licence bought from J. Howden in 1919. The licence was granted because direct supplies became difficult due to the war (*Shashi Shiryo*). Licences for auxiliary machinery were likewise probably bought to replace direct imports when demand for them had become great enough. Some technologies were 'discovered' by engineers on their missions abroad. This was the case with electric welding which was imported in accordance with a suggestion by Ito Kumezo, who, upon seeing the technique in use during his mission to Europe, became convinced of its advantages (Shiba 1920). Still others were in response to requests by IJN. Vickers' L-type submarine and its diesel engine, Yarrow's torpedo boat and boiler and Thornycroft's motor boat were of this category.[20] Shipping companies' preferences served as the motive for choice in some cases. The licence for Sulzer's diesel engine was bought when the shipyard received orders for three diesel vessels from OSK which preferred the adoption of Sulzer's engines.

Often, the contracts for purchases of licences contained the provision that the licenser firm would instruct the representatives sent from Mitsubishi Nagasaki Shipyard in the technology being licenced. In these cases, a group of engineers and workers was usually sent. The engineers studied design know-how, while the workers were trained in the skills of operation and manufacturing. Also, as in the case of turbines, the engineers of licenser firms came to assemble the first few products imported as part of licence agreements. These missions facilitated the assimilation of technologies imported through licensing.

Journals, books and professional societies

Technological knowledge from abroad could also be gathered from books and technical journals published abroad. This channel of technology imports was utilized fully by the Nagasaki Shipyard. Major journals in the field of shipbuilding and marine engineering were subscribed to. In 1915, the shipyard started to compile periodically a volume of excerpts from the foreign journals to distribute to the engineers and technicians of the shipyard (*Shashi*). Only one of these volumes, named *Bijou, Review of Reviews*, has remained at the shipyard. This volume, the third in the series covering 1917–19, contains thirty excerpts from not only technical journals in shipbuilding and marine engineering but also from management related journals. The forty-member editorial committee consisted mostly of engineers (Nagasaki Shipyard 1919).

The engineers themselves made efforts to gather information through foreign books and journals. According to Fukao Junji, 'the products of the shipyard were varied and mostly were those manufactured for the first time in Japan. The engineers both in design and manufacturing departments had to study directly from foreign books. They read technical journals thoroughly and bought foreign books with their own money' (Fukao 1979: 47). Yokoyama recounted how he studied books on turbines by Martin, Stodola and Goudie to learn design know-how (Yokoyama 1955).

New technological developments taking place abroad could also be learned through professional journals published in Japan. A major part of the periodicals of both the Society of Engineering Sciences and the Society of Mechanical Engineering, founded in 1879 and 1897 respectively, was devoted to excerpts, abstracts or translations of professional books and articles published abroad. Also, like the lecture Ito Kumezo gave to the meeting of the Society of Mechanical Engineers, members of professional societies who went abroad often gave similar lectures on what they saw and studied. This was another channel through which information about new developments could be learned.

Thus, a wide range of channels for importing technology was utilized by the Mitsubishi Nagasaki Shipyard. At early stages, practices adopted by the government doubtless served as models. The most notable feature of the way technologies were imported at Nagasaki was that the kinds of channels of technology imports employed evolved according to the changing degree of technological sophistication of the shipyard. Also, each channel was used in such ways as to suit the needs of the shipyard. Thus, long-term employment of foreigners for general operations of the shipyard gave way to short-term contracts for the introduction of specific technologies. The aim of overseas missions evolved from general inspection of the foreign ship-building industry to searching for technologies to import and training in the technologies imported under licence agreements. A group of engineers and workers was usually sent to the licenser firm as part of the contract to be trained in design and manufacturing know-how. Overseas missions and licensing contracts were thus complementary. These two modes were further complemented by imports of machinery. The first product for which a manufacturing licence was purchased was imported from the licenser firm for the purpose of 'reverse engineering'. Gathering of information through foreign professional journals and books also aided the shipyard's efforts to absorb foreign technology. Participation in professional societies also served this purpose. These interacting modes of importing technology were thoroughly exploited to accumulate the necessary technological capabilities. The engineers and workers of the shipyard were enthusiastic students, especially when sent abroad. They often studied managerial and organizational practices in foreign shipyards and managed to pick up various technologies other than the main subject of their missions that raised the efficiency of operations at the shipyard.

4

EDUCATION AND TRAINING AT MITSUBISHI NAGASAKI SHIPYARD

THE DEVELOPMENT OF FORMAL EDUCATION

The diffusion of education

Education had already diffused well in Japan before Meiji modernization. As a result, the 'literacy rate in Japan in 1879 was considerably higher than in most of the underdeveloped countries today, and it probably compared favourably even then with some contemporary European countries' (Dore 1965: 291). By the beginning of the Meiji era, 40 per cent of adult males were literate. The rate was 100 per cent among the *samurai*, 70–80 per cent for large city merchants and 20 per cent for the peasantry. Also, by this time, 40 per cent of all boys and 10 per cent of girls were enrolled in schools (Levine and Kawada 1980).

The Tokugawa educational system had already developed institutions of formal education beyond the primary level. While *terakoya*, Tokugawa primary schools, were for imparting basic intellectual skills for the general public, higher institutions, *gogaku* and *hanko*, were mainly for training *samurai* for administrative work, although some commoners were also admitted to *gogaku*.

Levine and Kawada (1980) point to the practical and vocational orientation of the Tokugawa schools. The classical Confucianist base for education evolved during the Tokugawa era to pursue more practical subjects. Also, the development of *kokugaku* and *rangaku* steered education towards 'scientific rationalism, receptivity to innovation and vocational preparation' (Levine and Kawada 1980: 45). The merchant and artisan classes had a well-developed system of apprenticeships for all kinds of trades.

Boys spent nine to ten years after *terakoya* as apprentices before becoming independent tradesmen.

The Meiji government viewed education as an important base for industrial development, and launched an ambitious programme for modernizing it. With the Educational Order of 1872 the government attempted to institute a three-tier educational system with eight years of compulsory education. Under the programme, 15,760 primary schools, 256 secondary schools and eight universities were to be founded. Although the government made the most use of *terakoya* and *gogaku* already in existence, the programme fell short of achieving its aim. Only half of the primary schools were built, fewer than half of the secondary schools and only one university. From the mid-1880s, the government set out on a more realistic programme with four years of compulsory education. One secondary school and one normal school were to be built in each prefecture. There was still only one university.

The most notable achievement of the Meiji education programme was the rapid diffusion of primary education. By the turn of the century 90 per cent of compulsory school-age children were enrolled, and this ratio kept rising despite the fact that, in 1907, compulsory education was extended to six years. Another feature was the diversification of the post-primary level education into several tracks. For boys these were: (1) academic track leading to university, (2) terminal seven-year secondary vocational oriented course, and (3) five-year secondary level leading to polytechnical institutes or normal schools. Girls also were separated into an academic track leading to normal schools and vocational tracks.

In contrast to primary education, and despite the multitracking, secondary and tertiary level enrolment was very slow to increase. It took until 1920 for the secondary level enrolment to reach 25 per cent of the 15–20 age group. By 1935 the percentage had risen to about 40. The tertiary level enrolment grew very gradually to 3 per cent of the 20–24 age group by 1935 (Levine and Kawada 1980). Enrolment trends reflected the distribution of expenditure devoted to each level of education. Primary education consumed three-quarters of all educational expenditures up to the turn of the century, while secondary education received less than 10 per cent. Although the percentage devoted to secondary education increased after 1900, the percentage remained at around 20 per cent until 1935. Tertiary education, in the meantime, received 8–18 per cent (Japan, Ministry of Education 1963). Therefore, national educational policy up to the 1930s concentrated resources on the diffusion of primary education.

This course of the development of formal education generated an adequate supply of literate labour by the turn of the century. Far less adequate were the secondary and tertiary level graduates to be recruited as technicians and engineers for the rapidly growing industries. Until 1935 enrolment in the technical education track at the secondary level accounted for less than 5 per cent of the slowly growing secondary enrolment, while over 60 per cent on average were in general secondary schools. In absolute numbers, enrolment in technical schools increased from 1,581 in 1895 to 48,572 in 1935. The demand for secondary level graduates in the industrial sector, in the meantime, increased much more rapidly than the supply. Also, the secondary technical education curricula could not keep up with the changing knowledge and skill requirements of the rapidly developing modern industries. The tertiary level enrolment trend in science and engineering was somewhat similar to that of the secondary technical track. Between 1880 and 1935, the percentage enrolment in these subjects remained steady at 12–15 per cent of total enrolment. The absolute number enrolled increased from 962 in 1880 to 14,232 in 1935 (Japan, Ministry of Education 1963). However, what was notable in Japan compared to Britain was that engineering was instituted as an important part of university education from the very beginning of industrialization.

Within the limits of its resources, the government attempted to further industrial education by a series of reforms. Up to the mid-1880s, the government ministries undertaking modern industrial enterprises founded education and training institutions as part of their enterprises. Kobusho founded the Imperial College of Engineering as well as training schools for workers within telegraph and railroad enterprises. Naimusho started an agricultural school and the Ministry of Finance set up a commercial school. Most of these, however, were soon upgraded to become part of universities or specialized institutions of higher education, thus creating a gap for secondary level industrial education. The Ministry of Education in turn now attempted to establish industrial and vocational curricula within secondary schools through the educational ordinances of 1886 and 1894. In

1899, a separate secondary level vocational track was established by the Vocational School Ordinance. Furthermore, in 1903 another ordinance started to promote *semmon gakko* (polytechnics) for higher level specialized training in technical fields, medicine, law and commerce. As a result of these ordinances, the number of secondary vocational schools and polytechnics multiplied, including a number of institutions or courses in naval architecture and marine engineering. However, enrolment in technical fields did not rise substantially. Moreover, as Levine and Kawada point out, these institutions at the secondary level 'proved unable to provide the skills needed by Japan's rapidly expanding modern industries . . . they served principally to recruit and channel youth who became clerical and administrative personnel, particularly in small and medium size enterprises, rather than skilled manual operatives for enterprises with new and complex technologies' (Levine and Kawada 1980: 103). It was left to the industrial enterprises themselves to compensate for inadequacies of the formal educational systems in providing prospective workers, technicians and engineers with relevant training. The early government enterprises had already set a precedent for within-enterprise education and training. Many large private industrial enterprises like Mitsubishi followed the pattern.

Formal educational programmes in naval architecture and marine engineering

Despite the inadequate diffusion of secondary and tertiary technical education, it is worth noting that specialized education in naval architecture and marine engineering was instituted from the early stages in the diffusion of advanced level education. These specialized courses provided a supply of engineers and technicians for large shipyards like Mitsubishi Nagasaki. At the secondary level, Koshu Gakko (Technician School) and the Ominato Zosen Totei Gakko (Shipbuilding Apprentice School) had courses in naval architecture when they were founded in 1889 and 1896 respectively. These became formal secondary vocational schools under the Vocational Education Ordinance of 1899. In both, the curriculum consisted of daily daytime practical training and classroom teaching in the evenings in a three-year post compulsory education programme. Some other secondary technical schools eventually offered courses in mechanical engineering, and produced graduates who went to work in private shipyards.

Universities in Japan stressed applied science and engineering in their educational programmes from the very beginning. The faculty of science of Tokyo University, the only university in Japan until 1897, had civil and mechanical engineering, applied chemistry and mining courses at the time of its founding in 1877. In 1884, in accordance with the request from IJN, naval architecture was added. In 1886, the Imperial College of Engineering of Kobusho merged with Tokyo University, now called the Imperial University, and the faculty of engineering was set up which offered specialist courses in civil, mechanical and electrical engineering, naval architecture, applied chemistry, mining and metallurgy, and architecture. Of the 191 naval architecture graduates up to 1907, 41 per cent went to work for private shipyards, while IJN and the government together claimed 36 per cent (Zosen Kyokai 1973a). In 1897 a specialist course in marine engineering was also set up.

University education became even more responsive to the manpower needs for industrialization when Tohoku and Kyushu imperial universities were founded with faculties of engineering in 1909 and 1910 respectively. The founding of these universities was made possible by a substantial donation from the Furukawa firm.[1] Because of the geographical proximity to the Mitsubishi Nagasaki Shipyard and the Sasebo naval yard as well as to the Yawata Steel Mill, the government saw fit to set up a naval architecture course at Kyushu Imperial University in 1920 (Zosen Kyokai 1973b). Lectures in marine engineering were given within the mechanical engineering course at both Kyushu and Tohoku as well as at Kyoto Imperial University, founded in 1897.

Semmon gakko also played a significant role. Tokyo Polytechnique, originally founded as Tokyo Craftsman School in 1881 to train foremen but eventually upgraded to a polytechnic, had a mechanical engineering course which produced graduates for industrial enterprises. Although relatively few, those who went to work in marine engineering were mainly recruited by Mitsubishi (Zosen Kyokai 1973a). Osaka Polytechnic, founded in 1896, set up courses in naval architecture and marine engineering in 1900. Their curricula were almost the same as those offered by imperial universities, but placed slightly greater emphasis on practical training. The several polytechnics that were founded in accordance with the 1903 Semmon Gakko Rei (Polytechnical Institutes Ordinance) all had mechanical engineering courses, some of which offered lectures in marine engineering.[2]

IJN programmes in education and training also produced manpower for private shipyards. IJN had continued its courses for training engineers, technicians and workers until 1883 when it requested the setting up of a naval architecture course at Tokyo University, at which time the engineers' course was abolished. The technicians' course was also abolished in 1907, when it was hoped that secondary technical schools would be able to supply the necessary number of technicians. This did not turn out to be the case, and the shortage of technicians became acute during the first world war boom. Under the circumstances, the training programme for technicians was revived in 1919 (Zosen Kyokai 1973b). Some of those trained in IJN programmes were recruited to private shipyards.

WITHIN-ENTERPRISE TRAINING PROGRAMMES FOR WORKERS AND TECHNICIANS AT THE NAGASAKI SHIPYARD

On-the-job training of workers

During the pre-Mitsubishi days of the Nagasaki Shipyard, there was no formal system of on-the-job training of workers. Operations of the yard under the supervision of foreign engineers were considered to provide learning opportunities for workers and engineers, and training at this time was not yet a purpose on its own (Nakanishi 1982). Traditional artisans, e.g. shipwrights, blacksmiths and founders, provided the source of skilled manpower, and they learned by direct participation in the operations of the yard.[3] The skills and capabilities they possessed as traditional artisans served as a basis for absorbing a different set of skills. These artisans brought with them a traditional master–apprentice system of training to the shipyard. By the 1870s it was possible for unskilled workers to become skilled through this mode of training.[4] The traditional mode of training persisted for quite some time at Nagasaki as well as in many other industrial enterprises in Japan. However, large modern technology-intensive enterprises, like Mitsubishi Nagasaki Shipyard, soon found the system far too inadequate to train workers in the rapidly changing skill requirements, and more direct modes of training came to be adopted.

The Mitsubishi Nagasaki Shipyard instituted the so-called *minaraiko* (on-the-job learners) system of training in 1890, in an attempt to train young workers directly. Under this system, boys of age thirteen and over who had completed several years of primary education were recruited and given on-the-job training for five years, after which they were obliged to work in the yard for at least three years. *Minaraiko* were trained daily on the job, mainly by foremen.[5] This scheme, however, did not immediately become the predominant form of training. For one thing, little systematic training of *minaraiko* was actually done. They were often reduced to assisting senior workers by performing minor chores; consequently, only those who had the eagerness to learn from observing senior workers could actually absorb new skills. For another, the nature of skills needed at the time in shipbuilding was still undiversified, requiring workers to perform a number of different manual operations which called for accumulation of experience rather than specialized training. Also, when the need for more specialized skills started to be felt, there was not yet a sufficient number of engineers and technicians who could train the workers (Sumiya 1971, Hyodo 1971). As a consequence, the management had to depend at least partly on foremen to recruit and train workers. The shipyard subcontracted foremen to do a certain amount of specific jobs and paid them in bulk; the foremen in turn recruited, trained and paid the workers to do work under their supervision (Mitsubishi Nagasaki Zosensho Shokkoka 1928, Mitsubishi Jukogyo Kabushiki Kaisha 1956).

There was another obstacle to having direct control over the training of workers. With the onset of full-scale industrial expansion in the 1890s, which caused a sudden boost in demand for skilled labour, the mobility of workers became extremely high (Table 4.1). Since the early days of modern shipbuilding in Japan, workers had moved among the several modern shipyards in order to acquire new skills. This 'roving' from yard to yard was itself a form of training which became all the more fashionable as the demand for skilled labour increased in the second half of

Table 4.1 Rate of mobility of workers at Nagasaki Shipyard

	(1) Number incoming	(2) Number outgoing	(3) Number at end of year	(1)+(2)/(3) (%)
1898	2,457	2,862	3,430	155.0
1899	2,507	2,379	3,558	137.4
1900	2,485	2,251	3,792	124.9
1901	5,253	3,836	5,209	174.4
1902	3,340	3,356	5,193	128.9
1903	2,894	2,429	5,658	94.0
1904	1,708	2,074	5,292	71.5
1905	3,801	2,348	6,745	91.2
1906	6,020	3,894	8,871	111.8
1907	5,812	5,014	9,669	112.0
1908	4,023	4,681	9,011	96.5
1909	603	3,911	5,703	79.2
1910	1,069	1,393	5,379	45.8
1911	2,471	1,433	6,417	60.8
1912	2,527	1,621	7,323	56.6
1913	3,331	2,125	8,529	64.0
1914	2,098	2,424	8,203	55.2
1915	2,576	1,497	9,282	43.9
1916	5,684	2,787	10,269	82.5
1917	6,456	4,598	11,283	98.0
1918	5,591	6,334	11,715	101.8
1919	7,448	5,106	14,205	88.3
1920	6,456	6,222	15,173	83.5
1921	6,433	5,176	16,430	70.7
1922	537	6,111	10,856	61.2
1923	326	3,333	7,849	46.7
1924	400	1,475	6,774	27.7

Source: Nenpo 1898–1924

the 1890s. The workers moved from yard to yard seeking better skills and better pay. Workers moved not only among civilian yards, but also to and from naval yards. In this way advanced naval technology embodied in these workers diffused to civilian shipyards. In 1912, out of 2,527 newly recruited workers, 847 were from other civilian and naval yards, machinery factories and iron and steel mills (Mitsubishi Goshi Kaisha Shomubu Chosaka 1914). Such high mobility of workers was an obstacle to on-the-job training.

It was quite some time before the Mitsubishi Nagasaki Shipyard established control over its labour force in terms of training. In the meantime, however, the yard did take measures to improve the situation. By the first decade of the century the oncoming wave of new foreign technologies imported under licence agreements began to make the skill requirements of the workers more specific and specialized. This, in turn, made training workers an increasingly important issue. One solution was the founding of Mitsubishi Kogyo Gakko (Industrial School, hereafter abbreviated to MKG) which aimed at training technicians. Consequently, on-the-job training courses were double-tracked into that for *minaraiko* and that for graduates of MKG or those who had undergone an equivalent level of education. The latter were called *shugyosei* (student workers). The two tracks served as modes of training for young recruits.

Other measures followed. In 1908 the subcontracting of foremen was abolished. Instead, direct payment systems were adopted.[6] The management adopted reward schemes for workers who stayed for more than a specified number of years. The training of *minaraiko*, who were long left as assistants to senior workers, gradually became more systematized. By 1912 one to two hours of supplementary classroom education was given at special classes for *minaraiko* at MKG. This was increased to three years in the new rules for *minaraiko* adopted in 1917 (*Shashi Shiryo*). According to a *minaraiko* recruited in 1917, the curriculum included English, Japanese, technical drawing and elementary algebra, which helped him to understand design drawings. The same worker, however, pointed out that, even at this time, senior workers did little on-the-job training (Ogawa in *Kaiso 1*). This, however, soon saw improvement, for the revised rules for *minaraiko* and *shugyosei* in 1919 provided for a 'systematic and orderly training' by trainers selected from engineers, technicians and foremen in each factory of the shipyard (*Shashi Shiryo*: 1, 194). One worker, appointed as a trainer in 1921, recounts the difficulties in forming training methods, for trainers were left without any guiding references, but some trainees acquired good skills after several months (Otaguro in *Kaiso 1*). Training was obviously more effective than letting workers learn by themselves. Thus, it was a long and gradual process until the Nagasaki Shipyard was able to develop effective direct training systems for workers.

Mitsubishi Kogyo Gakko and the training of *shugyosei*

Another ambitious attempt at institutionalizing in-firm education and training programmes was the founding in 1899 of a formal within-enterprise secondary technical school, Mitsubishi Kogyo Gakko.[7] The government enterprises of the 1870s, and notably the Yokosuka Naval Yard, had already established formal within-enterprise schools; however, as one to be founded by a private enterprise in the heavy industrial sector, MKG was the first of its kind (Sangyo Kunren Hakusho Henshu Iinkai 1971). Founded in the same year as the enactment of the Vocational School Ordinance, MKG was reflective of the need for secondary vocational education acutely felt nation-wide at the time. For the Nagasaki Yard, the school was started when the first real expansion phase of the yard was taking place. The shipbuilding encouragement law had been passed, and *Hitachi* had just been built. At this time, the educational level of workers and technicians was still low, while increasingly sophisticated technical knowledge was demanded of them. The founding objective of MKG, which states,

the development of shipbuilding industry affects not only the profits of the firm, but also national strength . . . the most urgent matter for its development is the training of technicians who possess appropriate skills and knowledge in shipbuilding technology . . . to develop their knowledge in application of engineering in order to form the basis of the development of this industry which in turn will serve the public interest of the nation.

(Mitsubishi Kogyo Kyoikukai 1922: 1–2)

reflects the general nationalistic sentiment of the time and the awareness of the importance of education and training for the development of the shipbuilding industry.

MKG admitted, by examination, boys of over ten years who had completed lower primary school and provided them with five years of education free of charge. As the length of compulsory education became longer, the length of schooling was shortened to three years, and the age of admittance raised to twelve years and above. The curriculum placed stress on secondary level general education and included reading, expository writing, mathematics, general science, English, technical drawing and physical education for the first two years. In the third year, specialized subjects such as naval architecture, mechanical and electrical engineering were added.[8] There were practice sessions in the factories also. Full-time secondary level teachers were employed for general education, but specialist subjects were taught by engineers, technicians and foremen. Among them were a number of graduates of MKG now working in the shipyard.

A list of textbooks in use at MKG around 1912 includes specialized textbooks in English on naval architecture and mechanical engineering.[9] This indicates that the content of technical education was comparable to that given in England at the time and that the students were subject to rigorous training in understanding English. Since all the blueprints and specifications used at the yard were in English, to have technicians and workers who could not understand English reasonably well was a serious problem.[10] The curriculum of MKG was designed to overcome the problem.

In contrast to *minaraiko*, graduates of MKG were not obliged to work at the yard for a certain number of years. If they did stay, they were given further education and training as *shugyosei* (student workers).[11] An hour a day of classroom teaching in English, mathematics, naval architecture, and mechanical and electrical engineering was continued for the training period of five years.[12] The rest of the time, *shugyosei* were trained on the job. They were obliged to work for the yard for three years after the training period. While the *minaraiko* system aimed at training skilled workers, *shugyosei* were apparently trained to become technicians. As discussed in the previous section, it took a long time for the *minaraiko* system to become an effective way of training workers. How successful were MKG and the *shugyosei* system? There is little doubt that the level of education at MKG was quite high and adapted to the technological needs of the rapidly developing heavy industrial sector in comparison to what formal secondary educational institutions could offer at the time. A professor of Tokyo Polytechnique reporting on MKG in 1906 commented that the quality of general education was as good as other secondary schools, while the content of technical education was much better (Makino 1906). Among the graduates were not only those who stayed on to work at the yard but also those who obtained jobs in other shipyards and machinery factories, those who moved on to commercial and other occupations and those who went on to higher level education (Table 4.2).

For the Mitsubishi Nagasaki Yard, the success of MKG as an

Table 4.2 Careers of MKG graduates

Careers	1904–12 graduates as of 1912	1904–12 graduates as of 1922	1913–22 graduates as of 1922
Recruited to the shipyard at graduation	284 (88.9)		
Working at Nagasaki Shipyard	166 (51.8)	84 (26.2)	538 (67.9)
Working for other Mitsubishi enterprises	3 (0.9)	12 (3.8)	16 (2.0)
Working for other firms	15 (4.7)	84 (26.2)	41 (5.2)
In other occupations	40 (12.5)	19 (6.0)	22 (2.8)
In military service	13 (4.1)	0	18 (2.3)
Undergoing advanced level education	19 (5.9)	0	41 (5.2)
Others*	64 (20.0)	121 (37.8)	116 (14.6)

* Emigrated, deceased or not known.
In ( ), % of the total number of graduates.
Source: Mitsubishi Kogyo Kyoikukai 1922, Mitsubishi Goshi Kaisha Shomubu Chosaka 1914

educational institution was a mixed blessing. The graduates naturally aspired to get good positions in the yard, and if they couldn't, many left to get suitable jobs elsewhere. As Table 4.3 shows, although most remained at the yard to become *shugyosei* upon graduation, many of them left later. For graduates up to 1912, fewer than 30 per cent on average were remaining ten years later. The management of the shipyard analysed the situation in 1914 as follows:

they (MKG graduates) possess excellent knowledge and skills . . . and it is important for the shipyard that they remain to work in the yard, but the reality is far from this ideal . . . the reason is that most MKG graduates are desirous of becoming draughtsmen, and few wish to work in factories . . . there is a good prospect for draughtsmen to eventually obtain engineer status, but in factories work is rough and the hope of becoming an engineer is limited.
(Mitsubishi Goshi Kaisha Shomubu Chosaka 1914: 62)

MKG graduates aspired eventually to become engineers rather than being content to remain as technicians. It was the shipyard that had to adapt to this situation and most MKG graduates eventually did become engineers (Masumoto 1926). Of the sixty MKG graduates up to 1909 who remained in the yard

Table 4.3 MKG graduates working at Nagasaki Shipyard

Year of graduation	Number of graduates	Number recruited at shipyard at graduation	Number remaining in 1912	1922	1928
1904	22	20 (90)	8 (36)	4 (18)	3 (14)
1905	31	27 (87)	16 (52)	10 (32)	5 (16)
3.1906	36	33 (89)	16 (44)	10 (28)	7 (20)
12.1906	38	30 (79)	16 (42)	8 (21)	6 (16)
1907	21	19 (91)	8 (38)	7 (33)	5 (24)
1908	37	31 (84)	12 (32)	5 (14)	5 (14)
1909	35	29 (83)	16 (46)	11 (31)	5 (14)
1910	24	22 (92)	12 (50)	5 (21)	1 (4)
1911	42	41 (98)	31 (74)	11 (26)	6 (14)
1912	34	32 (94)	31 (91)	13 (38)	7 (21)
1913	29	29 (100)		12 (41)	7 (24)
1914	56	52 (93)		26 (46)	14 (25)
1915	64	61 (95)		41 (64)	21 (33)
1916	77	69 (90)		41 (53)	29 (38)
1917	78	66 (85)		43 (55)	22 (28)
1918	85	78 (92)		54 (64)	29 (34)
1919	86			54 (63)	35 (41)
1920	77			55 (71)	35 (46)
1921	91			67 (74)	34 (37)
1922	154	119 (77)		119 (77)	72 (47)
1923	156				69 (44)
1924	146				70 (48)
1925	103				59 (57)

In ( ), % of the number in graduating class.
Sources: Mitsubishi Goshi Kaisha Shomubu Chosaka 1914b, Mitsubishi Kogyo Kyoikukai 1922, *Nenpo*

in 1922, fifty-one had become engineers, and the rest were probably promoted later. Of the seventy-eight MKG graduates whose career patterns in the yard are more or less known, all became engineers in eight to fifteen years after finishing the *shugyosei* training period.[13]

Mitsubishi Shokko Gakko

MKG was, in a way, a bit too successful. Rather than training technicians, as it originally aimed, the school trained engineers, although in contrast to engineers recruited from tertiary level graduates, MKG graduates did spend several years as workers and technicians before becoming engineers. This situation was acceptable to the management as long as the shipyard was expanding, and the mobility of even the engineers was high. However, the when recession hit in early 1920s the shipyard decided to abolish MKG to establish the Mitsubishi Shokko Gakko (Mitsubishi Workers' School, hereafter abbreviated as MSG). The formal reason for this transformation was that engineers and technicians could now be supplied by the growing number of graduates of formal educational institutions (Mitsubishi Jukogyo Kabushiki Kaisha 1956). It is true that by this time formal secondary and tertiary technical education had expanded considerably, but other reasons probably contributed also. One is that, since 1918, the educational activities of the Mitsubishi Shipbuilding Company (hereafter abbreviated as MZKK) had come under the control of a within-firm Mitsubishi Technical Education Foundation which in 1919 founded a workers' school at the Kobe Shipyard. Since the trustees of the foundation were the senior directors of the firm, it was obviously the opinion of most of them that a workers' school was more appropriate. According to Shiota Taisuke, who was a trustee of the foundation in 1920–22, MKG graduates were inferior in skills to other experienced workers in the factories although superior in knowledge, but their knowledge was inferior to the knowledge and ability of engineers who graduated from tertiary institutions. Their skills and knowledge were useful in design sections, but much less so in the factories; hence, the decision to lower the level of education to establish a school for workers (Shiota 1938).[14]

MSG first admitted students in 1923 while MKG graduated its last students in 1925. The aim of MSG was clearly defined as the training of workers who upon graduation would work for the Nagasaki Shipyard, and it recruited boys under sixteen years of age who had completed elementary education. Students were divided into three groups from the beginning, according to what they would specialize in as workers in the shipyard, and practical training was a major part of the first year of a three-year curriculum. Considerably more time was devoted to practical training than in the curriculum of MKG. The time spent on practical training differed according to groups. The first group, for riveters and other jobs requiring little technical knowledge, spent forty-four out of fifty-three hours per week on practical training; the second, for welders, carpenters, boilermakers, founders, blacksmiths and fitters, thirty-six out of forty-nine, and the third, for draughtsmen, eighteen out of forty-four hours (Mitsubishi Nagasaki Zosensho Kinrobu 1978).

Out of 2,097 graduates of the MSG up to 1935, only eighty-six became draughtsmen and the rest became workers in the factories (Mitsubishi Nagasaki Zosensho Kinrobu 1978). Unfortunately, less is known about the careers of MSG graduates than MKG graduates. Of the graduates of MSG up to 1935, 21.9 per cent remained in the yard in 1949. This rather low figure is probably due to the fact that many workers were dismissed immediately after the second world war in 1945–46, and the figure in 1944 was probably much higher; however, there is no data for the period before 1949. Career patterns of only thirteen MSG graduates are known. Interestingly enough, all of them followed similar career patterns as later graduates of MKG, i.e. they did achieve engineer status in about fifteen years after the *shugyosei* training period. Too few career patterns are known to generalize (many others may have remained as workers most of their career) and the promotion to engineer status was probably caused by the shortage of staff and workers during the second world war boom. In any case, even if MSG graduates became engineers, most remained in the same factories that they started in, and they accounted for a significant part of the labour force while they were workers.

For what percentage of the work force did the graduates of the within-enterprise training programmes account? Table 4.4 shows the number of apprentice (*minaraiko* and *shugyosei*) and apprentice graduate workers in various work places of the shipyard.[15] Unfortunately, there is no data for *minaraiko* and *shugyosei* separately; however, together they accounted for nearly 25 per cent of the total work force. It is evident that the ratio of apprentice workers is much higher in design departments, the laboratory and the machinery factory than in other work places. The management allocated more apprentices to these relatively knowledge-intensive departments so that they could be trained from very early in their careers. As pointed out previously, most MKG graduates became technicians and engineers. In 1922, out of 266 engineers of the yard, 54 (24.1 per cent) were MKG graduates, and out of 320 technicians, 116 (36.3 per cent).[16] Unfortunately, there is no data remaining for MSG graduates before the war, but their percentage share in the work force in 1930[17] can be estimated by making a few assumptions.

Table 4.4 Apprentice* (graduate) workers in the yard (as of 10.1924)

Work place	(1)** Total number of workers	(2) Number of apprentice graduate workers	(3) Number of current apprentices	(2)+(3)	(2)+(3)/(1) (%)
Machinery factory	3,360	1,105	282	1,387	41.3
Hull factory	2,850	229	77	306	10.7
Outside factory	1,405	187	97	284	20.2
Laboratory	82	18	16	34	41.5
Experimental Tank	12	3	0	3	25.0
Hull design	81	23	19	42	51.6
Machinery design	108	33	57	90	83.3
Other places	840	13	6	19	2.3
Total	8,738	1,611	554	2,165	24.8

* includes both *minaraiko* and *shugyosei*.
** includes current apprentices.
Source: Nenpo 1924

MSG graduated 2,097 by 1930. Supposing that all of them were working in the yard in that year, MSG graduates would account for 26.1 per cent of the total work force of 8,032 in that year. This data indicates that the *minaraiko* and *shugyosei* training programmes together with MKG and MSG succeeded by the 1920s in supplying a significant part of the staff and work force of the shipyard.

TRAINING ENGINEERS AND SHORT-TERM TRAINING PROGRAMMES

Recruiting and training engineers

There were no long-term training schemes for engineers within the shipyard. The engineers, when they were recruited, were considered to be well prepared to take part in the operations of the shipyard. Those who were given the status of engineers or assistant engineers at the time of recruitment were usually new graduates of naval architecture or mechanical/marine engineering courses of universities or polytechnics. Although much fewer in number, there were also engineer recruits who had specialized in metallurgy, chemistry, physics and electrical engineering. They were recruited to do specialized research in jikkenba, the laboratory. Adequate information is lacking to give exact numbers, but graduates of Tokyo Imperial University seem to have dominated in number.[18] Naval architecture graduates were given jobs in hull design and the hull factory while marine engineering graduates went to machinery design or the machinery factory. They remained in their respective specialities during the course of their career; thus, their formal education was in fact useful.

In addition to university and polytechnic graduates, some IJN engineer officers were also recruited to Mitsubishi Nagasaki Shipyard in mid-career or after retirement. Many of them came to hold important posts in the firm. Maruta Hidemi[19] and Kawai Shuntaro[20] became managers of the shipyard in 1906 and 1928 respectively. Takeda Hideo, an engineering admiral, was recruited as the chairman of the board of directors of MZKK in 1918. He also held senior director posts in Mitsubishi Internal Combustion Company and Mitsubishi Electric Company as well as the Nippon Kogaku firm. Some retired engineer officers were recruited as advisers during the 1910s when Nagasaki Shipyard started to build large naval vessels for IJN. There were also some who were recruited as engineers in mid-career.

The memoirs of engineers indicate that early recruits were given substantial jobs soon after recruitment. Shiota Taisuke, who replaced a foreigner upon recruitment in 1890, was immediately appointed the chief of the hull drawing office. He was placed in charge of designing and drawing plans for *Suma* (1,592Gt, the first steel ship of over 1,000Gt, completed in 1895), while Hamada Hyo designed and drafted the engine (Shiota 1938). In contrast, later recruits had to go through a period of doing minor jobs before they actually took part in designing or building. Seo Saburo,[21] recruited in 1925, recollects that, although appointed to the turbine design section, he was made to do routine design calculations and order estimates for some time before taking part in designing turbines (Seo in *Kaiso 2*). This difference was probably caused by the scarcity of educated engineers in the early years as well as by the need at later stages to acquaint new recruits with the increasingly complex working of the shipyard. Also, over time, the technology probably had become more firm-specific. In order to meet this change, in 1923, a six-month probationary period was adopted for new recruits from universities and polytechnics, and by 1927 this was extended to one year. During this period the engineer probationers were made to acquaint themselves with the work of all the design sections and factories of the shipyard. Trainers selected from experienced engineers were assigned for the purpose of guiding and evaluating the probationers. The final recruitment of a probationer as an engineer had to await the decision of a selection committee who evaluated his performance during the year (*Shashi Shiryo*). Thus, during the probationary period, engineer recruits went through a certain amount of training which familiarized them with the operations of the shipyard before they proceeded to do actual work.

In general, formal education prepared the engineer recruits well for the needs of the shipyard, but in some cases further education and training became necessary especially when new technologies were introduced. As seen in the previous chapter, missions abroad were often sent for the purpose of having engineers and workers trained in technologies being imported. These training missions were sent not only to shipyards and factories overseas, but also to naval yards and universities within Japan. Engineers, technicians and workers were equally involved in these missions. Table 4.5 summarizes these internal training missions as they appear in the records of the shipyard. Engineers were sent usually in connection with the introduction of new technologies. Suzuki Eitaro[22] was sent to Yawata Steel Mill for the purpose of studying metal analysis operations for the newly created laboratory in 1904. Motora Nobutaro's[23] mission was in preparation for launching model testing and research on resistance in the Experimental Tank. Kiuno Jozo[24] and Mase Tokuzo[25] were sent to study diesel engines which were soon to be manufactured at Kobe. Okuda Katsumi[26] and Kagami Kohei[27] were sent to do some background research for the development of the MS diesel engine which had just been launched. The table also shows that quite a few were sent to naval yards in the 1910s which is indicative of the close cooperation between the Nagasaki yard and IJN at this time. From 1917, two or three technicians started to be sent regularly to Kyushu Imperial University to study naval architecture or mechanical and electrical engineering for a period of two years. All of them

Table 4.5 Study and training missions within Japan

Name	Position in the shipyard	Period	Where sent	Purpose
Suzuki, E.	Engineer	7–10.1904	Yawata steel mill	Study methods of chemical analysis of steel
Motora, N.	"	9.1910–8.1913	Tokyo Imperial University	Study mathematics and physics for model testing and research on resistance
Kuga, H.	"	7–.1913	IJN	To assist in making drawings for a warship
Masaki, J.	"	"	"	"
Adachi, S.	"	"	"	"
?	"	"	"	"
Kiuno, J.	Asst. engineer	9.1914–3.1916	Tokyo Imperial University	Research on internal combustion engines
Mase, T.	Engineer	2.1916 (short period)	IJN	Study diesel engine being manufactured at Yokosuka yard
Kimura, G.	Foreman	8.1916 (short period)	"	"
Ito, K.	Engineer	"	"	Study French submarine being manufactured at Kure yard
?	"	"	"	"
?	"	"	"	"
?	Foreman	"	"	"
?	"	"	"	"
?	"	"	"	"
Kasahara, K.	Engineer	12.1916 (short period)	Yawata steel mill	Study electric motors for submarine
50 workers		12–.1916	IJN	To be trained in steelmaking
Hiroe, T.	Technician	1–.1917	"	Study ordnance manufacturing at Yokosuka yard
Takahashi, K.	Foreman	"	"	"

Name	Position	Dates	Institution	Study
Horikawa, T.	Technician	9.1917–6.1920	Kyushu Imperial University	Study electrical engineering
Murata, E.	"	9.1917–8.1919	"	Study mechanical engineering
Yamaguchi, K.	"	"	"	"
Tanaka, M.	"	9.1918–12.1920	"	"
Masuda, T.	"	"	"	"
Yamaguchi, H.	"	9.1919–11.1921	"	"
Matsuo, K.	"		"	
Sadakata, K.	"		"	
Tanaka, T.	"	9.1920–10.1922	"	Study electrical engineering
Yamazaki, G.	"	"	"	Study mechanical engineering
Kida, K.	"	4.–1921	"	"
Torisu, T.	"	4.1922–3.1924	"	Study naval architecture
Tanaka, T.	"	"	"	Study mechanical engineering
Hashimoto, Z.	"		"	Study electrical engineering
Takeda, R.	Technician	4.1923–3.1925	Kyushu Imperial University	Study naval architecture
Kakita, T.	"	"	"	Study mechanical engineering
Kaida, N.	"	"	"	Study electrical engineering
Jimbo, N.	"	4.1924–2.17.1925	"	Study naval architecture
Urakawa, I.	"	4.1924– 2 years	"	Study mechanical engineering
Uchino, S.	"	4.1925– 2 years	"	Study naval architecture
Yamaguchi, S.	Engineer	4.1925– 2 years	Tokyo Imperial University	Study mechanical engineering
Aoyama, S.	"		"	Study ship propulsion and stabilizing
Okuda, K.	"	1928	Tokyo Imperial University Aeroscience Institute	Study cylinder scavenging
Kagami, K.	"	"		"

Sources: Shashi, Nenpo

were graduates of MKG. Although not mentioned in the records of the shipyard, there probably was a programme to send selected MKG graduate technicians to study at a university.

Short-term training programmes

In order to meet the skill requirements of new technologies, the shipyard organized short-term programmes for mid-career workers and technicians. The most notable of the short-term programmes was that for training electric welders, which started in 1921. This programme subjected trainees selected from workers in various places to a six-month course consisting of daily practical training and an hour of lectures. The period was divided into three terms, and the content of the lectures and practical training became more sophisticated after each term. Moreover, if a trainee performed satisfactorily in the examination given at the end of each term, he was given a pay rise. The trainers, selected from engineers, developed the curriculum which included basics of metallurgy, chemistry and electrical engineering. The first course selected ten workers and technicians of 17–28 years of age, and, as far as records show, this programme operated at a rate of once a year on a similar scale until 1937.

It is said that at the end of this training period, thus far entirely inexperienced workers could perform as well as experienced electric welders. In addition, trainees had become more attentive and observant, more careful in handling tools and had mastered all the technical terms so that they could easily understand the instructions of engineers (Jikkenba 1923). This programme started when the shipyard was trying to promote the use of the electric welding technique within the yard. Its use diffused well in the 1920s, and by the early 1930s there was more demand for electric welders than the training programme could supply (Sasaki 1931). Undoubtedly the training programme played a significant role in this rapid diffusion of the technique.

Another short-term training programme for workers was launched in 1933. After a long recession period, the need to recruit workers arose when the economic situation started to pick up again, and the number of orders was more than the shipyard could handle. In order to meet this situation, the shipyard recruited workers from nearby small factories and provided them with a training programme of one to three months. These workers, although experienced, possessed 'unsystematic methods of operation' and re-training was needed. Trainers who were selected for this purpose trained them in operating skills, technical knowledge and rules of the factories (*Shashi Shiryo*).

The within-enterprise training activities at Mitsubishi Nagasaki Shipyard were designed to compensate for the inadequacies and peculiarities of formal education and the labour market. For the training of workers and technicians, the shipyard made use of the traditional indirect modes of training, while attempting to institutionalize more direct training systems such as *minaraiko* and *shugyosei* schemes. It took until the 1910s for the direct training programmes to become effective because of the persistence of traditional labour practices and high labour mobility. MKG was an attempt to fill the gap created by the lack of secondary technical education, and was designed to educate prospective technicians. Profiting from the resources of the shipyard, its curriculum was more relevant to the needs of the heavy industrial sector than those of other technical schools. The school was transformed to train skilled workers in the early 1920s. These training programmes generated workers, technicians and engineers who by the mid-1920s accounted for about one-fourth of the technical manpower of the shipyard. Notable was the fact that these people tended to be allocated to areas like design, the machinery factory and the laboratory. This suggests that the nature of the technological capabilities needed in these knowledge-intensive work places required long training in firm-specific knowledge and skills.

Despite limited enrolment, naval architecture and marine/ mechanical engineering courses in universities and polytechnics provided satisfactory training for prospective engineers of the shipyard, and there was no long-term training for them. However, when the shipyard was attempting to assimilate new technologies, they were sent out to receive special training within Japan as well as overseas. Technicians and workers were also sent. In this way, training was directly linked to the acquisition of new technological capabilities. Short-term training programmes such as the one for electric welders were also designed to facilitate the assimilation of new technologies. The fact that within-enterprise training programmes were elaborated over a long period of time indicates that they were necessary not only to complement inadequacies of formal education but also to meet technological demands of the industry which constantly needed to import and assimilate increasingly sophisticated technologies.

5

RESEARCH AND INVENTIVE ACTIVITIES AT MITSUBISHI NAGASAKI SHIPYARD

NATIONAL EFFORTS IN INDUSTRIAL RESEARCH

Government policy towards research activities was in line with its overall industrial policy of the period. Up to the turn of the century its interest was in promoting traditional industries, public works, agriculture, forestry and fisheries. The government founded experimental stations and research institutes to do testing and research in these areas, as seen in Table 5.1. This list is indicative of the government's lack of interest in promoting research on modern industries at this stage of industrial development in Japan.

The policy line shifted in the first decade of this century, as the government started to take an active interest in promoting modern industries. This is exemplified in the founding in 1900 of Kogyo Shikensho (Industrial Research Institute). The idea of founding a government industrial research institute originated with Kogyo Iken in 1884, as discussed in chapter 2. More directly, the founding of this institute resulted from the Noshomusho mission sent in 1890 to survey industrial research in Europe and the consequent recommendation to found a research institute to promote modern industries made by the Noshomusho High Conference in 1898. The conference was charged with industrial policy making for post-Sino-Japanese War Japan, when the country faced the first real urge for modern industrialization.

Kogyo Shikensho provided testing and research services for small chemical manufacturing enterprises and undertook research on lacquer and paper manufacturing; in short, its main interest in the beginning was the improvement of traditional

85

Table 5.1 Government research institutes founded before 1900

	Name	Notes
1871	Hokkaido Development Research Institute	
1872	Naimusho	
	Naito Shinjuku Laboratory	Experimental station in agriculture and sericulture
1874	Tokyo Hygienic Laboratory	
1875	Tokyo Meteorological Observatory	
1875	Kobusho	
	Telegraph Department Electric & Glass Laboratory	Tests on telegraph and telephone equipment and glass. Renamed Electric Research Institute in 1891 and started research on industrial use of electricity in 1897
1878	Tokyo Astronomical Observatory	
1882	Geological Survey Institute	
1888	Geographical Survey Institute	
1892	Research Unit on Prevention of Earthquake Damage	Became Tokyo University Seismological Institute in 1925
1893	Fishery Research Institute	
1895	Yokohama Raw Silk Laboratory	
1899	Epidemics Research Institute	Became attached to Tokyo University in 1916
1899	Mizusawa Latitude Observatory	

Sources: Hiroshige 1973, Tsushosangyosho 1979

chemical industries by adopting modern methods. During the first decade of its existence, research on the modern chemical industry was added to the activities of Kogyo Shikensho. In 1903, research on ceramics and glass was started; in 1906, synthetic dyes; and in 1909, electro-chemicals (Tokyo Kogyo Shikensho 1951).

Another development seen at this time was that the government started to give subsidies for the founding of and research in local public industrial testing stations. A part of these subsidies also went to research activities in private industrial enterprises. Although this was indicative of the government's anxiety to promote industrialization, the amount of subsidies was very small. The real spur for the government to promote modern industrial research came with the first world war as reflected in the number and kind of government institutes founded after 1914 (Table 5.2). Although research institutes for traditional industries still kept being founded, the number of those related to modern industries increased significantly. Due to the stoppage of imports from Germany and other European countries, especially in chemicals and iron and steel, measures had to be sought to stimulate and facilitate domestic production of these materials. By promoting industrial research, domestic production capability was expected to improve. In accordance with this policy, the Temporary Nitrogen Research Institute was founded to do research on the industrial production of ammonia using Haber's nitrogen fixation method.[1] The government added a research department to the Yawata Steel Mill, and founded a Steel Research Institute at Tohoku Imperial University in 1919. The latter institute expanded its scope to include research on metals other than steel to become the Metal Research Institute in 1922. This was made possible by donations from the Sumitomo and Mitsubishi firms and the Kobe Steel Company. This illustrates one significant outcome of the expansion of research activities at this time, the creation of a strong government–university–industry link in research. National universities were increasingly given the role of doing research of interest to the government as reflected in the number of research institutes founded as part of national universities after 1916. Private industries generously gave financial support to these institutes when their interests were also served.

Another body that exemplified the close government–university–industry link was the Rikagaku Kenkyusho (Institute of Physical and Chemical Research, hereafter referred to by its short name, Riken). The idea of founding a 'national scientific research institute to enhance national wealth by industrial development' (Hiroshige 1973: 92) was suggested to the government by a chemical engineer, Takamine Jokichi,[2] in 1913. Although considered premature at that time, the idea was taken up eagerly after the start of the first world war. In 1915, a planning committee for the founding of Riken consisting of government officials, scholars and industrialists was set up. Private industries and the government as well as the Imperial household contributed to the founding fund. Founded in 1917, Riken was to 'integrate pure and applied research for the development of industries; also, by training researchers and

Table 5.2 Government research institutes founded during 1900–35

	Name	Notes
1900	Industrial Research Institute	
1903	National Bureau of Weights and Measures	
1910	Railroad Research Institute	Attached to Ministry of Railroads
1914	Sericulture Research Institute	
1916	Livestock Research Institute	
1916	Yawata Steel Mill Research Department	Expanded in 1919 to become a research institute
1916	Inspection Office for Ship Machinery Instruments	
1916	Aeronautics Research Institute	Attached to Tokyo Imperial University
1917	Research Institute for Prevention of Coal Mine Explosions	
1917	Institute of Physical and Chemical Research (Riken)	
1918	Silk Industry Research Institute	
1918	Temporary Nitrogen Research Institute	Attached to Noshomusho
1918	Osaka Industrial Research Institute	
1919	Tea Industry Research Institute	
1919	China and Porcelain Research Institute	
1920	Fuel Research Institute	Attached to Noshomusho
1920	Ocean Meteorological Observatory	
1920	High Altitude Meteorological Observatory	
1920	Nutrition Research Institute	
1920	Monopoly Bureau Research Institute	
1920	Animal Disease Research Institute	
1922	Forestry Research Institute	
1922	Metal Research Institute	Attached to Tohoku Imperial University, originally founded in 1919 as Steel Research Institute
1924	Printing Office Research Institute	
1925	Seismological Research Institute	Attached to Tokyo Imperial University
1926	Chemical Research Institute	Attached to Kyoto Imperial University
1928	Industrial Arts Education Institute	
1931	Thermal Spring Therapy Research Institute	Attached to Kyushu Imperial University

Table 5.2 Continued

	Name	Notes
1932	Research Institute for Japanese Spiritual Culture	
1934	Building Materials Research Institute	Attached to Tokyo Polytechnic
1934	Microbial Disease Research Institute	Attached to Osaka Imperial University
1935	Telecommunications Research Institute	Attached to Tohoku Imperial University

Does not include research institutes attached to colonial governments.
Sources: Hiroshige 1973, Tsushosangyosho 1979

encouraging inventions, enhance intellectual productivity to consolidate the basis of wealth and strength of our country' (Tsushosangyosho 1979: 236). National university professors were appointed as researchers at Riken. The institute was indeed a 'national enterprise' which responded to the policy of strengthening government–university–industry links for industrial development. Fundamental research was done at Riken, but greater emphasis was placed on industrial research which could be commercialized. By 1937, more than 60 per cent of Riken's income came from subcontracting firms which commercialized its innovations.

Links with the army and navy in research were also strengthened during this period. The Temporary Balloon Research Committee, set up jointly by the army and IJN in 1909, became the Aeronautic Research Institute of the Tokyo Imperial University in 1916. Officers and engineers of the army and navy could be appointed as researchers at this institute, and military research could be done. Industry–military links also became close. The Nippon Kogaku Kogyo was set up by Mitsubishi upon the request of the navy to develop and manufacture optical weapons and instruments. The Nagasaki Arms Manufacturing Company branched out of the Nagasaki Shipyard in 1917 in response to the naval need for torpedoes. The Mitsubishi Shipbuilding Company's involvement in starting the manufacturing of submarines, aeroplanes and internal combustion engines during the first world war was in accordance with the request of the navy. Kawasaki Shipbuilding also became similarly involved. Other large manufacturing firms also developed links with the army and navy.

The expansion of research activities led the government to take measures to facilitate innovative activities. These were the revisions of standardization and patent laws effected in the early 1920s. In order to simplify the situation, in which three different systems of standards (traditional Japanese, yard-pound and metric) were in use, in 1919 Noshomusho set up a research council on the unification of standards which recommended the adoption of the metric system only. This was enacted in 1921. The ministry at this time also launched a long-term project to establish industrial standards (Japan Engineering Standard) which was continued until 1941. Patent law, which had been adopted in 1885 and once revised in 1909, was again revised in 1921, giving equal rights to the inventor and the employer of the inventor – in effect, making the law more 'democratic' than before (Tokkyocho 1955).

Government financial support of scientific and engineering research also expanded during this period. The only grant given to scientific and engineering research before the first world war was that of the Imperial Academy which was based on donations by large industrial concerns – Mitsui, Mitsubishi, Sumitomo and Furukawa. In 1917, Noshomusho set up a fund to encourage inventions. Exhibitions, competitions and lectures, as well as individual inventive and innovative activities, could receive grants under this programme. The Ministry of Education also started a grant scheme in 1918 for research in science, engineering, agriculture and medicine. A grant programme for encouraging industrial research was organized also by the cabinet in 1921. The original objective of the scheme was to encourage military industries in the civilian sector; however, from 1926 other industrial research could also receive this grant.

Table 5.3 summarizes the amount in grants given by these programmes. The total amount continued to increase into the early 1920s, but from then until 1932, due to the recession, the amount tended to decrease. However, despite the economic situation, the government maintained an interest in promoting research. This position is reflected in the recommendations of government committees and research councils which dealt with industrial policy making in the second half of the 1920s.[3] These committees and research councils were concerned with stimulating and rationalizing industries in recession, and the fact that they were anxious to promote research as part of this indicates

Table 5.3 Government funding of research and inventive activities

	Noshomusho grant for encouragement of inventions (yen)	Ministry of Education grant for scientific research (yen)	Cabinet grant for industrial research (yen)	Imperial Academy (yen)	Gakushin (yen)	Government expenditure at current prices (million yen)
1913	–	–	–	1,300	–	339
1914	–	–	–	2,460	–	354
1915	–	–	–	2,540	–	366
1916	–	–	–	3,000	–	361
1917	30,255	–	–	4,536	–	423
1918	70,000	145,000	–	6,754	–	582
1919	70,000	145,000	–	5,737	–	881
1920	70,267	145,000	–	6,737	–	1,085
1921	70,400	145,000	–	8,788	–	1,120
1922	70,000	150,000	–	11,640	–	1,198
1923	66,880	135,000	–	25,031	–	1,164
1924	66,880	135,000	–	17,120	–	1,187
1925	46,816	65,000	–	21,500	–	1,037
1926	46,816	65,000	250,000	49,000	–	1,133
1927	76,816	65,000	250,000	48,400	–	1,391
1928	76,816	65,000	250,000	53,200	–	1,688
1929	76,816	105,000	200,000	42,950	–	1,612
1930	62,351	97,000	200,000	42,850	–	1,452
1031	52,998	73,000	10,000	41,470	–	1,685
1932	72,590	73,000	10,000	42,965	–	1,839
1933	92,590	73,000	15,000	55,850	512,574	2,046
1934	103,498	73,000	18,000	50,630	676,170	2,005
1935	113,498	73,000	15,000	44,635	678,699	2,117
1936	122,917	73,000	15,000	44,160	727,112	2,183
1937	137,717	73,000	15,000	43,100	890,579	2,609
1938	124,934	73,000	–	43,730	1,325,428	3,046
1939	148,534	73,000	–	45,940	1,580,256	3,402
1940	142,926	73,000	–	45,530	1,992,784	4,821

Sources: Tsushosangyosho 1979, Hiroshige 1973, Ohkawa *et al.* 1974

that, as stated by the Resource Research Council in 1929, there was by this time a clear realization that 'encouraging scientific research and promoting its application is a basic prerequisite for development of industries' (Tsushosangyosho 1979: 352).

Given the economic situation of the time, the policy of research promotion was not easy to implement; however, in late 1932, Nippon Gakujutsu Shinkokai (Japan Association for Promotion of Science, hereafter referred to by its short name, Gakushin) was founded. The direct move for setting up this body came from academic scientists and engineers, some of whom were members of the House of Peers, who argued that scientific research was indispensable for 'improving the economic situation and to keep up in the world-wide industrial and economic competition', and for 'resource-poor Japan the only way to survive the competition is to excel in "original" [i.e. research-based] industries'. They also argued that the promotion of research was a basis of national prosperity and a constituent element of national prestige (Hiroshige 1973: 119–20). Whether or not they were really nationalistic, many of them felt the need to make the research system more efficient, and here their interests coincided with that of the government.

Gakushin's research grant scheme was notable in several aspects. First, the total number of grants made available was considerably larger than previous government schemes. In fact, as seen in Table 5.3, it was about double the total of other government grants in 1933. By 1940 Gakushin's grant alone had quadrupled while the number of other grants remained at about the same level. Second, although research in natural sciences, engineering, agricultural and medical sciences as well as human and social sciences was eligible under this grant scheme, a large percentage went to engineering (Table 5.4 (b), 5.4 (c)). Third, an increasingly large amount was given to cooperative research rather than individual research (Table 5.4 (a)). Committees were organized to coordinate cooperative research which brought together researchers from government, private and military research institutes. Topics pursued were often those linked to industrial and military application or those of interest to the government.[4] Thus, through Gakushin, the government succeeded in directing resources for industrial (and military) development.[5]

Table 5.4 (a) Gakushin research grants in yen (%)

Year	(1) Total	(2) Cooperative research	(3) Individual research
1933	512,574	63,683 (12.4)	448,891 (89.6)
1934	676,170	218,592 (32.3)	457,578 (67.7)
1935	678,699	248,619 (36.6)	430,080 (63.4)
1936	727,112	327,200 (45.0)	399,912 (55.0)
1937	890,579	587,661 (66.0)	311,918 (35.0)
1938	1,325,428	1,015,128 (76.6)	310,300 (23.4)

Table 5.4 (b) Break-up of individual research grants according to field in %

Field	1933	1934	1935	1936	1937	1938
Human and social sciences	16.0	16.0	15.8	16.0	17.1	16.0
Natural sciences	29.7	23.6	29.2	18.4	20.3	19.2
Engineering sciences	40.7	44.2	37.1	37.3	36.6	37.8
Agricultural sciences	5.6	5.4	7.2	9.6	8.8	7.6
Medical sciences	7.1	9.3	10.3	13.6	12.2	9.7
Interdisciplinary fields	0.9	1.4	0.3	5.0	5.0	9.6

Table 5.4 (c) Break-up of cooperative research grants according to field in %

Field	1933	1934	1935	1936	1937	1938
Human and social sciences	28.4	11.0	16.3	12.9	10.7	6.4
Natural sciences	0	20.2	10.9	12.9	28.3	10.3
Engineering sciences	39.5	43.0	40.8	47.5	42.0	62.2
Agricultural sciences	0	1.3	2.1	2.1	1.6	0.9
Medical sciences	32.1	24.7	29.9	24.9	17.4	20.0

Source: Hiroshige 1973

Research in the military sector, especially in the navy, became active and varied during this period. Up to the Russo-Japanese War, naval research was concerned chiefly with straightforward absorption of imported technology rather than going further to develop its own technology. After the war, however, IJN turned its interest increasingly towards the latter and set up research bodies to investigate various technical matters, such as wireless communication, electrical machinery, optical instruments, firearms, aeroplanes, fuels and engines. An Experimental Tank was built in 1908. The expansion of research activities continued through and after the first world war. Links with government research institutes as well as private industrial enterprises also strengthened. In the 1920s, despite disarmament agreements (or, on the contrary, because of them) IJN further consolidated its research system. The Experimental Tank and the aeroplanes research institute were merged to form the Naval Technical Research Institute which aimed to do basic technical research. At the same time, a research section was set up in all naval yards and factories to do research directly related to naval construction and ordnance manufacturing, and to complement research work of the Naval Technical Research Institute (Tsushosangyosho 1979, Zosen Kyokai 1973b). Military research consumed a substantial part of government expenditure on research. A survey for the year 1930 estimated that research expenditure of the army and navy was roughly equal to the expenditure for all other government research institutes put together (Hiroshige 1973). The navy, being more technology intensive than the army, probably accounted for a greater part of this sum.

Research also became an integrated activity in some private industrial enterprises. In-house research was started by large electricity, mining and chemical firms in the 1890s. Large shipyards and steel mills also set up research sections in the following decade. The government research activities could not yet respond to the needs of these enterprises. The first world war stimulated research in industrial firms, and the number of in-house research departments increased steadily, as seen in Table 5.5. However, the scale of most of them was very small and the facilities were generally poor.[6] Since private industries were more sensitive to recession, some were closed down or reduced their activities during the 1920s; however, firms of those industries that despite recession tended to expand, such

Table 5.5 Number of research bodies founded by industrial enterprises

	No. founded	Cumulative
1881–1902	6	
1904–13	35	
1912	34	34
1913	7	41
1914	6	47
1915	10	57
1916	15	72
1917	19	91
1918	18	109
1919	13	122
1920	17	139
1921	10	149
1922	8	157
1923	2	159

Source: Tsushosangyosho 1979: 175, 242

as electricity and chemicals, strengthened their research capabilities. Although private industrial research in general was considerably limited compared to government and military R&D, a few like the Mitsubishi Shipbuilding Company succeeded in setting up research activities on a fairly large scale.

Finally, let us see in quantitative terms what all the national efforts in industrial research amounted to. Unfortunately, there are no statistics on R&D for this period; however, the extent of engineering research can be assessed by a government survey conducted in 1930. The figures in Table 5.6 show how small in scale the research institutes and R&D expenditure in 1930 were compared to 1970. However, it is notable that, in contrast to the great difference in absolute amounts, the difference in per cent share of R&D expenditure to GNP is much smaller.

Table 5.6 R&D efforts in engineering

	1930	1970
Number of research institutes		
total	349	11,595
national	73	
local public	83	
private	193	11,132
Number of researchers		
total	2,729	129,681
national	829	
local public	551	
private	1,349	93,679
R&D expenditure	¥ 15,720,000	¥ 748.7 billion
	(¥ 7.5 billion	(¥ 627.1 billion
	in 1970 value)	in private)
As % of GNP	0.11%	1.05%

Sources: Hiroshige 1973, Tsushosangyosho 1979, Ohkawa and Shinohara 1979
Originally a survey conducted in 1930 by Shigenkyoku (Resource Bureau).

Although limited in scale, both the government and private industrial enterprises made serious attempts to promote research on modern industries before the second world war. This was because there was a clear realization that research was conducive to industrial development and ultimately to national wealth and strength. Two features of the pre-war government research policy are especially noteworthy. First is the overwhelming preoccupation with engineering and industrial research compared with the arts and more basic scientific research. Second is that, even during the recession in the 1920s and 1930s, the government tried to enhance industrial research as much as possible and to make it increasingly efficient by creating a strong government–university–industry–military link. However, government-sponsored research could not meet all the research needs of private industrial enterprises; hence, large firms in mining, electricity and chemicals set up their own laboratories. In shipbuilding Mitsubishi took the lead by setting up a laboratory at Nagasaki in 1904.

THE ROLE OF IN-HOUSE RESEARCH BODIES

Jikkenba, the laboratory at Nagasaki and the Experimental Tank

Research as a distinct activity at the Nagasaki Shipyard started as a small chemical analysis laboratory in the foundry shop in 1904. This eventually developed into an independent research laboratory for the entire shipyard. The need for a chemical analysis laboratory arose out of the sudden expansion of heavy industries following the start of the Russo-Japanese War, which brought about certain technical changes in the industrial sector, one of which was that machinery parts which thus far had been made of cast iron started to be replaced by cast steel. Chemical analysis of steel was a necessary part of the production of cast steel (Yano 1966).

For the new chemical analysis laboratory, the shipyard hired an applied chemist, Suzuki Eitaro, for the job. He was immediately sent to the Yawata Steel Mill to be trained in chemical analysis of steel for three months, and the laboratory started operation upon his return. It should be mentioned that in order to start the production of cast steel in the foundry shop, the shipyard hired two British engineers on short term for the purpose (R. Flicker and J. Thomas, see Figure 3.1). Soon, material testing (tensile strength) was added to the chemical analysis work. These two were the main activities of the laboratory until 1916. In the meantime, operations diversified to include chemical analysis of metals other than steel. For example, in 1907, the laboratory did analysis for Stone's manganese bronze, which the shipyard manufactured under licence. Eventually, the laboratory provided testing services for various materials in use in the shipyard, even for non-metal materials, if such tests could be done with the equipment and personnel of the laboratory.

The laboratory gradually became more active, and in 1916 it was given a new building. It is said that the manager of the yard, during a mission to Europe in 1913, was so much impressed on seeing the laboratory of the Krupp firm in Germany that he decided that a comparable facility was desirable at Nagasaki (Yano 1966). Also, due to increasing naval orders, more work was demanded of the laboratory. After 1916, the laboratory, now called Jikkenba (literally meaning factory for experiments), quickly expanded its staff, facilities and activities. Since there are no records of R&D expenditures, the extent of research activities at Jikkenba has to be estimated by other means. Table 5.7 shows the number of engineers, technicians and workers (of the years for which records are available) attached to the laboratory between 1904 and 1935. There was a sudden and large increase in staff in the second half of the 1910s. This was due to the deliberate expansion of the laboratory as well as to the war boom. At this time the number of staff of the entire shipyard also increased. In the 1920s, the number initially decreased then quickly stabilized at between eighty and ninety. This indicates that in terms of the number of employees, Jikkenba did not suffer the continuous decrease during the recession that was the fate of most other parts of the yard. Between 1930 and 1933, when the shipyard dismissed a large number of staff and workers, the number working in Jikkenba in fact increased. The number of engineers and technicians working in Jikkenba changed only slightly between 1923 and 1935. These figures are indicative of the importance the shipyard attached to research during the years of recession. The steadiness of the activities of Jikkenba is reflected also in the number of reports written by Jikkenba staff between 1921 and 1935. An average of about 100 reports were produced at a fairly steady pace during these years.

Thus, in quantitative terms, Jikkenba became a very active part of the shipyard during the first thirty years of its existence. Also, Jikkenba greatly diversified its functions, especially after 1916. University trained specialists were recruited to follow new lines of research. Chemical analysis, which had been concerned mainly with metals and inorganic materials, started the analysis

Table 5.7 Number of laboratory employees and reports

	(1)	(2)	(3)	(4)	(5)		(1)	(2)	(3)	(4)	(5)
1904	3	1	0	2	–	1920	–	14	23	–	–
1905	–	–	–	–	–	1921	156	12	16	128	76
1906	5	2	1	2	–	1922	107	13	13	81	124
1907	–	–	–	–	–	1923	88	8	7	73	87
1908	7	3	2	2	–	1924	98	8	8	82	81
1909	–	–	–	–	–	1925	–	9	7	–	99
1910	–	–	–	–	–	1926	81	10	6	65	118
1911	–	–	–	–	–	1927	82	11	5	66	98
1912	9	3	2	4	–	1928	89	11	5	73	119
1913	–	–	–	–	–	1929	88	11	5	72	76
1914	–	–	–	–	–	1930	86	12	7	67	130
1915	–	–	–	–	–	1931	85	9	6	70	96
1916	20	3	9	8	–	1932	87	9	6	72	95
1917	–	5	–	–	–	1933	102	9	6	87	77
1918	67	5	9	53	–	1934	106	8	6	92	70
1919	150	6	–	–	–	1935	114	8	6	100	94

(1) Total number working in laboratory
(2) Number of engineers
(3) Number of technicians
(4) Others (workers, clerks, etc.)
(5) Number of reports compiled
Sources: Yano 1966, Mitsubishi Zosen Kabushiki Kaisha Staff List, Kubo 1972

of organic materials such as coal, fuel and lubricating oils, paints and asbestos. In 1919, a metallurgy laboratory was created and research on electric steel casting was started in 1920 by a newly recruited electrical engineer.[7] This research was in preparation for electric steel casting which the shipyard started a few years later. The metallurgy laboratory also started research on corrosion of metals for which a chemist[8] was employed. A notable achievement in metallurgy research at Jikkenba was the development of an alloy, NM (nickel-manganese) bronze. Research on this had been started by Ogata Masaya and a few other engineers in the foundry shop, for the purpose of finding suitable brass material for making propellers which was of good strength and easy to cast. They brought in various materials to Jikkenba for tests (Yano 1966, Sasaki 1925). Soon Sasaki Shintaro,[9] the director of Jikkenba, joined this effort, and the research culminated in the development of a new alloy in 1920 which was patented. It was further discovered that, by slightly changing the ratio of constituent elements, the metal was also suitable for other uses including turbine blades.

Material strength testing, which had so far done relatively routine tensile strength testing, started other kinds of research on material strength. This was done by Takaba Ichitaro,[10] who developed methods for strength testing of various metals. A major problem the shipyard faced around 1920 was the frequent failure of turbine blades caused by the fatigue of blade materials of the turbines built at the yard. The material testing laboratory installed three fatigue testing machines to examine this problem; also, it worked with turbine design and manufacturing sections to develop new material for turbine blades. Whenever accidents occurred or problems arose in the shipyard, and if material strength was in question, they were always brought into this laboratory for investigation.

Another line of research on material strength was pursued by Okuda Katsumi, recruited in 1925. He had chosen to be a researcher when he specialized in applied physics at Kyushu Imperial University. He had started research on stress analysis using optical elasticity methods as a postgraduate, a topic that he was allowed to pursue as a researcher at Jikkenba with an MKG graduate assistant. Okuda was eventually awarded a doctor of engineering degree for his research in this area. Okuda made another significant contribution by involving Jikkenba in the research for the development of the MS diesel engine. This, he recollects, led to the fulfilment of his ambition to start research on machinery which Jikkenba had so far neglected (Okuda 1960). The experimental set-up to study scavenging and fuel injection was built at Jikkenba, and members of both the laboratory and diesel design team worked on the set-up together.

Electric welding was an area in which Jikkenba involved itself deeply. This was due to the efforts of the director of Jikkenba, Sasaki Shintaro, who was also responsible for making Jikkenba as active and as versatile as it was during the 1920s and 1930s. Sasaki, whose research on electric welding was assisted by an MKG graduate technician, Ichibangase Kiyoshi, was concerned not only with doing research on electric welding, but also with promoting the use of the technique in the shipyard and eventually in Japan. In fact, his research interest was in improving the technology so that its value could be recognized and its use promoted. Thus, when IJN prohibited the use of electric welding following a few accidents caused by faulty welding, Sasaki wrote a report (Sasaki 1921) analysing the shortcomings of the method employed thus far and how to avoid them. IJN did eventually resume its use. Jikkenba's involvement in electric welding was not limited to doing research. It also started the manufacturing of electrodes, and, as discussed in the previous chapter, it gave training courses for electric welders in the shipyard.

Jikkenba was also held responsible for inspecting weights and measures used at the shipyard and was in charge of taking photographs at the time of the launching of ships. There was also a microscope room attached, where microscopic observation of metal sections was done. Thus from 1916 onwards, despite the recession in the 1920s and 1930s, Jikkenba continued to be a very active part of the shipyard. The shipyard was anxious for new technological developments since, because of the recession, it had to explore new areas of production like diesel engines and turbo-generators.

Research activities at the Nagasaki Shipyard were not limited to Jikkenba. It was also an integral part of other departments of the shipyard, especially machinery design. Turbine and diesel engines, boilers and auxiliary machinery were all being manufactured under licence. The machinery design sections did research to adapt and improve the imported technologies. This was often done in cooperation with Jikkenba.

There was another department within the shipyard whose main function was testing and research, the Experimental Tank built in 1908. This technology was imported from Wm Denny & Bros' shipyard in Dumbarton. As steamships increased in size and speed, the accurate estimation of necessary power and the determination of a suitable hull shape were becoming increasingly important questions in the second half of the 1800s. A model testing technique was first introduced in Britain, and in 1883 Wm Denny & Bros' shipyard in Dumbarton built a tank. The technology diffused rapidly to other firms and other countries. At Nagasaki it was Maruta Hidemi,[11] the manager of the yard in 1906, who proposed the building of the tank. He was an acquaintance of one of the Denny brothers, Archibald, from whom he probably learned the usefulness of the apparatus. This decision was taken at the time that the Nagasaki Shipyard was building *Tenyo*, the first turbine vessel, and it was expected that vessels would further increase in size and speed.

The model testing technology was imported by sending two engineers, Kawahara Goro[12] and Shiba Koshiro,[13] to Dumbarton.[14] The equipment and machines were purchased from the firm of M. J. Kelso on the advice of the Denny firm. Denny sent a draughtsman, A. Morris, to supervise and instruct model testing methods. Operation was started immediately after the tank was completed in 1908. Nagasaki was the first private shipyard to install a tank. A total of twelve engineers, technicians and workers were stationed at the tank. The number increased to twenty-two by 1922 and remained around that figure. As with Jikkenba, the Experimental Tank did not suffer a decrease in staff during the 1920s and 1930s.

The two engineers sent to Denny eventually left their jobs at the tank, and it was Motora Nobutaro who did significant research work at the Experimental Tank. Motora was sent to Tokyo Imperial University to study theoretical physics in preparation for testing and research at the tank. He pursued research on both theoretical and practical aspects of model testing. In 1916, he derived an equation for the analysis of the efficiency of the model propeller (Motora 1916). He effected improvements on both the resistance dynamometer and the propeller dynamometer which improved the accuracy of measurement and made the handling of the instruments easier (Motora 1927).[15] The most remarkable of his achievements was the invention of the Motora type stabilizer. In 1918 the Nagasaki Shipyard bought the licence for the Sperry gyroscope, which was the most popular type of stabilizer at the time. Its performance was good, but the instrument was heavy and complex in structure. Motora, based on a series of experiments on rolling motions of model ships, devised a stabilizer that was better able to eliminate rolling than the Sperry gyroscope and lighter in weight. The invention was patented in Japan in 1920 and subsequently in other countries. The stabilizer was adopted for most large commercial vessels at Nagasaki. For reasons not well documented, the instrument eventually gained more popularity abroad, where improvements were effected on the original invention. The Denny-Brown stabilizer was developed after purchasing patent rights of the Motora type (Yano 1966, Matsushita 1960). As model tests became standard practice in the second half of the 1920s, the Experimental Tank at Nagasaki became an increasingly active part of the shipyard.

Mitsubishi Shipbuilding Company Research Institute

The Mitsubishi Shipbuilding firm's deep commitment to research is reflected in the founding of an institute specializing in research on technology related to shipbuilding, the Mitsubishi Zosen Kabushiki Kaisha Kenkyusho (Mitsubishi Shipbuilding Company Research Institute, hereafter abbreviated as MSCRI), between 1918 and 1933. The idea of founding this institute came from Iwasaki Koyata, the president of the Mitsubishi Goshi Kaisha, the shareholding firm of the Mitsubishi concern. This was clearly in line with the national trend at the time to expand scientific and industrial research capability to fill the gap created by the difficulty of importing technology during wartime. Iwasaki requested Suyehiro Kyoji, the professor of naval architecture at Tokyo Imperial University, who was eventually appointed as the director, to draw up a plan for a research institute in 1917.[16] He was sent on a mission to the USA to inspect industrial research institutes and to buy machines and instruments for MSCRI.[17] The institute, formally founded in 1918, was expected to achieve innovations that could substitute for technology imports. This was to be done mainly through applied research, but the firm expected some basic research to be done, and its newly recruited staff included theoretical physicists and chemists in addition to mechanical, electrical and chemical engineers. Although researchers had quite a bit of freedom to pursue research topics of interest to them, they were also expected to respond to requests from the shipyards.

The main areas of research were machinery and metal engineering. New machines were invented such as a new type of turbine rotor balancing machine, a material testing machine, a refrigerator and a cryptograph machine as well as a machine for analysing wave shapes. In metal research, notable achievements were the development of a new alloy, Iidaka metal, for use as turbine blades, a new method of metal rolling, and arc welding of cast iron. Research on metals using X-ray, which was of importance in advancing electric welding technology, was also pursued. Patents were obtained for many of the inventions. Those that were commercialized were manufactured at Nagasaki or other shipyards and factories (Mitsubishi Jukogyo Kabushiki Kaisha 1956, Zosen Kyokai 1973b). Results of research at MSCRI which were not directly related to productive operations of the firm were published in professional journals in Japan and abroad. MSCRI researchers gave lectures on their research findings at Mitsubishi Technological Research Meetings, and the institute published reports regularly (*Shiryo Iho*).

There was a close cooperative relationship between MSCRI and the shipyards. Some innovations were joint efforts of the institute and a shipyard; e.g. the refrigerating machine developed in 1924 was invented jointly by a MSCRI researcher, Iguchi Haruhisa, and three engineers of the Kobe shipyard.[18] Shipyards manufactured machines and materials when requested by MSCRI; the latter in turn did experiments upon requests from shipyards. There were cooperative research activities with other research institutes; also, MSCRI did research in response to requests from the army and navy. Research on metal rolling was a joint research with Riken and the invention of a cryptograph machine was in accordance with a request from the army. As far as the Nagasaki Shipyard is concerned, MSCRI had a role to play in the research for improving turbines. The development of Iidaka metal and balancing machines was in response to the request of the Nagasaki Shipyard's turbine design section to search for better material for turbine blades and to devise an improved system for turbine rotor balancing.

Records indicate that, in the 1920s, the Mitsubishi Shipbuilding Company attempted to stimulate research efforts of the firm in order to explore new areas of production. In 1924, the firm set aside a part of its annual profit to create a fund for research in the accounts of the head office.[19] This fund was to be used for research that would contribute to the diversification of the firm's productive activities. The shipyards as well as MSCRI could draw from this fund with the permission of the head office. Unfortunately, records do not indicate on what research the fund was used, but most research activities of MSCRI, and the new product innovations undertaken at shipyards, e.g. the diesel engine project at Nagasaki, were probably funded by this.

In 1933, however, MSCRI was donated to Riken. The reasons for this are not documented in the records of the firm. The most immediate reason was certainly the recession, which hit the firm the hardest in 1931–32, but there must have been other causes for this move, since the firm attempted to expand rather than diminish its research activities despite the unfavourable economic situation in the 1920s. Most probably, the firm decided to consolidate research efforts at the shipyards and concentrate on research of immediate relevance to productive activities. This would explain the sustained activity level of Nagasaki Jikkenba despite the crisis faced by the firm in 1931–32. Another possible reason is that the research at MSCRI, although partly commercialized, fell short of achieving major innovations that could replace technology imports, which the institute originally aimed at.

The fact that the Mitsubishi Shipbuilding firm had three specialized research bodies within the firm – Jikkenba, the Experimental Tank and MSCRI – indicates that in-house research occupied a place of vital importance in the firm. Of these the contrasting fates of Jikkenba and MSCRI are quite striking. The former grew from a small chemical analysis laboratory to a large versatile centre for research. Its activities stayed close to and responded well to the needs of production in the shipyard. Since ships and engines were being built by importing technology, the need for research was in problem solving and trouble shooting in the process of assimilating foreign technology. Indeed, research related to turbine and diesel engines and electric welding, all of which were imported technologies, accounted for a major part of Jikkenba's activities. The indispensability of Jikkenba is reflected in the fact that it remained active throughout the recession in the 1920s and 1930s. MSCRI, in contrast, was founded with the aim of achieving major technological breakthroughs; however, actual achievements were more in improving existing technologies than in creating new ones. MSCRI was given up after fifteen years of existence. The difference in the course of the evolution of these two in-house research bodies illustrates that the kind of research needed for the firm at this stage of industrial development was in assimilating and improving existing technologies through minor technological changes. Achieving major breakthroughs at this stage was very difficult and not really necessary.

MANAGEMENT OF RESEARCH AND INVENTIVE ACTIVITIES

Policy towards inventive activities

The research activities often culminated in inventions. In fact, even before the founding of the research laboratory, engineers at Nagasaki started to obtain patents for new instruments, materials and machines they invented in their work. These inventions induced the shipyard to institute rules for the inventive activities of its employees in 1907. The rules stipulated that the Mitsubishi firm, not the inventor, was the one entitled to apply for and utilize patent rights obtained for inventions of the employees. The firm was to give compensation and, in some cases, awards for such inventions when they proved to be useful and profitable. This policy was preserved in the revised rules of 1922 which made an addition that any research with the objective of inventing something was to receive advance approval from the firm.

This conservative policy towards inventive activities was the cause of dissatisfaction of potential inventor-employees[20] and may have had the effect of depressing inventive activities. In order to stimulate inventions while adhering to the above rules, the firm first introduced a separate award scheme in 1915 for inventions by its employees. This scheme was borrowed from the one in practice at William Denny Bros' shipyard in Britain.[21] Unfortunately, in the records of the firm, the details of the operation of this scheme do not remain, but there are references to awards actually given for inventions and improvements. For example, a money award was given to a *kumicho*, Yamamoto Shichiro, in 1915, for inventing tools to make coils which cut both cost and time making them[22] (*Shashi*). There is little doubt that the intent behind this scheme was to encourage inventive activities as much as possible while preserving the right to patents obtained for inventions of the employees. The scheme was applied to workers as well as engineers and technicians. Inventions that were patented averaged thirty per year between 1912 and 1935, including several that also secured patent rights abroad (Mitsubishi Jukogyo Kabushiki Kaisha 1956).

There were inventions and improvements other than those that were subject to patent rights. These were usually those that made tools more efficient, those that improved manufacturing processes or introduced mechanization in production. Workers and technicians improved hand tools they used. Such improvements were sometimes able to replace tools that had thus far been imported. Hori Yasuemon recounts that, after his improvement of the hammer he used every day, the importing of the tool was stopped (Hori in *Kaiso 1*). Construction processes were mechanized during the 1910s by the adoption of pneumatic compressors, gas cutting and electric welding. In the 1920s and 1930s, the need for operational innovations that would raise productive efficiency and reduce cost came to be acutely felt because of the recession. Numerous improvements and inventions to produce these effects were introduced by engineers as well as workers. Mimura Tetsuo, chief engineer in the hull factory, arranged assembling operations to be done as much as possible in the factory, for this saved considerably more time than assembling at the construction site (Mimura in *Kaikyuroku 2*). Honda Tomozo, an MSG graduate worker, in 1932 devised a method to make most of the pipes on land rather than at the construction site which also economized on time (Honda in *Kaiso 2*). Fukao Junji, the chief engineer in the machinery factory, rearranged the factory layout which facilitated the transporting of materials, eased and made safer access to machines and improved lighting. He also saw to it that the machine tools were always in good condition and well adjusted so as to ensure precision in the manufacturing process (Fukao in *Kaiso 2*).

These inventions and improvements were encouraged not only by the firm but also by the chief engineers of individual factories who sometimes gave awards from their own pockets for inventions and improvements of their subordinates. Fuji Kensuke, the chief of the power station, carefully examined every invention and improvement and gave awards to those that were adopted, which included fairly trivial items like improvement on lamps and safety signs, which nonetheless contributed to raising efficiency (Morimoto in *Kaiso 2*). Mimura held marking competitions and awarded the winners which aided the upgrading of the marking skill of the workers (Mimura in *Kaikyuroku 2*).

Technological research committees

In order not only to stimulate research and inventive activities, but also to channel them for the profit of the firm, there was a need to diffuse the fruits of these activities, solve problems and to coordinate them within the firm so that they would continue to be useful. The technological research committees that were set up on various topics of interest to the firm served this purpose. The first one remaining in the records is the Electric Welding Research Committee which held its first meeting in Kobe in 1920, and at Nagasaki the following year to discuss common research problems and exchange information.[23] The meeting held in 1935, in addition to research issues, discussed the question of adopting standards and a uniform examination system for workers in electric welding skills (*Shashi Shiryo*).[24]

The second committee created was on casting technology which met for the first time in 1921. The direct motive for convening this committee was the faulty casting of turbines built for the naval cruisers *Tama* and *Kiso* for which the Nagasaki Shipyard received complaints from IJN. Hamada Hyo, the chairman of the committee, explained the goal of the committee as follows:

> to exchange information and discuss common problems in order to improve casting technology. . .the stage whereby we could learn and borrow everything from abroad has passed. . .now it is necessary to do research ourselves. . . for example we had not succeeded in satisfactory production of manganese-bronze ingots since we bought Stone's licence (in 1904), until the stoppage of imports during the first world war forced us to do serious research after which we finally succeeded in its domestic production. . .in order to achieve something we need to apply scientific knowledge to eliminate problems encountered.
>
> (*Shashi Shiryo*: 23,212)

Such needs and objectives were shared by other committees. The committee on casting met once in a year and a half to discuss problems in the casting of various metals, ways to cut costs and increase efficiency of production. According to the rules of the committee adopted in 1935, the committee was to share experiences in casting at different shipyards of the firm and select topics for further survey or research with the purpose of improving casting technology. Members were chosen by the managers of the shipyards and appointed by the president of the firm. Sub-committees were to be set up whenever necessary.

Exchange of information and coordination of research efforts by the shipyards of the firm to improve welding or casting technologies were the main functions of the above two committees. The Internal Combustion Engine Research Committee organized in 1928 was slightly different, in that its main job was to guide the development of a new type of diesel engine. Mitsubishi had purchased the licence to manufacture Sulzer marine diesel engines in 1924; however, this engine found itself at a disadvantage in both cost and performance in the competition with Burmeister and Wain engines being built by other firms. The committee was set up to look into this problem. At its first meeting, it was decided that R&D for a new type of marine diesel engine was to be launched at the Nagasaki Shipyard. The committee discussed and decided what kind of research was to be done, and the problems encountered at each stage of the development of what was to become the MS diesel engine. The committee met every two to five months until the completion of the MS engine.

These three committees and the committees on tools and marine 'coal burning' (i.e. steam) engines were the ones set up before 1935. The records indicate that more were set up afterwards and many of them added several sub-committees;[25] therefore, technological research committees became a well-established means to guide and coordinate research and innovative activities for further technological developments of the firm.

Mitsubishi Technological Research Meeting and links with universities, research institutes and professional societies

Mitsubishi Goshi Kaisha, under the initiative of its Shiryo-ka (Information Department), held a monthly Mitsubishi Technological Research Meeting in 1924–25.[26] This meeting was to promote the exchange of information and coordinate research activities of firms within the Mitsubishi concern including the related firm of Asahi Glass Company. It also attempted to encourage communication and cooperation with researchers and research institutes outside Mitsubishi (*Shiryo Iho*: 172, 1924). Topics discussed at these meetings were those of common interest to participants and were chosen from the following areas: fuels, iron and other metals, engines, machines and tools, chemicals, and other topics related to industrial production. (*Shiryoka Nenpo* 1924). At each meeting, researchers from

Table 5.8 Lectures at Mitsubishi Technological Research Meetings

30.6.1924	On electric welding and arc welding of cast iron Haramishi Mototeru (Mitsubishi Goshi Kaisha) Sato Shunichi (MSCRI)
21.7.1924	Substitute fuel for gasoline Tanaka Yoshio (Professor, Faculty of Engineering, Tokyo Imperial University)
29.9.1924	New method of making electrolyzed metal sheet Hatta Shiroji (MSCRI) Okochi Masatoshi (Director, Riken)
28.10.1924	Refrigerating machine using carbon dioxide gas Iguchi Haruhisa (MSCRI)
25.11.1924	On making oxides of tungsten, and tungsten steel Yasui Koji (Mitsubishi Mining Research Institute)
15.12.1924	On glass Misumi Aizo (Chief, Technology Department, Asahi Glass Co.)
31.1.1925	Transformation of iron and steel industry and research Honda Kotaro (Professor, Metal Research Institute, Tohoku Imperial University)
27.2.1925	X-ray analysis of metals Kakinuma Usaku (MSCRI)
27.4.1925	? Namba Motohiro (Director, Asahi Glass Research Institute)
16.5.1925	On soda industry Nishikawa Torakichi (Professor, Kyushu Imperial University)
26.6.1925	Manufacturing of duralumin Goto Seiji (Professor, Toyko Imperial University)
5.10.1925	Metal materials in use at Nagasaki Shipyard Sasaki Shintaro (Mitsubishi Nagasaki Shipyard)

Source: *Shiryoka Nenpo* 1924–25

within and outside Mitsubishi were invited to give lectures. Table 5.8 lists the lectures given at these meetings.

The table indicates that Mitsubishi was anxious to promote exchange of information and cooperation with universities and other research institutes. Such exchanges on research matters were frequent and often on an informal basis. For example, when *Tenyo-maru*, at the time of its trial run, was found unable to correct its tendency to list, the shipyard asked Shiba Chuzaburo, the professor of naval architecture at Tokyo Imperial University, to examine the problem (Itami in *Kaikyuroku*

1). Honda Kotaro, a professor of the Metal Research Institute of Tohoku Imperial University, held a summer lecture session from 1920 to which two or three engineers, technicians or workers from Nagasaki were sent. The memoirs of some of these people show that they took advantage of the opportunity to discuss and seek advice on problems they were encountering in their jobs at the shipyard (Fukao 1979, Tanaka in *Kaikyuroku 1*, Ichibangase in *Kaiso 3*). Many instances of contacts with Professor Honda appear in the memoirs of staff. Since the Metal Institute was partially funded by large industrial concerns like Mitsubishi, its link with the industrial sector was probably very close. Another university that had close industrial links was Kyushu Imperial University. As discussed in Chapter 4, its naval architecture course was set up because of its proximity to Nagasaki and Sasebo, which implied that the university expected to utilize professional resources of the two yards. Nagasaki engineers were invited one after another for several-year periods of lectureships. A Nagasaki engineer, Nomura Shogo, left the shipyard to take a professorship there. Sasaki Shintaro, the director of Jikkenba, gave weekly lectures at the university on metallurgy. He influenced some metallurgy students there to come to work at Nagasaki. Some who did, later came to play important roles in the introduction and development of automatic welding technology as engineers or researchers at Nagasaki.[27] Sasaki was also a member of the Gakushin committee on electric welding. Engineers also actively participated in professional societies: Society of Naval Architects, Society of Mechanical Engineers and the Welding Society. Many Nagasaki engineers gave lectures at their meetings and/or published in their periodicals. Such professional activities facilitated the exchange of information and enhanced research activities.

In Japan, therefore, there already existed a fairly well-defined policy towards research before the second world war. It was moulded to be responsive to the needs of industrial development. Research was viewed as a means to enhance industrialization, and government policy gave priority to and concentrated resources on research directly related to industrial development. Industrial research was complemented by the strengthening of government–university–industry–military links. What is noteworthy is that the policy of stimulating industrial research was sustained throughout the recession periods of the 1920s and 1930s. Research was regarded as having the potential to produce innovations that could improve the economy.

At Nagasaki Shipyard, research was already instituted at the beginning of the century. This was a natural outcome of the need to assimilate and improve foreign technologies. Jikkenba grew increasingly active as it provided a variety of research services for design and manufacturing departments. No major breakthroughs were achieved, but the minor technological changes that resulted from its research activities facilitated the assimilation and improvement of imported technologies. Therefore, since before the war, industrial research in Japan was clearly and overwhelmingly geared towards 'adaptive' research or 'improvement engineering'. At Nagasaki this was encouraged down to the worker's level, and gave rise to technological changes in production engineering that raised efficiency, reduced costs and/or substituted for imports. Research activities were enhanced rather than depressed during the recession in the 1920s and 1930s, and the firm instituted measures to make in-house research more effective. Technological research committees coordinated research and facilitated the diffusion of information within the firm. Cooperation with universities and research institutes outside the firm was encouraged through the Mitsubishi Technological Research Meeting and other informal links.

6

INDIGENOUS TECHNOLOGICAL DEVELOPMENTS AT MITSUBISHI NAGASAKI SHIPYARD

This chapter traces the development of three technologies at Mitsubishi Nagasaki Shipyard – the steam turbine engine, electric welding and the diesel engine – in order to examine exactly how firm-level efforts in technology imports, training and research influenced the development of specific technologies. In marine engineering, the steam reciprocating engine was replaced by the steam turbine during the first two decades of this century because of the latter's superiority over the former in speed and power. From the 1920s, diesel engines in turn started to replace the turbine for reasons of fuel economy for ships that did not require high speed. Electric welding started to replace riveting around the time of the first world war. The new technology had an advantage over the traditional one in achieving greater strength and weight reduction, which were significant as ships and their engines increased in size and power. Moreover, the technology required less labour and materials. These three were the leading innovations that influenced shipbuilding technology in this century.

STEAM TURBINE ENGINES

Importing the technology and the development of design capability

A major innovation of the last years of the nineteenth century was the steam turbine engine for electric power generation and marine propulsion. As compared to steam reciprocating engines, turbines were smaller and lighter but could produce more power. The marine application of the turbine was first demonstrated by C. A. Parsons, whose turbine-propelled *Turbinia*'s speed surprised the spectators at the Spithead Naval Review in 1897. This was thirteen years after Parsons had succeeded in building a turbo-generator. Two types of turbine were developed – reaction, like the Parsons, and impulse, which was developed also around this time by DeLaval, Curtis, Zölly and Rateau. In the reaction turbine, steam is expanded along a rotor drum which has alternating rows of moving and fixed blades around the periphery. When expanding through this, the steam reacts against the blades to make the drum rotate. In the impulse turbine, the steam expands through a series of nozzles to strike upon a row of blades on the circumference of a wheel. The expansion takes place in a number of stages by pressure or velocity compounding. Impulse turbines have shorter high speed rotors than reaction turbines, but the latter utilize steam more efficiently. In Britain the steam turbine was adopted immediately for naval and merchant vessels. The Admiralty put it in the destroyers *Viper* and *Cobra* in 1900. By 1903, the steam turbine was propelling two cross-Channel steamers, and the next year, the cross-Atlantic passenger liners *Victorian*, *Virginian* and *Carmania*, and in 1906 it was adopted for the 43,000Gt Cunard liners *Lusitania* and *Mauritania*.

The Mitsubishi Nagasaki Shipyard was quick to react to these developments. It purchased manufacturing and sales licences for Parsons' marine and land turbines in 1904. It was the first firm in Japan to import turbine technology and it was even ahead of IJN in this.[1] Orders for either marine or land turbines had not as yet been received. Why did the shipyard import the technology at such an early stage? The only Mitsubishi record on this point is Shoda Heigoro's letter to the assistant managers of Nagasaki of December 1903 expressing the intention of the firm to obtain Parsons' licence before other firms or IJN, and suggesting sending a letter to the A. R. Brown firm to negotiate with Parsons' firm to that effect (Iwasaki Denki Hensankai 1971). Shoda, therefore, was convinced of the future of turbines. He had been to Europe in 1889 and 1898. The latter mission had the specific purpose of ordering ships for NYK's European line, including materials for *Hitachi* to be built at Nagasaki, through the firm of A. R. Brown. He probably gathered knowledge of marine turbines at this time which doubtless included the news of *Turbinia* of the preceding year. The knowledge of the development of marine turbines had reached Japan by 1901[2] but in his lecture on 'Recent Progress in Marine Engineering', Shiba Chuzaburo, the professor of naval architecture at Tokyo Imperial University, made a careful statement about it in July 1902, saying 'the adoption of steam turbines for marine propulsion is a problem which needs to be thoroughly investigated' (*Kogaku Kaishi 243* 1902).

When the contract with Parsons was exchanged in 1904, the shipyard sent an engineer, Esaki Ichiro, and a foreman, Araki Eisaburo, to Parsons' factory to be trained in designing and manufacturing turbines.[3] In 1905, the firm succeeded in pursuading Toyo Kisen Kaisha (Oriental Steamship Company, TKK) to adopt turbines for its San Francisco liners *Tenyo* and *Chiyo*. The shipyard ordered turbines for these two ships to be made at Parsons, and recruited two Parsons' engineers on short term to have the turbines assembled and installed.[4] This most certainly was to provide an opportunity for engineers and workers to study turbines before the shipyard actually undertook to build one. The Nagasaki Shipyard built Parsons' marine turbines for the first time for the Imperial Volunteer Fleet vessel *Sakura* in 1909. The shipyard likewise imported a 500kW turbo-generator and turbines for the naval vessel *Mogami*, before building the first naval turbines and turbo-generator in 1908 and 1910 respectively. Parsons designed them and provided all the drawings.

Purchasing a licence and building turbines according to the design and drawings supplied by the licenser was only the first step in the course of the development of turbine designing and manufacturing technology at Nagasaki. What followed were years of ceaseless efforts to learn more and improve so that something better could be built. What Mitsubishi imported from Parsons in 1904 was far from a mature technology, but one that continued to evolve. In the 1910s, single and double reduction geared turbines were introduced. Efficient speed of rotation of turbines is much faster than that of propellers, therefore turbine efficiency is increased when the turbine's rotational speed is slowed down by gears. Another change was the incorporation of impulse stages in combination with reaction stages within the reaction turbine. Reaction turbines became longer as steam pressure rose. The incorporation of impulse

Table 6.1 Marine turbines for mercantile ships built at Nagasaki

	Number	Output (S.H.P.)	Type
1908–10	6	38,000	Parsons direct coupled (imported)
	3	9,000	Mitsubishi-Parsons direct coupled
1911–13	6	28,000	Mitsubishi Parsons direct coupled
	3	11,900	Mitsubishi-Parsons single geared
1914–16	7	20,640	Mitsubishi-Parsons impulse-reaction single geared
1917–19	4	13,000	Mitsubishi-Parsons impulse-reaction single geared
1920–22	6	28,800	Mitsubishi-Parsons impulse-reaction double geared
1923–25	2	9,600	Mitsubishi-Parsons impulse-reaction double geared
	5	18,200	Mitsubishi impulse single geared
1926–28	2	8,000	Mitsubishi impulse double geared
1929–31	2	6,500	Mitsubishi-Zölly double geared
1932–34	6	23,300	Mitsubishi-Zölly double geared
1935–37	4	31,200	Mitsubishi-Zölly single geared
	12	69,680	Mitsubishi-Zölly double geared

Source: Mitsubishi Nagasaki Zosensho 1957

stages enabled the turbine to remain reasonably short since impulse stages could lower steam pressure at shorter rotor length; also impulse stages are more efficient at high pressure. The Nagasaki Shipyard kept up with these changes, and by the mid-1920s the shipyard was capable of designing and building Mitsubishi-type combined high-pressure impulse and low-pressure reaction turbines or all-impulse turbines, single and double geared, for merchant and naval vessels, as well as turbo-generators (Tables 6.1, 6.2, 6.3).

Many problems were encountered in the process. Some were caused by inexperience and errors in design which were corrected as soon as the exact causes were spotted. Also, there were long-term problems. One was the search for a more suitable material for use as turbine blades which became an issue of gravity as steam pressure and temperature increased. Another was devising a good mechanism for balacing turbine rotors. Considerable research was done on these. Yokoyama Kozo, who spent most of his career at Nagasaki designing and building turbines, has written two accounts of the development of turbine technology at Nagasaki (Yokoyama 1955, 1958). The following draws information from his accounts.

115

Table 6.2 Steam turbines for naval vessels built at Nagasaki

	Number	Output (S.H.P.)	Type
1908–10	3	8,000	Parsons direct coupled (imported)
	3	27,000	Mitsubishi-Parsons direct coupled
1911–13	7	49,500	Mitsubishi-Parsons direct coupled
1914–16	7	111,000	Mitsubishi-Parsons direct coupled
1917–19	7	89,000	Mitsubishi-Parsons direct coupled
1920–22	22	389,500	Mitsubishi HP impulse/LP reaction single geared
	8	134,000	Mitsubishi HP mixed/LP reaction single geared
	12	450,000	Gihon HP impulse/LP reaction single geared
1923–25	10	217,500	Mitsubishi HP impulse/LP reaction single geared
	6	36,500	Mitsubishi HP mixed/LP reaction single geared
	8	180,000	Gihon HP impulse/LP reaction single geared
1926–28	4	102,000	Mitsubishi HP impulse/LP reaction single geared
	4	100,000	Kampon impulse single geared
1929–31	4	130,000	Kampon impulse single geared
1932–35	4	152,000	Kampon impulse single geared

Source: Mitsubishi Nagasaki Zosensho 1957

When the Nagasaki Shipyard started to build turbines, designing was done by Parsons which also supplied the basic plans. Design know-how was learned only gradually, for, according to Yokoyama, those who possessed the know-how did not share it.[5] When Yokoyama was placed in charge of making drawings for turbines, he started studying design know-how himself from books.[6] The first turbines that Nagasaki engineers had a part in designing were those of *Anyo* (built 9.1911–6.1913). After this, more and more designing was done at Nagasaki, although all the designs had to be sent to Parsons for checking and approval. The first marine turbines designed entirely at Nagasaki were the single reduction geared turbines of combined impulse-reaction type for the IJN destroyer *Sawakaze* in 1920. As for turbo-generators, the first ones designed entirely at Nagasaki were the all-impulse turbines for Okinawa Electric Company in 1924. Therefore, during the twenty years after licensing, design capability was accumulated,

Table 6.3 Turbo-generators built at Nagasaki

	Number	Total capacity (kW)	Type
1908–10	10	5,000	Parsons all-reaction single cylinder
1911–13	11	6,150	Parsons reaction (with impulse stages) single cylinder
1914–16	17	7,750	Parsons reaction (with impulse stages) single cylinder
1917–19	31	92,900	Parsons reaction (with impulse stages) single cylinder
1920–22	32	19,034	Parsons reaction (with impulse stages) single cylinder
1923–25	6	10,200	Parsons reaction (with impulse stages) single cylinder
	20	2,261	Mitsubishi all-impulse single cylinder
1926–28	23	1,847	Mitsubishi all-impulse single cylinder
		(HP)	
	3	18,000	Mitsubishi combined HP impulse/ LP reaction
	5	13,850	Mitsubishi-Zölly single cylinder
	3	67,500	Mitsubishi-Zölly two–cylinder
1929–31	9	75,850	Mitsubishi-Zölly single cylinder
	5	95,640	Mitsubishi-Zölly two–cylinder
1932–35	23	72,590	Mitsubishi-Zölly single cylinder
	16	348,700	Mitsubishi-Zölly two–cylinder

Source :Mitsubishi Nagasaki Zosensho 1957

new techniques were absorbed and improvements were made in building turbines.

Single reduction geared turbines were adopted for *Anyo*. Esaki Ichiro designed them; Yokoyama and an MKG graduate Okano Sanshichiro made the drawings. Despite some problems with shaft bearings caused by inexperience with shafts rotating at high speeds, the turbines worked well at the trial run. However, soon after the ship was put into service, the turbine gear teeth broke. The cause was not easily detected. Yokoyama, after his return from Britain, carefully investigated the accident and discovered the cause to be the erroneous pitch of the gear teeth.[7] When this was corrected, no similar problems arose. The shipyard at this time sent an engineer and two workers to Parsons to study gear hobbing.

A further increase in efficiency of turbines could be achieved by double gears which would make steam turbines suitable for ships of slower speed. Parsons invented double geared turbines several years after single gears were introduced. At Nagasaki, this was adopted for the NYK passenger cargo ship *Hakone* in 1922. With this ship the bolts holding the gear wheels broke. Investigation into this was done jointly by the turbine design section and Jikkenba. The cause was the mechanism by which gear wheels were held together. Double reduction geared turbines were presenting similar problems in Britain where they were becoming unpopular to the extent that they were rarely adopted. At Nagasaki, the mechanism was redesigned which eliminated accidents of this kind, and double gears continued to be adopted. This continued use of double gears was observed by the British journal *Marine Engineer* in 1935 as 'very curious' (Yano 1966).

Another change was the incorporation of impulse stages in the reaction turbine, and the adoption of combined high-pressure impulse and low-pressure reaction turbines and all-impulse turbines. In principle, all-reaction turbines are more efficient than impulse turbines, but the use of impulse stages enabled the turbine size to be smaller, hence reducing the weight of the engine. Impulse stages had been incorporated in the reaction turbine since 1915, but this was different from building all-impulse turbines. Since Parsons' turbines were reaction turbines, the Nagasaki Shipyard had little experience with all-impulse turbines when IJN found the Parsons-designed high-pressure turbine of the destroyer *Sawakaze* too long to fit into her engine room and requested Nagasaki to change it to an all-impulse turbine. Nagasaki designed one on the basis of the plans of Brown-Curtis impulse turbines supplied by IJN. Many problems arose with this turbine, but it was an excellent opportunity to study impulse turbines. By 1924, the shipyard could design its own all-impulse turbines. The ferry boats *Tsugaru* and *Matsumae* completed in 1924 were fitted with all-impulse turbines designed at Nagasaki. The 500kW generator for Okinawa Electric completed the same year was also an all-impulse turbine. For naval vessels, Nagasaki continued to build its own combined high-pressure impulse–low-pressure reaction turbines until IJN developed its own Kampon-type impulse turbines in 1927.

According to Yokoyama, an optimally efficient turbine is the combined high-pressure impulse and low-pressure reaction type (impulse stages incorporated also in the reaction turbine). Outside naval vessels, the shipyard designed and built this type of turbo-generator for the South Manchurian Railroad in 1926. This design proved to be of better efficiency than other types available at the time. A notable feature of this turbine was the use of stainless steel as the material for turbine blades. No problems arose when the turbine was put into service, and the shipyard was awarded a certificate of excellence.

By the mid-1920s the Nagasaki Shipyard had developed adequate capability to design a turbine of its own type. This ability, in turn, made the shipyard critical of Parsons' designs. For the warship *Tosa*, Nagasaki designed its own high-pressure impulse–low-pressure reaction turbine, but also requested Parsons to do a design of it for reference.[8] When the two designs were compared, Nagasaki's was 100 tons lighter and smaller in volume than Parsons' at equivalent capacity. Not only had Parsons' technology been thoroughly absorbed, but the shipyard was well on its way to going a step further.

Research on blade material and rotor balancing

As the rotational speed of turbines increased and the steam pressure and temperature rose, finding metal material of greater strength and better resistance to corrosion for use as turbine blades became a crucial issue. The problem took an urgent turn when the manganese bronze blades of *Sawakaze* broke on the trial run. Brass had been the predominant material for turbine blades since the licence agreement with Parsons in 1904. IJN was using mainly phosphorus bronze in accordance with Brown-Curtis practice. By the mid-1910s, because of the introduction of the use of super-heated steam, a number of other materials came to be used: manganese bronze, nickel and monel metal. Nickel steel was relatively weak to corrosion; monel metal was very expensive. For *Sawakaze*, manganese bronze blades were used according to Parsons' specifications, but several blades broke on the first trial run. These were changed to white copper steel, but more broke on the second run. Nagasaki and IJN engineers met to investigate the problem. The cause could be attributed not to the design but to the blade material. This time all blades subject to the same level of stress as the ones that broke were changed to white copper steel.

This event prompted the Nagasaki Shipyard to launch a search for better material for turbine blades. The materials available at the time were unsatisfactory in one respect or another, of strength, anti-corrosiveness or cost. Jikkenba, as well as the turbine design department, became involved in this search. A number of alloys of nickel steel and brass were tested at Jikkenba which invented a device to measure the level of stress exerted on turbine blades[9] (Takaira in *Kaiso 2*). The shipyard also requested MSCRI to do research on this, and a MSCRI researcher, Iidaka Ichiro,[10] invented an aluminium alloy named after him. Iidaka metal was comparable to monel metal in tensile strength, although slightly inferior in anti-corrosiveness. An advantage of this metal was its lightness. The shipyard adopted it for the turbines of ferry boats *Tsugaru* and *Matsumae* in 1924.

Another fruit of the research on blade materials was the discovery that NM bronze, developed at Nagasaki as a material for propeller blades,[11] proved to be an excellent material for turbine blades. This metal was comparable to Iidaka metal in strength and more resistant to corrosion, although heavier. NM bronze was adopted for turbine generators of Okinawa Electric as well as for new turbines of *Tenyo* in 1924. Both Iidaka metal and NM bronze proved to be better materials for turbine blades than other materials available at the time.

The research on this subject went further. After the *Sawakaze* incident, IJN launched research on stainless steel as blade material, and by 1923 it was starting to be used to replace worn-out blades. Noting this, the Nagasaki Shipyard sent Sasaki Shintaro, the director of Jikkenba, and two other engineers to Kure Naval Yard to study the making of stainless steel. Research on stainless steel was also started at Nagasaki, and tests proved its suitability as blade material. This was adopted for turbines of the South Manchurian Railroad in 1926, probably for the first time in the world. Stainless steel soon became the predominant material for turbine blades.

Another problem to be solved to improve the performance of turbines was devising machinery for the dynamic balancing of turbine rotors. Static balancing by trial and error was the original method of balancing turbine rotors. According to Yokoyama, he first saw a dynamic balancing machine at Vickers Shipyard in Barrow-in-Furness in 1912. He sketched the machine from memory and had one built at Nagasaki for the balancing of turbines for *Kirishima*. This device needed improvement as rotational speed increased. So, when the Nagasaki Shipyard asked MSCRI to do research on turbine blades, it also requested research on a rotor balancing device. Suyehiro Kyoji, the director of MSCRI, in response, invented a balancing machine in 1921 which was immediately built and used at Nagasaki. This machine was able to eliminate rotor vibration considerably more than the machines available at the time and made balance testing much easier. A few years later, another MSCRI researcher, Kuno Itsuo, invented a balance testing machine using optical rays, which further improved the accuracy of balance testing.

Impulse turbines

The Nagasaki Shipyard's experience with turbines was mostly with the reaction type until the 1920s, since Parsons' was of this type. By the 1920s, the demand for impulse turbines had increased, especially for naval vessels. The Washington armaments reduction agreement of 1922 placed a tight restriction on the size and weight of naval vessels and, as a result, impulse turbines were preferred because of their smaller size and weight. Nagasaki at this time had more orders for naval vessels, since the recession had cut orders for merchant vessels, and the building of turbine generators had not started on a significant scale.

The shipyard was able to design and build impulse turbines, but since the shipyard's experience with them was very limited, it was seen fit to purchase a licence for them from a foreign firm in order to 'incorporate their knowledge and experience, do further research so as to utilize imported knowledge to the utmost' (Yokoyama 1958). The available technologies were surveyed: the Rateau turbine of Metropolitan Vickers, the Zölly turbine of Escher Wyss, the Brown-Boveri and Brown-Curtis. The Brown-Boveri turbine was a reaction type, and there were difficulties in establishing a contract with Brown-Curtis, so the choice was between the Rateau or Zölly turbines. The two Nagasaki engineers, who at the time were on a mission in Britain, were sent to Metropolitan Vickers to inspect the Rateau turbine.[12] Reports were submitted to the head office, which decided to import Zölly turbine technology. One reason for the choice, according to Yokoyama, was that at this time more theoretical German technology was preferred to empirically oriented British.

The licence to manufacture the Zölly turbine was purchased from the Escher Wyss firm in 1925, and three engineers and a foreman were sent to the Escher Wyss Works in Zurich to study its design and building.[13] This technology was imported so that the shipyard would be better equipped to build impulse turbines for naval vessels; however, soon after the contract with Escher Wyss, IJN developed its own all-impulse turbine. All the naval turbines were to be built according to the IJN design, and Nagasaki never had the chance to adopt Zölly turbines for naval vessels. With merchant vessels, diesel engines were gaining in popularity; moreover, orders for them were slack because of the recession. New markets for turbines had to be explored, and this was sought in electric power generation which was a rapidly growing industry in the 1920s. The firm adopted the policy to expand the manufacturing of turbo-generators, and the Zölly turbines came to be built mainly as generators.

The Nagasaki Shipyard had built turbo-generators so far only as a 'side' business. Only relatively small-capacity generators were built, and since the shipyard built 500kW turbo-generators for the first time in 1908, all the turbo-generators were designed by Parsons until the all-impulse turbines for Okinawa Electric Company were built in 1924. In contrast to marine turbines, for which the shipyard sent a mission to study design and building immediately after the contract in 1904, the mission with the purpose of studying turbo-generators was sent only ten years later in 1914.[14] In the 1920s, after the generator for Okinawa Electric, a Mitsubishi-type combined impulse-reaction turbine was developed and a few generators of this type were built, but the largest had the capacity of only 8,000kW.

The Zölly turbines were adopted for the first large-capacity generator for which the shipyard received an order, the 12,500kW generator for the Yawata Steel Mill, completed in 1927. This was designed by Escher Wyss. Several turbine generators after this were designed at Nagasaki, but the design adhered quite strictly to the original Escher Wyss model. This strict adherence was the decision at the managerial level of the firm, which, for Yokoyama, was quite contrary to his expectations. What he had hoped to see was a selective incorporation of the Zölly design and practice to improve what the shipyard could design. The result of the straightforward adoption of the Escher Wyss design was the frequent occurrence of breakdowns and troubles. Research on the problems revealed that the cause often lay in some aspects of the design. Yokoyama says that although the Zölly turbine was advanced in theory, it was designed so as to minimize weight and size for the purpose of cost cutting, which on the one hand was an attractive feature, but on the other a source of problems.

One advantage of the frequent encounter with troubles was that they were opportunities to learn more and improve. When it was realized that the Zölly design was not entirely satisfactory, the shipyard started to modify it and soon proceeded to do the entire designing. In 1933, when the 18,000kW generator was built for the Yamaguchi Prefectural Railroad, so many aspects of the Zölly design had been changed that, according to Seo Saburo, the turbine had become one of the Mitsubishi type (Seo in *Kaiso* 2). Seo recounts that 'both Yokoyama and Yoshida[15] never approved of blind adherence to the Escher Wyss design. They always tried to make something better. The young engineers were always encouraged to try to surpass foreign technology' (Seo in *Kaiso* 2: 114). By the mid-1930s, the Nagasaki Shipyard was able to build some of the world's largest-capacity turbo-generators.

ELECTRIC WELDING

Importing and the diffusion of the technology

The value of welding technology for shipbuilding and mechanical engineering is quite obvious. It can replace such processes as riveting, caulking and smithing; also it can bring about greater strength and tightness of the joined parts than these processes. It economizes on the amount of materials used; hence, the weight of the finished product can be reduced. Like steam turbines, welding technology developed first in the last fifteen years of the nineteenth century and the first decade of this century. Several methods were invented: gas welding and two methods of electric welding (resistance welding and arc welding).[16] Within the last technique three methods using different types of electrode appeared. These employed carbon electrodes, bare metal electrodes and flux coated metal electrodes respectively. The method that came to be utilized most widely was the last method, arc welding using flux coated metal electrodes. Carbon electrodes, because of the high temperature induced, were not suitable for welding relatively thin steel plates, and compared to bare metal electrodes, flux coated metal electrodes could produce better strength since oxidation could be avoided during welding. Before the flux coated electrode was developed, gas welding, invented in France in 1901, saw more widespread use than electric welding, since the low temperature of gas compared to arc welding required less skill. However, with the advance of flux coated electrodes and the demand for welding steel plates of varied thickness, arc welding gained popularity towards the end of the first decade of this century.

The Nagasaki Shipyard purchased a licence for the arc welding method using flux coated metal electrodes from the Swedish firm of Elektriska Swetning Aktieboraget in 1914.[17] This method was developed by Oskar Kjellberg of Sweden in 1907. As with turbines, Mitsubishi was the first in Japan to import this technology. The knowledge of this technology was brought to Nagasaki by Ito Kumezo, who was sent to Europe several times during the 1910s to survey new technological developments, especially internal combustion engines (Shiba 1920). In 1914, a machinery shop engineer, Inakaki Tetsuro,[18] a boiler shop foreman and a foundry shop worker were sent to Sweden for three months' training in the Kjellberg method. The shipyard imported a welding machine and electrodes from the Elektriska Swetning firm the following year, and practice started with instruction by those trained in Sweden. Manufacturing of electrodes started in the boiler shop. In preparation for this, Jikkenba did the chemical analysis of the flux of the Kjellberg electrode (Yano 1966). Electric welding at the Nagasaki yard was first used for repairing and strengthening parts of machines in the boiler and foundry shops. Soon it found application in the making of superheater headers of boilers, water feeders and condensers. By 1916, it started to be used in hull construction, mainly for strengthening and mending iron and steel plates (Shiba 1920, Sasaki 1931).

The first world war enhanced the use of arc welding, especially in America, where there was a soaring demand for cargo ships because of the need to transport goods and arms to Europe. The United States Shipping Board's Emergency Fleet

Corporation, set up to meet this demand, adopted electric welding on a wide basis for repairing, renovating and building ships because of its advantage in the speed of construction. This prompted Lloyd's Register of Shipping to institute rules for the application of electric welding in shipbuilding. Noting these developments, the Nagasaki Shipyard sent Mimura Tetsuo to America in 1918 to survey the application of electric welding in shipbuilding. He visited shipyards and factories where electric welding was used and attended research meetings (Mimura in *Kaikyuroku 2*). After his return he was placed in charge of constructing the hull of the 421Gt ferry boat Suwa, Nagasaki's first all-welded boat, in 1920. This and the 362Gt cargo boat *Fullargar*, built in Britain in the same year, were the first all-welded ships in the world. *Suwa* operated as a ferry boat for more than ten years without any problems with its welded parts. This proved that electric welding was well resistant to corrosion by sea water, an aspect that could not easily be tested in the laboratory.

Although the use of electric welding was greatly enhanced because of the war, the technology itself had not undergone much qualitative improvement (Sasaki 1931).[19] The technique needed to be improved in order for it to be used more in shipbuilding and machinery making. At Nagasaki a laboratory to do research on electric welding was set up within Jikkenba in 1918. Sasaki Shintaro, the director of Jikkenba, had a passion for promoting the use of electric welding, and the development of the technology in Japan owed much to his efforts. Sasaki comments that when electric welding technology was first imported, most people at the shipyard were dubious of the reliability of the technique; however, by 1920 most members of the firm were convinced of its advantages (Sasaki 1931). The setting up of the firm-level research committee on electric welding in 1920 was an indication of the desire of the firm to advance this technology. The use of electric welding technology at Nagasaki continued to increase despite the recession in the 1920s. The technology underwent considerable improvement and elaboration as the technique was applied to more types of metals and more parts of machinery and ships. Electric welding was a new technology, and, in view of the economy it brought to machinery and metal structure building in terms of materials and work time, its application was well able to expand even during a recession.

A decisive reason for the increased use of electric welding was the restriction placed on the weight of naval vessels as a result of the Washington arms reduction agreement of 1922. Since electric welding could reduce the weight of vessels by 20 to 30 per cent compared to riveting, its application was desirable. IJN thus far was not an eager advocate of electric welding. In the early 1920s, electrically welded plates often cracked when tempered. Seeing this, naval inspectors at the Nagasaki yard had prohibited its use on naval vessels (Sasaki 1931). However, the advantages of electric welding could no longer be ignored after the arms reduction agreement, and IJN adopted the policy to utilize it as much as possible.

The use of electric welding on naval vessels increased steadily at the Nagasaki yard after 1922 until with the 8,500Dt cruiser *Misumi* (completed in 1935) 70 per cent of its hull was welded (Kakita 1961). In the same year, however, several destroyers whose hulls were likewise welded 'split in half' during a naval drill in stormy weather. The cause was attributed to the hastily increased use of electric welding. IJN restricted its use in hull construction after this event; however, its use for machinery and other equipment on naval vessels continued to increase.

The application of electric welding on merchant vessels and machinery building was naturally stimulated by the expansion of its application for naval vessels. By the early 1930s, masts, bulkheads, deck room walls and propeller shaft sleeves of merchant vessels were electrically welded. By this time it was commonly used to build tanks, and connect pipes and ducts. For machinery work, electric welding started to be used to build parts of turbines and diesels by the mid-1930s, e.g. mufflers for diesels, steam separators and condensers of turbines and turbine casings. Stainless steel blades of turbines could be repaired by electric welding. Parts of other machinery such as draught fans were also welded. In 1932 the shipyard built an all-welded cracking chamber for the refinery of Nippon Petroleum Company (Sasaki 1953, Kakita 1961, Yano 1966).

This widening range of the application of electric welding was due to the fact that, gradually, more kinds of metals could be welded. Mild steel was the predominant material in machinery making and shipbuilding, and electric welding was mostly applied to this metal. The use of other metals in machinery gradually increased and electric welding was applied to them also. By 1922 cast iron could be welded. As naval turbines expanded in power, so did the size of turbine casings. The casting of large iron casings could not easily be done and casting defects were often found. Electric welding was a suitable method of correcting these defects. Research was done until tests proved that welded parts were as strong as the cast iron itself and electric welding was used for cast iron structures as a normal procedure. By 1926, copper alloys such as brass and gun metal could be welded. This made possible the welding of propeller shaft sleeves which were made of gun metal. Electric welding was applied to aluminium alloys and stainless steel by the early 1930s as well as to Ducol steel plates, which were increasingly used for naval vessels (Sasaki 1953).

Research and the training programme for electric welders

The increasing versatility of electric welding was due to the research done at the shipyard on electric welding. The lecture Shiba Koshiro gave at the Society of Naval Architects in 1920 indicates that the shipbuilding department was doing research on the applicability of electric welding to hull construction by 1920 (Shiba 1920). Mimura recounts his research efforts in applying electric welding to naval vessels (Mimura in *Kaikyuroku* 2). Research on electric welding, however, was done mostly at Jikkenba by Sasaki Shintaro and his assistant Ichibangase Kiyoshi. Sasaki started metallurgical analysis of electrically welded parts and studied its relationship to mechanical properties, a line of research that he continued for many years. One of his research achievements in the early 1920s was the discovery that the use of hydrogen gas at the time of welding produced uniformity in the welded parts of steel plates, which thus far had been difficult to achieve. This method was patented and the improvement it brought to electric welding helped in winning the confidence of IJN in electric welding (Sasaki 1953, Yano 1966). Ichibangase did a series of studies on various kinds of electrodes available at the time.[20] The boiler shop had been making electrodes since 1915, according to the Kjellberg method, but Jikkenba took over this job in 1923. Ichibangase recounts his efforts to improve the process of manufacturing electrodes. He invented a device to speed up the process and introduced mechanization in mixing the flux and drying the rods. Better-quality electrodes were always sought. Based on the study of the various electrodes available at the time, a Mitsubishi-type electrode was developed by the late 1930s. Electrodes for welding specialized metals, e.g. gun metal and stainless steel, were also developed (Ichibangase in *Kaiso 3*). Jikkenba did research on electric welding of cast iron, stainless steel and copper and aluminium alloys. The application of electric welding to these kinds of metals was the result of research, and a number of Jikkenba reports were written on the welding of these metals.[21]

The development of electric welding owed as much to the availability of trained welders as to research. As discussed in Chapter 4, the training programme for electric welders was created in 1921. This was modelled upon the training scheme in operation at the American Emergency Fleet Corporation.[22] Seven engineers from different work places were appointed as trainers. The programme put trainees to a six-month full-time training consisting of lectures and practical training. The lectures gave trainees basic knowledge in metallurgy, chemistry and electrical engineering, in addition to practical knowledge of electric welding.[23] Records show that the programme operated at a rate of once a year until 1937. For the first two sessions the number of trainees were ten and twelve respectively. Each session was usually recorded, as Jikkenba reports, but for some reason most of these records have not remained; therefore, the total number of trainees is not known. According to the report on the first two sessions of the programme, the training noticeably improved skill, knowledge and awareness. Sasaki assesses the effect of training in terms of the average tensile strength of the test pieces made by electric welders at the shipyard (Figure 6.1). The tensile strength improves for a few years from 1923 until 1925, then drops until it goes up again after 1928. Sasaki attributes the drop in the second half of the 1920s to the sudden demand for welders resulting from IJN's policy of large-scale adoption of electric welding for naval vessels. Since those not adequately trained were included, the average went down. The figure also shows the standard tensile strength of welders adopted by IJN and Nippon Kaiji Kyokai (Japan Marine Bureau), which are lower than the average of Nagasaki welders. These possessed better skills than welders elsewhere which, according to Sasaki, was due to the excellence of the training programme

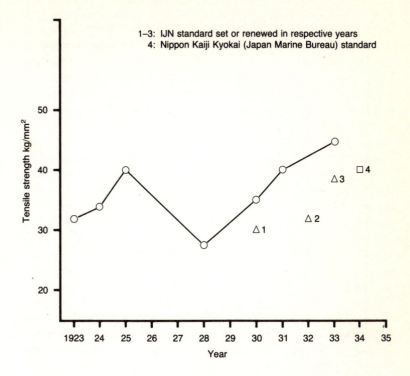

Figure 6.1 Average tensile strength of test pieces made by electric
welders at Nagasaki Shipyard
Source: Sasaki 1953

at Nagasaki. Assistant naval inspectors stationed at Nagasaki
took part in the shipyard's training programme. The Yawata
Steel Mill as well as IJN sent workers to attend the course.

Electric welding had become well integrated in the daily
operations of the shipyard by the mid-1930s. As seen so far,
research and training played an important role in its diffusion
within the yard. A quantitative indication of the development
of electric welding is seen in the increase in the number of
welders and the number of electrodes consumed at the
shipyard, shown in Figure 6.2. Both the number of welders
and the consumption of electrodes increased steadily. The rate
of increase of electrode consumption is greater than that of the

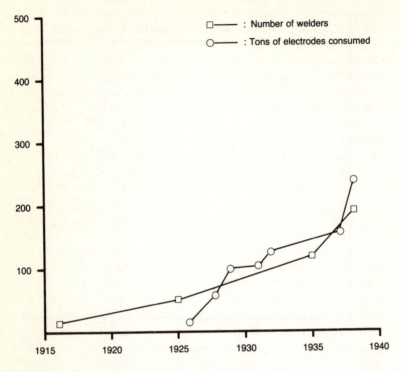

Figure 6.2 Number of welders and the consumption of electrodes at
Nagasaki Shipyard
Source: Kakita 1961, Sasaki 1953

number of welders.[24] This is indicative of the boom in demand
for welding in the second half of the 1920s. It should be noted
that the consumption of electrodes and the number of welders
continued to increase during 1930–32, the years when the
construction work of the shipyard as well as the number of
staff and workers decreased considerably due to recession. This
indicates that the increase in the use of electric welding during
these years was indeed great.

Electric welding, compared to turbines or diesels which leave
visible traces of technological development in the form of
machines, is a technology whose evolution is relatively difficult
to trace. It was seen that the range of its application expanded

130

both in quantitative and qualitative terms. Further and more visible evidence of the extent of its development at the Nagasaki Shipyard is provided by the fact that, by the second half of the 1930s, the shipyard was able to build thick boiler drums by electric welding. Boiler drums had been riveted, but as both temperature and pressure rose, riveting became increasingly unreliable. The solution to this was first sought in the adoption of unjointed solid drums, but this was much higher in cost. The Nagasaki Shipyard set up a research committee on high-pressure boiler drums in 1932 and started research on the welding of boiler drums.[25] Research on the welding of thick steel plates and appropriate types of electrode and X-ray studies of welded parts were done by members of Jikkenba and the boiler shop.[26] According to Sasaki, the building of the cracking chamber for Nippon Petroleum in 1932 was part of the preparation for building welded boiler drums. In 1938, Jikkenba built a test drum to conduct a breakdown test. This proved that the welded part of the drum possessed the same strength as the plates. The shipyard built its first all-welded boiler drum in 1940.

Another visible result of the development of electric welding at the Nagasaki yard was the successful attempt at building an automatic welding machine during the second world war. This attempt was in response to the need to construct transport vessels rapidly during the war, since automatic welding speeds up the welding process by twenty times (Yano 1966).[27] The development effort started with the attempt to build an imitation of the automatic welding machine of the American firm, Unionmelt, from its photograph found in the advertisement in the *Welding Journal*. This was in 1941, and by this time licence agreements with American firms were not possible because of the political situation. Several members of Jikkenba and the welding factory (created in 1938) were involved in this project. The electric welding research committee provided a firm-level forum for this project, and in 1942 a sub-committee was organized specifically to discuss the Unionmelt method. Literature survey and research on flux and control mechanism were done. By the end of 1942 the machine had been built and test runs produced smooth welded parts similar to the photographs seen in the original advertisement (Kanamori in *Kaiso 3*, Yano 1966). The manufacturing and the use of the machine on a commercial base was not realized because of the lack of appropriate parts and materials during the war, but the success in the experimental building of the automatic welding machine is a proof of the level of sophistication the electric welding technology at Nagasaki had achieved.

It is said that the rapid growth of the shipbuilding industry in post-war Japan was due to the excellence of welding technology. Automatic welding was in fact imported anew after the war, but the capabilities accumulated before the war made a definite contribution to the rapid development of the technology. In an interview with the author, Dr Kanamori Masao[28] emphatically said that pre-war developments were significant, and cited the example of low-temperature brittleness to illustrate the point. Automatic welding itself is an easy technique to use, but many problems arise when welded ships are actually put into service. For example, the stress on the welded plates of a hull at the surface of the water increases as the temperature drops since the part above the water level becomes increasingly brittle. This often causes cracks in the metal plates. Successful application of electric welding must take into account such phenomena. Because metallurgical research had been done since the pre-war days in relation to electric welding, the occurrence of such problems could be foreseen and avoided. Rapid development of the technology after the war was possible because of such a research base.

Dr Kanamori also emphasized the importance of professional societies and links with universities and other research institutes in upgrading the electric welding technology at Nagasaki. In order to pursue research on any topic at the shipyard it was necessary to know who was doing what and where. The Japan Welding Society (founded in 1925) provided this information and facilitated contacts with other researchers. Jikkenba engineers were always encouraged to visit universities and other research institutes whenever necessary. Researchers from outside frequently visited Jikkenba. In this connection, Sasaki Shintaro's activities are worth noting. As the director of Jikkenba, he made a substantial contribution in expanding its range of research. Sasaki's own research interests were in metallurgy and electric welding. As a researcher he was as active outside as at the shipyard. He was a regular lecturer at Kyushu Imperial University. He frequently went on lecture trips to other universities and professional societies. He published a great deal on these topics in professional journals. When Gakushin set up a committee on electric welding, Sasaki was chosen as a member. After the war the Welding Society of Japan created an award scheme which bears his name. His activities made a significant contribution to the development of electric welding not only for Mitsubishi but for Japan as well.

DIESEL ENGINES

Vickers' diesel engines

Innovations that influenced the development of shipbuilding and marine engineering in this century occurred coincidently. Invented by Rudolf Diesel in 1890, the internal combustion engine bearing his name started to be manufactured commercially during the two decades before the start of the first world war. A number of machinery manufacturers in Europe developed and built their own types of diesel engines: Burmeister and Wain (Denmark), M.A.N. and Krupp (Germany), Werkspoor (Holland), Fiat (Italy), Vickers and Doxford (Britain). Technically different types of engines were developed: two-cycle and four-cycle types, single acting or double acting, with air or airless injection systems. A two-cycle engine works once in every two movements of the piston while a four-cycle one works once in every four. In the single acting engine, fuel is injected into one (upper) side of the piston only while in double acting engines, fuel is injected alternately to both sides of the piston. The latter can produce more output. The air injection engine uses compressed air to inject fuel into the cylinder; the airless injection engine injects pressurized fuel into the cylinder without the use of compressed air. The former needs an air compressor, which is attached to the engine, while the latter does not. By 1910, diesel engines started to be adopted for relatively large merchant vessels. One of the earliest was the 2,500BHP four-cycle engine for the 4,950Gt Danish cargo vessel *Selandia*, put to service in 1912. Diesel ships could not produce the speed of turbines but their fuel consumption was much less and so diesel had a promising future for propelling cargo vessels.

Mitsubishi already had an interest in diesel engines in the first half of the 1910s. In fact, at the trial run of *Selandia* at Tynemouth in 1911, the Nagasaki engineer Esaki Ichiro, who was on a mission to Parsons' firm at Wallsend-upon-Tyne, was allowed to be on board, on the promise that he would not make public the details of the engine (Yano 1966). The following year, Ito Kumezo was sent on a year-long mission to survey internal combustion engine manufacturers in Europe with the specific purpose of selecting the appropriate firm from which to import diesel engine manufacturing technology. He visited most diesel manufacturers during this and on the following missions up to 1918, and went to some factories more than once.[29]

Despite Ito's mission, the initiative for importing diesel technology was not taken by Mitsubishi. It was in response to the request by IJN to manufacture submarines that the firm imported diesel engine technology as a part of the contract for submarines. Mitsubishi exchanged contracts with Vickers for the manufacture of Vickers' L-type submarine and its diesel engine in 1917. Whether it was IJN or Mitsubishi that chose Vickers is not clear from the records. It is most likely to have been a joint decision. Although IJN started to import submarines in 1905, the decision for large-scale adoption of submarines was taken only after the start of the first world war, and doubtless was stimulated by the remarkable activity of German submarines. IJN's own experience with submarines was still very limited. The ones imported up to 1914 were the American Holland type and Vickers' C type. IJN built and designed a submarine for the first time based on the Vickers C model in 1916. At the time of the first world war, therefore, IJN was still at a 'search' stage. IJN itself imported a Schneider-Laubeuf submarine and engine in 1917, and Sulzer's and M.A.N.'s diesel engines for submarines. A licence to manufacture Sulzer's submarine diesel engine was purchased in 1918. Kawasaki Shipbuilding bought the licence and started building Fiat-Laurenti-type submarines and engines. These 'sampling' activities proved for IJN that Schneider's and Fiat's engines were not as satisfactory as Sulzer, M.A.N. and Vickers types. After the war, IJN did considerable research to improve Sulzer- and M.A.N.-type diesel engines and eventually succeeded in developing its own Kampon-type diesel engine for submarines. Research on the Vickers type was left to Mitsubishi, whose efforts culminated in the development of a Mitsubishi-Vickers-type engine in 1934 which used crude oil as fuel, in contrast to the original Vickers' model which used petroleum (Nippon Zosen Gakkai 1977, Seisan Gijutsu Kyokai 1970).

Mitsubishi had its own reasons for buying Vickers' licence. Although no reference to this is found in the records of Mitsubishi, there was a prolonged negotiation between the two firms from 1912 to 1915 for a licence to contract ships and machinery to Vickers' design, which had remained unsigned. The correspondence between the two firms shows that it was difficult to arrive at terms of a contract that were satisfactory to both firms.[30] The submarine contract probably presented a satisfactory *dénouement* to the suspended negotiations with Vickers. Moreover, Vickers' L-type submarine had been adopted by the Royal Navy where it had already established a reputation for being reliable. The British Admiralty readily authorized this agreement.[31] Takeda Hideo[32] and Matsumoto Koji were sent on behalf of Mitsubishi at the final stages of negotiations and the signing of the contract in 1917. It was stipulated in the contract that Vickers would allow Mitsubishi to send representatives to their works to study construction of the submarine and its diesel engine. Ito Kumezo led the party of engineers and workers to Britain in late 1917 to be trained at Vickers' Ipswich works. The group consisted of eight engineers and several foremen and workers of the machinery factory.[33]

These engineers and workers had already accumulated some experience with diesel engines before going to Vickers. According to Shimizu Kikuhei,[34] who later played a key role in the development of the diesel engine at the Nagasaki Shipyard, it was in mid-1915 that he was told that the shipyard would soon have to build submarines and their diesel engines. At the time there was very little that he could consult in order to study design and building of diesel engines. Shimizu found out that the Society of Mechanical Engineers was planning sketch sessions of the diesel generator owned by the Tokyo Gas Company which had been imported from Germany. The Nagasaki Shipyard took advantage of this opportunity to send Shimizu, Kiuno Jozo, Tanaka Shigesaburo[35] and Nakamura Sadao[36] to Tokyo for a three-month mission to do a detailed sketch of this engine (Shimizu in *Kaikyuroku 1*).

When the plans of this four-cycle single acting 250hp, 150kW air injection system diesel generator were completed in late 1915, the firm decided to transfer the engineers and workers involved in the submarine project to the Kobe Shipyard, which was chosen as a more appropriate place because of the availability of deep sea nearby which was necessary for testing submarines. The diesel generator was built at Kobe in 1916. According to Shimizu, it took a few months after the completion of the engine for it to run smoothly. When satisfactory results were obtained, several engines of the same type were built (Shimizu in *Kaikyuroku 1*).

The members of the diesel building team were already experienced when they were sent to Vickers in late 1917, which undoubtedly aided their training there. One of them, Mase Tokuzo, had studied submarine engine building for a year at the Yokosuka Naval Yard before going to Vickers (see Table 4.5). At Vickers the engineers and workers studied the designing and building of submarines and diesel engines for nearly a year. The building of submarines started immediately after their return to the Kobe Shipyard in late 1918. The engines for the first three were imported from Vickers; later ones were built at Kobe. Submarine building became a major activity of this shipyard.

Although building diesel engines for submarines was the main job of the internal combustion engine department of the Kobe Shipyard, diesel generators, engines for aircrafts and cars were also built.[37] In 1920 the Kobe Shipyard bought the licence to manufacture diesel engines for merchant vessels as well from Vickers. This was a timely action since shipping companies started to adopt diesel engines to economize on fuel consumption as soon as the recession hit. OSK decided to adopt diesel engines for three China liners built at the Kobe Shipyard in 1924. The 600hp four-cycle single acting airless injection engines for these three vessels were purchased from Vickers, and assembled at the Kobe yard. In 1926, another two sets of the same type engines were built at Kobe according to plans supplied by Vickers, again for OSK ships. In 1928, it was decided that the Vickers design of the diesel engines for two other OSK ships were both too heavy and big. These were redesigned at Kobe.

Sulzer's diesel engines

The adoption of diesel engines for large merchant vessels became widespread after the first world war. It was in the interest of shipping firms to have diesel ships since they were considerably more economical in terms of fuel consumption than turbines.[38] After 1923, diesel engines were adopted for most large merchant vessels in Europe. Shipping companies in Japan were also anxious to adopt diesel engines for large passenger and cargo ships. Soon after OSK ordered Vickers' diesel engines for their China liners, NYK asked for an estimate for diesels for a 7,000Gt liner. Mitsubishi recommended Vickers' engines but NYK rejected them on the grounds that they were much heavier than others and Vickers had so far no experience in building large-capacity diesel engines. The shipping firms' preferences were Sulzer's engines in the two-cycle range and Burmeister Wain's in the four-cycle range. This prompted Mitsubishi to consider buying Sulzer's licence, since the firm already possessed four-cycle technology. When negotiations were started with OSK for three South American liners, Mitsubishi negotiated simultaneously with Sulzer to purchase a licence for the two-cycle engines for adoption in these vessels. When the order was confirmed for the OSK liners, Mitsubishi exchanged contracts with Sulzer for the manufacture of two-cycle single acting air injection marine diesel engines. The contract provided for sending a technical staff of five for a year to study the design and building of the engines. The Nagasaki Shipyard sent Inagaki Tetsuro and Akiba Yoshie,[39] two other engineers and a foreman from the machinery factory to the Sulzer firm in 1924.

During their stay, engines for the first two of the OSK vessels were built at the Sulzer factory. These were adopted for *Santos* and *La Plata* in 1925–26; the engines for the third, *Montevideo*, were built at Nagasaki. In order to design diesel engines, the Nagasaki Shipyard created a special section for them in September 1924 and transferred seven engineers and four technicians from other sections of the machinery design department. Another engineer was recruited from Mitsubishi Internal Combustion Engine Company.

The building of Sulzer's engines started in late 1925. The shipyard soon found out that the Sulzer engine was not entirely satisfactory. Minor technical problems frequently arose, the most common one being the burning of shaft bearings (Kagami in *Kaiso 2*). It was more expensive than the Burmeister and Wain four-cycle engine which was becoming more popular with shipping firms than the Sulzer. Technically, the major problem with the Sulzer engine was the necessity to attach an air compressor because it had an air injection system. Air compressors were, by the nature of their structure and function, subject to frequent breakdowns.[40] Even if they functioned well, they reduced the efficiency of the engine by consuming 8 to 10 per cent of engine output. It lengthened the engine and increased its weight. Air compressors could, of course, be disposed of if an airless fuel injection system could be developed. At this time it was difficult to burn fuel completely by airless injection in large diesel engines; however, the system had already been developed for small engines. In fact the Vickers engine had an airless injection system; therefore, in principle, it was possible to adopt it for large two-cycle engines. It was a question of time, but the Sulzer firm had no intention of developing this immediately (Shimizu and Kawai 1934, Yano 1966).

MS diesel engine

The Nagasaki Shipyard probably started considering improving the Sulzer diesel engine very soon after it started to build it. By early 1927, the future of diesel engine building at the Nagasaki yard was a subject of deep concern, and the Head Office of the firm convened a meeting of specialists from Nagasaki and Kobe to discuss the matter. The question took an urgent turn when it was learned that NYK and OSK had decided to adopt the Burmeister and Wain engines for their new Australian liners in June 1928. This was thought to place Sulzer's engines at a further disadvantage in securing orders in the future. In August 1928 Mitsubishi decided to develop 'better and cheaper' engines and created an intrafirm Internal Combustion Engine Research Committee (hereafter abbreviated as ICERC) to guide this development effort (*Shashi*).

Prior to this, some preparatory moves were made. In November 1926, Shimizu Kikuhei, who had worked with the Vickers diesel engines at Kobe, was asked to go to Nagasaki to work with the Sulzer engines. At this point the firm was already aware of the need to improve the Sulzer engines. When Shimizu saw the Sulzer engine, he became convinced that there was room for improvement. Hamada Hyo, then the chairman of the board of directors of MZKK, consulted Shimizu about the possibility of improving the Sulzer engine. Shimizu replied that it would be possible to apply the airless injection system to two-cycle diesel engines (Shimizu in *Kaikyuroku 1*). The Nagasaki yard immediately conducted some preliminary experiments to find out the feasibility of the application of airless injection to two-cycle engines. In early 1928, to one cylinder of the Sulzer 6ST60 model being built for *San Louis*, a cargo vessel, Vickers' airless injection system was attached, and tests were conducted. These tests confirmed that application of airless injection was possible (Kawai 1940).

Research efforts to develop what was to become the MS two-cycle single acting airless injection diesel engine proceeded in a systematic fashion thanks to the method devised by Shimizu, who was held responsible for this project, and to the guidance provided by ICERC. The basic idea behind MS was to inject fuel oil directly by pressurizing it by a pump thus eliminating the necessity of using compressed air. For this, three basic problems had to be solved: devising a new method of scavenging the cylinder, including reshaping the scavenge port; reshaping the combustion chamber; and devising the airless injection system. Shimizu proceeded to design the basic features related to these aspects of the new engine, and in the first phase of the development effort, research was to be done to test whether Shimizu's ideas would work. In the second stage, an experimental engine was to be built to determine the exact shapes and dimensions of the new engine. Results of the experiments conducted were to be reported at ICERC meetings where they would be discussed and the next step of the research decided. In the first stage, the Sulzer engines being built at the shipyard were to be used at their trial stage to conduct necessary experiments. The following recapitulates what was actually done in the development effort.

Scavenging experiments

The results of the application of Vickers' airless injection system to the engine of *San Louis* were discussed at the first meeting of ICERC, where it was decided that an experimental machine to study scavenging, to observe air current inside the cylinder and to measure scavenging efficiency was to be built. For this, Kagami Kohei[41] of the internal combustion engine section and Okuda Katsumi of Jikkenba were sent to the Aeronautics

Research Institute of Tokyo Imperial University to learn how to calculate scavenging efficiency and to learn about air currents in a diesel cylinder. On the basis of their mission report, at the second ICERC in November 1928, it was decided to have a real size experimental machine built which took scale effect into consideration. The machine was designed by Okuda and Kagami. Fujita Hideo[42] drew the plans. This experimental set-up was completed in January 1930. The first job was to study the behaviour of air current inside the cylinder with the newly designed scavenge port. Experiments were conducted by hanging strings and sending incense smoke or sawdust into the cylinder. It took a year to study this and to measure and calculate scavenging efficiency. On the basis of the results obtained, the exact shape of the port to be used on the experimental MS[43] engine built in 1931 was discussed at the tenth ICERC in March 1931.

Combustion chamber shape

Plans for studying the appropriate combustion chamber shape were discussed at the fourth ICERC in July 1929. Kawai Kiyoshi,[44] who had just returned from more than three years of study and training at Zurich Polytechnic and the Sulzer factory, was placed in charge of this and the research on the airless injection system. Some preliminary tests were conducted and the several shapes proposed by Nagasaki and Kobe yards were discussed at the sixth and seventh ICERC in February and May 1930 respectively. In August 1930, the sixth cylinder of Sulzer's 6ST68/120 engine built for *Hokuriku* was used to test three of the shapes proposed. One was found to be better than the other two. It was also found that the fuel injection pressure should be much higher than originally proposed. These results were discussed at the ninth ICERC in December 1930. In January of the following year, one cylinder of the engine built for *Koryu* was modified to raise fuel injection pressure, and a further five types of combustion chamber shapes and several nozzle shapes were tested. The results were discussed at the tenth ICERC in March 1931 when the features of appropriate combustion chamber shape and fuel injection nozzle were determined.

Airless injection system

When the preliminary experiment with the engine of *San Louis* had proved that airless injection was possible with the two-cycle engine, ideas as to the exact system of airless injection to be adopted were discussed in the ICERC meetings. The eighth ICERC meeting in August 1930 decided to test what was to become the MS airless injection system with its accumulator-type fuel pump and its unique fuel valve control system, which was done in February 1931 with successful results. The tenth ICERC meeting in March 1931 decided then to test this system further by converting all cylinders of *Koryu* to this airless injection system, which was started in April 1931. Because of problems with the fuel pump, the experiment lasted several months, but satisfactory results were obtained in the end.

Thus by the tenth ICERC meeting in March 1931 the key problems in the development of the new engine, scavenging and airless injection systems and the shapes of scavenge port and combustion chamber, had been solved. The project then moved on to build a single cylinder experimental engine which was completed in September 1931. Experiments were conducted with this for several months, the results of which determined the exact dimensions of the scavenge port and combustion chamber, injection nozzle diameter, injection angle, injection time, etc. The order for the first MS diesel engines had in fact been received in February 1931. They were built at the same time as the final experiments were being conducted and were completed in July 1933. The OSK cargo *Nankai* fitted with them was put into service in January 1933.

This newly developed MS diesel engine was of better performance than the Sulzer-type engine. The successful application of the airless injection system did away with the troublesome air compressor. Because of this, engine efficiency improved by 6–7 per cent (Fujita 1985). Moreover, the absence of an air compressor made the engine shorter and reduced its weight. *Nankai*, a New York cargo vessel with MS engines, consumed 120 tons less fuel oil per return voyage to New York than her sister, *Kinai*, fitted with Sulzer engines (Kurosaki in *Kaiso* 2). Its scavenging system with small scavenging pumps attached to each cylinder effectively reduced engine length in comparison to Sulzer's system which had one large pump

Table 6.4 Marine diesel engines built at Nagasaki

	Number	Output (BHP)	Type
1925	2	4,600	Sulzer single acting (imported)
1926	2	4,600	Sulzer single acting (imported)
	3	6,900	Mitsubishi-Sulzer single acting
1927	3	6,900	Mitsubishi-Sulzer single acting
1928	4	16,000	Sulzer single acting
	3	6,900	Mitsubishi-Sulzer single acting
1929	13	48,300	Mitsubishi-Sulzer single acting
1930	10	38,800	Mitsubishi-Sulzer single acting
1931	1	1,500	Sulzer single acting
	3	7,000	Mitsubishi-Sulzer single acting
1932	4	14,400	MS
1933	4	16,200	MS
1934	5	35,300	Mitsubishi-Sulzer double acting
	1	4,200	MS
1935	2	7,500	MS
1936	2	16,000	MSD (double acting)
1937	3	12,000	MS
	3	24,000	MSD

Source: Mitsubishi Nagasaki Zosensho 1957

attached to one end of the engine. The scavenge port was of an entirely new design which produced better scavenge efficiency. The accumulator-type airless injection system with control valve and the newly shaped combustion chamber produced better combustion efficiency and was simpler in structure and easier to handle. Compared to the Sulzer engine, the MS had a simpler structure which made it less vulnerable to breakdowns. After the MS engine had been developed, all marine single acting diesel engines built at Nagasaki were of this type, and the building of Sulzer's single acting engines was stopped (Table 6.4).[45]

Even after the initial success with MS, research to improve it further was continued. Scavenging efficiency at the time of the building of the first MS was not much better than Sulzer's. Further research on this eventually clarified the effects of the shape of the scavenge port and the height of the piston. This was reported at the thirteenth ICERC in March 1935. The dimensions related to these were then changed. In the same year a smaller scavenge experimental machine was built, and as a result of research with it, methods to measure and calculate scavenge air flow and scavenge pressure were devised.[46] Further research on airless injection was also done by building an experimental machine for it in 1939. This enabled the clarification of differences at the time of injection between low-speed and high-speed engines. The original MS experimental engine also continued to be used. In 1935, this was remodelled to enable experiments in developing the double acting version of MS, the MSD, which was successfully built in 1936 (Yano 1966).

The research activities in developing and improving MS were done not only by the internal combustion engine section of the machinery design department, but also by Jikkenba. The latter indeed played a significant role in this effort. Okuda Katsumi and his assistant Takaira Fumio (1924 MKG graduate) were involved from the very beginning. The scavenging experimental machine was built and installed in Jikkenba, and the research on scavenging was done jointly by Jikkenba and the design team. Okuda devised a method of measuring and calculating stress on various parts of the engine (e.g. piston) using optical elasticity. This type of information was vital in designing. Vibration stress was also measured. Other measurements and analyses were done by Jikkenba, e.g. analysis of the exhaust gas of the experimental engine and measuring the fuel injection pressure. According to Dr Fujita Hideo, the successful development of the MS engine in a relatively short period of time owed much to these efforts by Jikkenba.

After the first MS had been built in 1932, Jikkenba's involvement with MS became even more intense and varied. When the shaft bearing of the MS of *Nankai*'s sister, *Hokkai*, burned, two Jikkenba workers invented a device to measure the temperature of shaft bearings. The experimental set-up to study fuel injection was installed in Jikkenba. Research on scavenging was continued, and the small experimental machine mentioned previously was built in Jikkenba. At this time another MKG graduate technician, Kumon Noboru, joined this research. In 1938 a major improvement to MS was introduced by Okuda when he invented a vibration stabilizing apparatus for the MS engines of *Argentina*.

The example of the diesel engine at the Nagasaki Shipyard thus shows in a rather remarkable way how originally imported technology can be transformed to produce an innovation of improved performance. What supported this was a systematic research and development effort guided by ICERC which had MZKK's foremost experts on the subject and members of the decision-making ranks of the firm. The actual research was done jointly by the internal combustion engine design team[47] of the machinery design department and Jikkenba. The latter played an important role.

The success of the project was due to the excellent team work of the engineers and technicians involved; however, as Dr Fujita stressed, the role of Shimizu Kikuhei was crucial.[48] He was the one who invented the basic features of the scavenge port, combustion chamber and fuel injection system. The simplified structure of MS was a result of Shimizu's designing ability. He was also responsible for setting down the procedures employed in the development effort: defining key problems to be examined, experimenting by using the Sulzer engines being built at the shipyard and the building of an experimental engine. This procedure, according to Dr Fujita, was as important a legacy as knowledge and experience for post-war diesel engine development. Mitsubishi developed another type of diesel engine, the Mitsubishi UE diesel engine, after the war. The same procedures were employed, and, because of the experience with MS, the project team was confident of its success (Fujita 1985).

The three technologies discussed in this chapter underwent considerable transformation after they were initially imported. The shipyard not only assimilated but also improved these technologies by accumulating minor technological changes. These were often brought about by problem solving and trouble shooting activities; for example, turbine gear hobbing and double gears were improved through such activities. The development of new materials for turbine blades and better machines for rotor balancing improved the performance of turbines. The diffusion of electric welding was made possible by the application of the technique to different kinds of metals, and the development of appropriate electrodes. In diesels, a good deal of problem solving had to be done to apply the airless injection system successfully to large two-cycle engines.

The shipyard exploited various channels of importing technology to develop these technologies. Careful 'searching' was done to choose suitable diesel engine and impulse turbine technologies. Machines were imported and training missions were sent as part of licence agreements. Engineers were recruited from the Parsons firm for the assembling of the first turbines imported. In the case of diesels, a 'reverse engineering' exercise was done by sketching and building an engine before manufacturing under licence started. Missions were sent to licenser firms more than once when necessary. Textbooks and journals were used as sources of information for learning design know-how of turbines and for imitating an automatic welding machine.

The training programme for electric welders was important in diffusing the technology within the shipyard. Missions for the purpose of training in specific techniques were sent to universities and naval yards as well as to overseas licenser firms. MKG graduates played significant roles as assistants to key engineers. The role of some engineers stands out in the course of the development of the three technologies: Yokoyama in turbine, Sasaki in electric welding and Shimizu in diesel (also Motora in stabilizer technology as discussed in Chapter 5). The appearance of such committed and talented engineers is an interesting and important phenomenon that warrants socio-historical investigation. What can be said here is that their university training was useful to their careers in that they had specialized in the fields in which they made significant contributions at the shipyard.

The role of research was overwhelmingly important in the development of the three technologies. Jikkenba and MSCRI did research on turbine blade materials and rotor balancing. Diffusion and improvement of electric welding owed much to research done at Jikkenba which ranged from basic metallurgical studies to research on electric welding of different metals and their electrodes. The laboratory worked closely with the diesel design team to do necessary research to develop the MS engine. Technological research committees facilitated the improvement and diffusion of electric welding and guided the MS development effort. Exchange of information and research cooperation extended beyond the firm to universities and other research institutes.

7

TECHNOLOGICAL LEARNING AND INDUSTRIAL DEVELOPMENT – CONCLUSIONS AND POLICY IMPLICATIONS

TECHNOLOGICAL LEARNING AND TECHNOLOGICAL STRATEGIES AT MITSUBISHI NAGASAKI SHIPYARD – CONCLUSIONS

Considerable accumulation of technological capabilities took place at Mitsubishi Nagasaki Shipyard in the pre-war period. Technology imports, within-enterprise training and in-house research played important roles in this technological learning process. New technologies were imported through appropriate channels; and they were then assimilated and improved through incremental technological changes. These, in turn, were made possible by various programmes of training and research. The combination and the evolution of the varied modes of technology imports, training and research constituted the 'technological strategies' of the shipyard in the pre-war period.

Because of the strategic and commercial importance of shipbuilding, it was government policy to close the gap with the world technological frontier and to make the industry competitive in the production of high-quality ships. Mitsubishi Nagasaki Shipyard responded to this by importing 'best practice' technologies through various channels. The extent and the manner of use of these channels were adapted to the changing degree of the technological sophistication of the shipyard. The channels were used in the way that fully utilized the technological capabilities already accumulated while developing new ones needed to assimilate more advanced technologies.

A variety of within-enterprise training schemes was instituted for workers, technicians as well as engineers, both long-term and *ad hoc*. The long-term schemes were geared to develop basic skills and knowledge for workers and technicians, since formal education at the time could not supply recruits with the suitable technological capabilities. Short-term and *ad hoc* programmes were designed to accumulate specific skills and knowledge required for the assimilation and improvement of new technologies.

Research activities stayed close to the needs of production. The testing and analysis of materials used at the shipyard constituted a major part of the research function. A good deal of problem solving and trouble shooting was done through research. These activities not only facilitated the assimilation of imported technologies, but also improved them by introducing minor technological changes. Both training and research were thus indispensable in accumulating technological capabilities to assimilate and improve imported technologies.

The most salient feature of the technological learning process at Mitsubishi Nagasaki Shipyard was the ubiquity of 'improvement engineering'. This was such a pervasive activity that it would not be an exaggeration to say that the engineers and workers were somehow conditioned to bring about improvements in whatever they did, whenever and wherever possible. Imported technologies underwent considerable improvements after initial importing through the accumulation of minor technological changes. In the case of the MS diesel engine, improvement efforts did not stop with minor changes but resulted in a major innovation. There were improvements not only in product engineering but also in production engineering. This ranged from the introduction of pneumatic compressors to the improvement of simple tools by workers. All of these contributed to the enhancement of productive efficiency.

The technological learning process at Mitsubishi Nagasaki Shipyard both complemented, and was complemented by, national-level efforts. Training missions were sent to universities and naval yards. There was cooperation with external research institutes. Professional societies provided sources of information. The shipyard recruited engineers from the graduates of naval architecture and marine/mechanical engineering courses in universities and polytechnics, as soon as these courses had been established. On the other hand, where national efforts were insufficient, for example in diffusing secondary technical education, the shipyard complemented the inadequacy by founding MKG. The institutionalization of in-house research was, in part, a result of the lack of relevant research efforts at the national level.

The shipyard was also responsive to national policies towards the shipbuilding industry. It built large, technologically sophisticated ships which the government tried to encourage through subsidies and tariff measures. The shipyard responded to the absence of a machinery industry by assuming the role of machinery maker. These efforts made the shipyard a difficult and complex enterprise. The government in turn attempted to ease the difficulty by regulating naval orders to smooth out the fluctuations in demand for commercial ships. Also, the diffusion of technology from the navy helped the shipyard to upgrade its technological capabilities. These complementarities and the mutual responsiveness between efforts at the firm and on a national level suggest that what Freeman (1987) termed the 'national system of innovation' already existed before the war.

The technological efforts within the framework of the 'national system of innovation' led the Japanese shipbuilding industry to achieve a high degree of technological sophistication by the first half of the 1930s. By this time, the 'best practice' technologies were well assimilated and improved, and the ships and the engines built at Nagasaki Shipyard were qualitatively competitive with those built in the most advanced shipyards of the world. The growth of the industry in the post-war period, i.e. the attainment of the position of the world's leader as early as the second half of the 1950s, would probably have been difficult without the accumulation of the technological capabilities in the pre-war period. As pointed out in the cases of electric welding and the diesel engine, the pre-war experiences were indispensable in bringing about the development of these technologies in the post-war period at Mitsubishi Nagasaki Shipyard.

The type of technological efforts made in the pre-war period was similar to those of the post-war period. In both periods, the technological development was characterized by active imports of technology and the predominance of 'improvement engineering'. This suggests that the present innovativeness of the

Japanese industry has been brought about by the continuation of the same technological learning process that started over a century ago. Technological learning, therefore, is a process that can be sustained and elaborated on for a long time, the cumulation of which can lead a country's industrial sector to a degree of technological sophistication that is highly competitive in the international economy. This is the implication of the Japanese experience for international transfer of technology, whether from developed to developing countries or among these two groups of countries. In any case accumulating technological capabilities is of utmost importance.

Two other features of the pre-war technological development process deserve attention. First, the 'technological strategies' both at national and firm levels were generated more out of trial and error experiences and the necessity to respond to immediate problems than they were the products of conscious, long-range planning. For example, the diminished reliance upon foreign technological assistance, which became apparent by the early 1890s at Mitsubishi Nagasaki Shipyard, was less a result of a conscious strategy to achieve technological self-reliance than of the necessity to save high salaries and the difficulty in forming good working relationships between the foreigners and the Japanese employees. MKG, the industrial school, although successful as an educational institution, had eventually to be replaced by MSG. MSCRI also had to be given up.

There were also trial and error experiences on the part of the government. It was the failure of the government enterprises of the 1870s, which were premature attempts at import substitution of heavy industries, that brought about the modified policy adopted from the 1880s of the simultaneous pursuit of export promotion of traditional and light industries, and the import substitution of heavy industries, which in the long run was effective in developing all sectors of industry. Within the import substitution strategy, the machinery industry was not subject to fostering for a long time. This is not a sound policy from the contemporary viewpoint which stresses its importance. This negligence, however, was compensated for by the response on the part of the large shipyards to assume the role of the machinery industry. For the government, this situation was less problematic than fostering the machinery industry independently, when the demand for machines was less certain than that for ships. For the shipbuilding firms, diversification made their enterprises large and complex, but this proved to be a source of strength during recessions, when productive activities other than shipbuilding could fill the gap in demand for ships. In retrospect, despite the errors made and the need to respond to immediate problems, the effective 'technological strategies' were selected, and the 'national system of innovation' functioned well in the pre-war period. This was because through trial and error the strategies were constantly adapted so as to sustain the process of the accumulation of technological capabilities to improve imported technologies.

The final point about pre-war technological development is that government intervention in technological matters was not very pronounced. The government attempted to promote the construction of large, technologically sophisticated ships by means of subsidies and tariffs, but the firms were free to choose the technologies to import to achieve this goal. The government did exercise some control through naval demand for specific technologies, but this accounted for a relatively small portion of the technologies imported at Mitsubishi Nagasaki Shipyard. This role of the government was rather restrained compared to the various controls on technology imports that the government exercised in the post-war period. This suggests that in the pre-war period the initiative of the firms was as important, if not more so, as government leadership in bringing about technological development. The importance of the role of the government in the pre-war period lay not so much in the direct fostering of the shipbuilding industry, but in indirect measures, e.g. setting model methods for importing technologies, diffusion of education and scientific infrastructure building.

SOME POLICY IMPLICATIONS OF THE JAPANESE EXPERIENCE

The implications for policy making of the experiences in technological learning in pre-war Japan follow directly from the above discussion. The most important is that, to bring about industrialization by importing technology, the accumulation of technological capabilities is an absolute necessity, and to do this, firm-level training and research activities are indispensable. Persistent technological learning accumulates technological capabilities that can upgrade the technological level of a late-comer country to a degree that in some respects surpasses that of the early starters.

However, sustaining the technological learning process is not easy. The 'technological strategies' had to be constantly adapted through trial and error experiences to sustain the accumulation of technological capabilities in pre-war Japan. This is probably inevitable in selecting the 'right' strategies. In the case of Japan the post-war technological strategies that turned out to be successful in making Japanese industries innovative and competitive probably owed something to the trial and error experiences in the pre-war period. The readiness to experience trial and error, and change strategies accordingly, is an important element in policy implementation.

The accumulation of technological capabilities is enhanced by complementarities between firm-level and national-level efforts. Such complementarities facilitate the effective utilization of the available technological manpower and research capacity which are often limited, especially in developing countries.

What does the Japanese experience imply about the role of protection and the capital goods industry, which are much discussed issues, in relation to technological learning in the developing countries? For the Japanese shipbuilding industry in the pre-war period, government subsidies and tariff measures had the effect of increasing the demand for large, technologically sophisticated ships. If it were not for these measures, the Japanese shipyards may not have had the opportunity to build high-quality ships until much later. However, protective measures did not in any way restrict imports of technology. As a result, technologies were imported extensively. This, however, did not hinder the accumulation of technological capabilities but rather enhanced it, by making available the 'best practice' technologies.

In pre-war Japan, the machinery industry was not fostered as an independent industry but developed as an integral part of the shipbuilding industry. As a result, the machinery industry itself grew only very slowly. This form of fostering the machinery industry had both advantages and shortcomings. This experience shows, however, that it is possible to develop a machinery industry through uses in downstream industries.

Finally, it should be noted that the conclusions and policy

implications of this study are based on the experiences of a leading firm in the shipbuilding industry. Examination of other industries is necessary to establish whether they are also valid for the industrial sector as a whole; however, there are reasons to believe that similar processes took place in other industries. Shipbuilding was one of the earliest industries to develop, and, as discussed in the earlier chapters, practices adopted by early industrial enterprises often served as models for later ones. Also, it may be remembered that several major machinery firms actually branched out of the Nagasaki Shipyard. It can well be assumed that these firms followed processes of technological learning that took place at Mitsubishi Nagasaki Shipyard.

APPENDIX

OVERSEAS MISSIONS FROM MITSUBISHI NAGASAKI SHIPYARD 1896–1935

Name	Status in shipyard	Date	Destination	Purpose
Maruta H.	Engineer	5.1896	Britain	Inspect shipbuilding industry
Miki M.	"	10.1896	"	"
Shiota T.	"	1.1897	"	"
Esaki I.	"	6.1897	"	Inspect machinery industry
Hamada H.	"	8.1898	Britain, USA	"
Kato T.	"	9.1898	Britain	Inspect shipbuilding industry
Mizutani R.	Assistant manager	"	Britain, USA	"
Yamada K.	Engineer	10.1899–4.1900	Britain	"
Koga Y.	"	10.1899	"	"
Sugitani Y.	"	2–9.1900	"	"
Yamamoto K.	"	5–11.1900	Britain, USA	"
Wakabayashi K.	"	"	"	"
Tomikawa N.	"	1–.1901 five years	Britain	Given leave at his will to study at Lobnitz shipyard in Renfrew
Saito G.	Foreman (kumicho)	9.1901–12.1909	Europe, USA	Given leave to study in shipyards
Inoue N.	"	1.1903	"	"
Maruta H.	Engineer	3.1902	"	Accompany Iwasaki Koyata, President of Mitsubishi, and

Name	Status in shipyard	Date	Destination	Purpose
				to inspect shipbuilding industry
Machida T.	"	5.1904	Britain	Given leave to study at Fairfields Shipyard
Esaki I.	Engineer	11.1904	Britain	Study turbine design and building at Parsons firm
Araki E.	Foreman (*koshi*)	"	"	"
Ito T.	Engineer	11.1904–10.1909	"	Given leave to study at Vickers
Saeki H.	"	11.1905	"	Study decoration of ship cabins
Kawahara G.	"	11.1905–12.1906	"	Study experimental tank at William Denny & Bros Shipyard
Maruta H.	Assistant manager	7–12.1906	"	Negotiate turbine contract with Parsons
Shiba K.	Engineer	9.1907–9.1908	"	Study experimental tank at William Denny & Bros Shipyard
Sugitani Y.	Assistant manager	3.1908	Russia	Negotiate order for a Russian volunteer fleet vessel
Crowe, D.	Dockmaster	1.1909	Shanghai, Tsingtao	Inspect ship repairing works
Abe S.	Engineer	2.1910	Hong Kong	Supervise repairing of cylinder for *Kiyo*
Yamamoto N.	Assistant manager	4–7.1910	Britain	Duties related to Japan–Britain exhibition
Maruta H.	Manager	5.1910	China	Canvass for orders for ships from Chinese Govt
Kato T.	Assistant manager	7.1910	China	Negotiations for an order for a gunboat
Fukagawa S.	Engineer	10.1910	Russia	To do an estimate for repairing a vessel in Vladivostok
Abe S.	"	2.1911	Britain	Study at Vickers (as assistant naval inspector for *Kongo*)
Akashio T.	"	"	"	"
Ono Y.	"	"	"	"
Esaki I.	Assistant manager	"	"	Study turbine design at Parsons firm

Name	Status in shipyard	Date	Destination	Purpose
Morikawa T.	Engineer	4.1911		Inspecting engineer for maiden voyage of *Canada*
Koga Y.	"	7.1911	Britain	Study casting at Vickers (assistant naval inspector for *Kongo*)
Fukase O.	"	8.1911		Inspecting engineer for maiden voyage of *Shunyo*
Okamoto T.	"	9.1911	Britain	Study boiler making at Vickers (naval inspector for *Kongo*)
Ito K.	"	11.1911–4.1912	"	Inspect machinery and shipbuilding industry
Tokudaiji N.	"	12.1911–7.1912	"	Study at Napier & Miller Shipyard
Yokoyama K.	"	1.1912–8.1913	"	Study at Vickers (naval inspector for *Kongo*)
Tamai K.	Engineer	2–7.1912	Britain	Inspect shipbuilding industry
Yamaguchi S.	"	3–8.1912	"	Study pumps and auxiliary machinery at G. J. Weir and Contraflow Kinetic Air Pump firms
Morikawa T.	Foreman (*koshi*)	"	"	"
Tokunaga T.	Foreman (*kogashira*)	"	"	"
Nakajima J.	Foreman (*kumicho*)	"	"	"
Haraguchi K.	Foreman (*kumicho*)	"	"	"
Matsumoto K.	Engineer	4–10.1912	"	Study at Vickers (naval inspector for *Kongo*)
Kamigo D.	"	4–9.1912	"	"
Kasahara K.	"	7.1912–1.1913	"	Study electric engineering at Vickers (naval inspector for *Kongo*)
Hori T.	"	7–12.1912	"	Study at Napier & Miller
Tadokoro M.	"	8.1912–1.1913	"	Study at Vickers (naval inspector for *Kongo*)

Name	Status in shipyard	Date	Destination	Purpose
Tokunaga Y.	"	8.1912–1.1913	"	"
Fukagawa S.	"	9.1912–2.1913	"	"
Kuga M.	"	10.1912–3.1913	"	Inspect building of coal carrier for Mitsubishi Goshi Kaisha at Napier & Miller Shipyard
Hirayama S.	Foreman (koshi)	10.1912–3.1913	Britain	Inspect building of coal carrier for Mitsubishi Goshi Kaisha at Napier & Miller Shipyard
Hirayama T.	Foreman	10.1912–3.1913	"	"
Ishuin K.	Engineer	11.1912–11.1913	"	Study at Vickers (naval inspector for Kongo)
Hirata Y.	"	"	"	Inspect fitting of Kongo at Vickers (naval inspector for Kongo)
Maeda R.	"	12.1912–6.1913	"	Study at Vickers (naval inspector for Kongo)
Shiota T.	Manager	12.1912–4.1913	Europe	Inspect shipbuilding and machinery industry in Europe
Ito K.	Engineer	12.1912–11.1913	"	Study diesel engine
Fukase O.	"	3–8.1913	Britain	Inspect building of a coal carrier at Napier & Miller Shipyard
Watase M.	"	"	"	"
Koyanagi J.	Foreman (kogashira)	"	"	
Esaki I.	Assistant manager	4–8.1913	"	Talks on the design of turbines for Hyuga at Parsons
Takashima S.	Engineer	12.1913–6.1914	"	Study decorative work for ships in London
Nambu T.	Engineer	9.1913	Britain	Inspecting engineer for Katori, and inspect shipbuilding industry in Britain
Kano A.	"	2–7.1914	"	Study gear hobbing at Parsons
Kimura D.	Foreman (kumicho)	"	"	"
Iwasaki S.	"	"	"	"
Inagaki T.	Engineer	5–12.1914	Sweden	Study electric welding at Elektviska Swetning Aktieboraget in Gotenburg

Name	Status in shipyard	Date	Destination	Purpose
Kishitake G.	Foreman (*kumicho*)	"	"	"
Nakao Y.	Worker	"	"	"
Sekino C.	Engineer	9.1914–5.1915	Britain	Study design and building of turbo-generators at Parsons' Heaton works
Nagai S.	Foreman (*kogashira*)	"	"	"
Takahashi K.	Foreman (*kumicho*)	"	"	"
Ito K.	Engineer	3.1916	Sweden	Study design and building of Jungstrom turbines
Yamaguchi S.	"	"	"	"
Omura K.	Foreman (*kumicho*)	"	"	"
Tokudaiji N.	Engineer	6.1916	USA	Inspect shipbuilding materials
Matsumoto K.	"	4.1917	Britain	Study submarines
Hayashi H.	"	10.1917	USA	Inspect Westinghouse factory
Ogata M.	"	10.1917	"	Inspect factories at Westinghouse firm
Inagaki C.	"	"	"	"
Ito K.*	Assistant manager (*Kobe*)	"	Britain, France	Head a group of engineers and workers to study submarines at Vickers and aircraft at Hispano Suiza
Yashiba Y.	Engineer	5.1918	Canada	Study electric propulsion
Mimura T.	"	6.1918	USA	Inspect new technological developments in shipbuilding including electric welding
Nishikawa K.	"	"	"	"
Owaki S.	"	"	"	Study organization of factories
Koyanagi S.	"	"	"	Study electric propulsion
Kasahara K.	"	3.1919	Europe, USA	Inspect electric industry
Haru N.	"	4.1919	"	Inspect shipbuilding industry

157

Name	Status in shipyard	Date	Destination	Purpose
Onnoike T.	"	"	"	"
Kimura Y.	Engineer	5.1919	Europe, USA	Inspect shipbuilding industry
Komatsu Y.	"	"	"	"
Seki M.	"	"	Britain	Study at Parsons firm
Inagaki T.	"	8.1919	"	Study at Vickers
Saito T.	"	5.1920	Europe, USA	Study decoration for *Katori*
Okuyama T.	"	"	"	"
Yamadaka G.	"	7.1920	USA	Study Sperry's stabilizer
Miyazaki K.	"	"	"	"
Oka K.	"	"	"	"
Motora N.	"	"	"	"
Sano Y.	"	2.1921	Britain	Study at Vickers, inspect materials for *Takao*
Fukami G.	"	6.1921	USA	Study Sperry's stabilizer
Fukushima K.	"	"	Europe, USA	Inspect shipbuilding industry
Hagi K.	"	"	"	"
Sakakibara T.	"	4.1922	Britain, USA	Study at Wm Denny & Bros Shipyard and inspect shipbuilding industry in USA
Inagaki T.	"	8.1924	Switzerland	Study diesel engine design and building at Sulzer firm
Akiba Y.	Engineer	8.1924	Switzerland	Study diesel engine design and building at Sulzer firm
Sato S.	"	"	"	"
Hiraoka M.	"	"	"	"
Ishimura G.	Foreman (*kocho*)	"	"	Study building of Sulzer's diesel engines
Yamaoka K.	Engineer	10.1924	"	Inspect diesel engines for *Santos* and *La Plata* at Sulzer
Mitamura Y.	"	1.1925	"	"
Eto S.	"	5.1925	"	"
Hayashi S.	Foreman (*kumicho*)	"	"	Study building of Sulzer's diesel engines

Name	Status in shipyard	Date	Destination	Purpose
Yano I.	Engineer	7.1925	Britain	Study boat building at Thornycroft firm
Yamashita O.	Foreman (*gocho*)	"	"	Accompany Yano to study Thornycroft's motorboat
Yoshimizu N.	Engineer	"	Switzerland	Study turbines at ETH (Zurich Polytechnic)
Yoshida K.	"	11.1925	"	Study turbine design and building at Escher Wyss firm
Muto Y.	"	"	"	"
Koezuka Y.	"	"	"	"
Ito T.	"	"	Germany	Study boiler making at DurrWerke
Kawai K.	Engineer	12.1925	Switzerland	Study diesel engine at ETH
Yamaguchi S.	"	2.1926	USA	Study industrial application of electrical machinery at Westinghouse firm
Watanabe K.	"	6.1926	Europe, USA	Study fitting equipment for *Asama* and *Tatsuta*
Kato T.	"	"	"	"
Sasaki S.	"	"	"	Inspect industrial research institutes
Nakamura M.	"	"	"	Study electric furnace
Akiba Y.	"	"	Switzerland	Inspect and study design of diesels for *Asama* and *Tatsuta* at Sulzer firm
Uemura Y.	"	4.1927		Inspect loading of shipbuilding materials
Kusunaga K.	Engineer	7.1927	Switzerland	Study passanger cabin decoration for *Asama* and *Tatsuta*
Oka S.	"	8.1927		Inspect *Aorangi* engines (large Sulzer diesels) in voyage between Vancouver and Honolulu
Sakakibara T.	"	"		"
Eto S.	"	"	Switzerland, Britain	Inspect engines and auxiliary machinery for *Asama* and *Tatsuta*

Name	Status in shipyard	Date	Destination	Purpose
Yokoyama K.	Engineer	9.1927	USA	Study boiler controlling system
Kawai K.	"	1.1928	Switzerland, Britain	Inspect engines and auxiliary machinery for *Asama* and *Tatsuta*
Masaki K.	"	2.1928	Europe, USA	Inspect electric generator for *Asama* and *Tatsuta* at Allen firm
Nishikawa K.	"	5.1928	Britain	Study cabin furniture making at Waring Gillow firm
Horikoshi H.	"	"	Europe, USA	Accompany Abe S. (director) to inspect shipbuilding industry
Inagaki C.	"	"	"	Study internal combustion engines
Tsukuda K.	"	9.1928	Britain	Study cabin furniture making at Waring Gillow firm
Tamai K.	"	11.1928	Europe, USA	Study state of the market for shipbuilding materials
Seta I.	"	1.1929	Europe	Inspect crankshaft for diesel at Skoda firm. Study turbine design at Escher Wyss firm
Ebi K.	"	3.1929	"	Inspect loading of materials for shipbuilding
Moriya S.	"	6.1929	Europe, USA	Study design and building of Sperry's stabilizer
Utsumi E.	Engineer	6.1929	Europe	Study design and building of Sperry's stabilizer
Koshinaka T.	"	9.1929		Inspect electrical machinery in operation on *Asama* on return voyage to USA
Moriyama S.	"	10.1929		Inspect *Asama* engines on voyage
Inagaki T.	"	3.1930	Europe, USA	Attend conferences on mechanical engineering

Name	Status in shipyard	Date	Destination	Purpose
Hiraoka M.	"	4.1930	Europe	Study casting at Sulzer and Escher Wyss firms. Inspect foundries in Europe
Muto Y.	"	3.1931	Switzerland	Study design of land turbines
Suzuki Y.	"	6.1931	Europe, USA	Study powder coal engines
Sato T.	"	5.1933	"	Accompany OSK engineers to do preliminary survey for new vessels
Kagami K.	"	"	"	"

* More than twenty engineers and workers went with Ito at this time: one party to Vickers' Ipswich factory, including Shimizu Kibuhei, and another to Hispano Suiza in France. Since this mission was sent from Kobe Shipyard, names of other engineers are not listed here. Exact number of workers sent is not known.
Source: Nenpo, Shashi, Shashi Shiryo, Mitsubishi Nagasaki Zosensho 1928

NOTES

CHAPTER 1

1 The 'latecomer' hypothesis was first proposed by Gershenkron (1952).

2 This type of argument is a corollary with respect to technology of the extreme and rigid 'structuralist' dependency argument of writers such as Frank (1967).

3 To be precise on terminology, *technological change* refers to the addition or modification of knowledge about a production process or product, and *technical change* refers to the physical change to the production apparatus or output. Here, technological change is used to refer to both, since technical change often accompanies technological change.

4 These studies belong to the IDB/ECLA Research Programme on Science and Technology. Similar studies have been done by Westphal and his colleagues for Korea (e.g. Westphal *et al.* 1984).

5 In the research done so far, the relationship between protectionism and the development of technological capabilities is still very unclear. This is caused in part by the lack of clear conceptualization of the issue. Effects of protectionism may vary according to the kind of measures taken (e.g. subsidies or tariffs, restrictions on imports of products or technologies), and the nature of infancy may vary according to the type of industry. These problems must be sorted out in a conceptual framework before any meaningful conclusions can be drawn. Since the question of protectionism is not a central interest of this book, this will not be attempted.

6 Views of scholars such as Rosenberg (1976, 1982), Nelson (1977, 1980, 1982), Freeman (1974, 1982) and Pavitt (1979, 1980, 1985) and their colleagues.

7 The two terms are often used interchangeably, and refer to the processes that generate technological changes necessary for the assimilation and improvement of imported technology. 'Technological capabilities' include the capability to select appropriate technology to import, knowledge and skills to operate a production process, and engineering and innovative capability to sustain, adapt and improve it.

8 Johnson (1982) does a critical review of these categories of work. He

adds another category, 'projectionists', which includes works that have attracted popular attention (e.g. Vogel 1979). These do not explain the Japanese case, but rather are attempts to focus on 'home country failings in the light of Japan's achievements, or at issuing warnings about the possible effects of Japan's growth on other parts of the world'.

9 Johnson (1982) categorizes this group separately, but it basically belongs to the 'unique institutions' argument.

10 Both these authors belong to a group of 'quantitative economic historians' who have based their work on the 'long-term economic statistics of Japan', a statistical data-collecting project that Ohkawa Kazushi and his colleagues undertook in the 1960s. Their research efforts have revealed important characteristics of the Japanese economic growth, e.g. 'trend acceleration' and dual structure. Although the topic of utmost interest for this group has been the analysis of the dual structure, some have recently taken an active interest in the study of technological change.

CHAPTER 2

1 T. C. Smith goes so far as to say that the knowledge of western technology acquired through *rangaku* is responsible for the rapid industrialization in Japan which failed to take place in other Asian countries (Smith 1955).

2 Capital investment in government enterprises until 1881 was more than one-third of the expenditure on the army and navy together, and 'when we consider the other claims on governmental incomes it is difficult to see how the government could have invested more than it did on industrial enterprises' (Smith 1955: 72).

3 Ever since the commercial treaties of the 1850s, Japan had been flooded by cheap imports. Cotton imports were rapidly destroying the traditional cotton industry. The only marketable exports at this stage were tea and raw silk.

4 For example, the blast furnace set up at Kamaishi by foreign engineers was both a technical and financial failure caused by the inability to adapt foreign technology to utilize domestic coking coal effectively (Nippon Steel Corporation 1973).

5 The diffusion of electric power replaced steam power in large factories, and made it possible for small-scale traditional manufacturing to mechanize. This contributed to the continued viability of small industries which is characteristic of industrial development in Japan. Also, electrification brought about a mushrooming of industries that used electricity as a primary input, e.g. chemical fertilizer industries in the 1920s (Nakamura 1983).

6 The average relative contribution of mining and manufacturing, construction and facilitating industries for the period 1888–1938 were: 38.4 per cent, 7.9 per cent and 15.2 per cent respectively. Also,

the figure for agriculture was 9.6 per cent and for commerce and services 28.9 per cent (Minami 1981).

7 Whereas mechanization in silk consisted of a simple replacement of hand reeling by machine reeling, requiring little change in the basic process, skills or scale, that of cotton spinning required the replacement by machine of the entire process with different sets of skills and an increase in the scale of production, making the change more difficult and expensive (Smith 1955).

8 According to Takahashi (1969), with the low tariff rates of the time, such measures to increase income capacity of investment were an absolute necessity to compete with imports.

9 See note 4.

10 Noro was a former student of Ohshima Takato, the Dutch scholar whose translation of a Dutch metallurgy book led to success in modern iron smelting by *bakufu* and some *han*. Noro was responsible for the early success of Kamaishi before the recruitment of British engineers (production of 3,000 tons of pig-iron per year). He had studied at the mining school in Freiburg, Germany. He had also revived the Kamaishi blast furnace in 1894, after the works had been sold to a private entrepreneur. Among the innovations Noro introduced at Yawata was a new method of blending Japanese coal to produce coking coal suitable for blast furnaces.

11 Kobusho was abolished in 1885 when all of its duties were transferred to Noshomusho or the other newly created Teishinsho (Ministry of Communications). Noshomusho, it may be noted, was the institutional precursor of the post-second world war Ministry of International Trade and Industry.

12 In 1896, a law to subsidize shipping (possession and navigation of vessels of over 1,000Gt) was also passed. Three years later, this law was revised to reduce the subsidy on imported ships to one half of that given to domestically built ones. These two laws worked hand in hand to promote both industries, although shipping was quicker to respond.

Up to this time, the government was anxious to replace traditional boats with western-type vessels. With this aim the government banned the building of large size traditional vessels in 1885, and adopted regulations for the obligatory survey of western-type vessels. This had little immediate effect since many small builders and owners avoided the obligatory survey by building boats that were traditional in appearance but whose internal structure was western style. The change to western-type shipbuilding did not take place until after 1896 when a survey for all vessels of over 20Gt became obligatory (Zosen Kyokai 1973a).

13 The raising of tariff rates on imported ships after the regaining of tariff autonomy in 1911 also had the effect of curbing imports and increasing demand for domestically built ships (Blumenthal 1976).

14 In this change the length of the period in which iron shipbuilding dominated was much shorter in Japan than in Britain, an example of latecomer advantage.

15 The number of firms having the capacity to build ships of more than 1,000Gt increased from five in 1913 to fifty-three in 1918, then diminished to nineteen by 1921. The number of workers in these firms increased from 26,000 in 1913 to 97,000 in 1918, and dropped to 63,000 by 1921. The number further decreased to fewer than 40,000 by the second half of the decade. Only four ships of over 1,000Gt were built in 1913; in 1918, 189 and in 1921, forty-one (Zosen Kyokai 1973b, Kaneko 1964).

16 Also, the fact that the project to build iron ships with iron produced at Kamaishi did not materialize, because of the failure of the blast furnace, lessened the significance of the yard for Kobusho.

17 Except for work done at government yards, repair works at the time were dominated by foreigners, which had raised the cost and made the duration of the work uncertain (Mitsubishi Jukogyo Kabushiki Kaisha 1956). Mitsubishi's partner, the Boyd firm, was a shipbuilder in Shanghai. It gave up its interests in this repair yard at Yokohama in 1879.

18 The sales price of the Nagasaki yard was about half the assessed value of the land and the physical facilities (Nakanishi 1983).

19 Shoda Heigoro, the manager of Nagasaki (1897–1906), is said to have told engineers of the shipyard to ignore cost considerations and build ships of good quality (Yadori 1932).

20 Odaka converted revenue for each year to 1934–36 prices and divided them by the average number of workers for each year.

21 The term 'engineers' at Nagasaki Shipyard is used in this book to mean those who held the job of *gishi*. They were usually university or polytechnic graduates trained in naval architecture, mechanical/marine engineering or other engineering specialities, or technicians who were promoted to this position in the course of their career at the shipyard.

22 At this time, the various enterprises of Mitsubishi became independent branch firms with the shareholding Mitsubishi Goshi Kaisha as the parent firm. Nine branch firms were set up by 1921 among which were Mitsubishi Electric Co. and Mitsubishi Internal Combustion Engine Co. (later Mitsubishi Aircraft Co.). The activities of these firms were originally part of the Nagasaki or Kobe yards, and their separation entailed transfer of staff and facilities from the shipyards. Some also went to Nippon Kogaku Kogyo (now the manufacturer of Nikon optical products) founded by Mitsubishi in 1917 in accordance with the naval requirements for optical instruments and weapons.

CHAPTER 3

1 In a few cases, e.g. the manager of the railroad construction enterprise, the salaries were even higher than the highest government official.

2 The group sent at this time included five naval officials, five workers (carpenters, blacksmiths, founders) and two seamen as well as two

students of political economy and two medical students (Watanabe 1977, Ishizuki 1972).

3 For example, Maeda Masana, the Noshomusho official who edited the *Kogyo Iken*, was sent to France twice during the 1870s, partly for studies and partly for Japan's participation at exhibitions.

4 An 1890 naval architecture graduate of Tokyo Imperial University, he later became the manager of the shipyard, then a director of MZKK.

5 Clark's contract was renewed twice and he stayed until 1905. This was probably for the construction of *Hitachi's* sister ships. (Letters re. J. S. Clark, Mitsubishi Research Institute.)

6 Morris' name appears on Denny's salary book which indicates that he began as an apprentice at Denny's in 1888, becoming a draughtsman in 1893. He stayed there until he left for Japan in 1907 (Wm Denny & Bros Co. archives UGD/3/B/2, University of Glasgow archives).

7 A. R. Brown first came to Japan as a seaman in 1869. He became a Kobusho employee as a lighthouse survey boat navigator, then transferred to Naimusho to form the marine bureau and assisted in drawing up regulations for it. His involvement with Mitsubishi started early in the 1870s when he acted as an agent to buy ships in England for Mitsubishi. He was given the job of supervising the construction of NYK ships in Britain when NYK was set up in 1885. In 1888 he set up his own firm in Glasgow to do business as an agent for NYK and Mitsubishi. In 1900 an engineer, G. MacFarlane, joined the firm which was then renamed A. R. Brown & MacFarlane Co. Ltd. The firm acted as an agent for Mitsubishi until Mitsubishi Trading Co. was set up in 1917 (Bush 1969). Some personal letters between Brown and Mitsubishi staff are found in the A. R. Brown firm archives at the University of Glasgow; however, the pre-war commercial papers are not found.

8 The few non-technical staff members sent on overseas missions are not included in the table.

9 Kato was an 1892 naval architecture graduate of Tokyo Imperial University, who later became assistant manager of the shipyard. His mission report has been kept by his son, Mr Kato Tomoo, also a former engineer at Nagasaki, who kindly lent it to the author for inspection.

10 A 1908 mechanical engineering graduate of Tokyo Imperial University, he spent most of his career at Nagasaki designing and building turbines.

11 An 1898 mechanical engineering graduate of Tokyo Imperial University, Ito's major contribution was the introduction of various foreign technologies which he inspected during his missions which included the diesel engine, Ljungstrom turbine and electric welding. He became a director of Mitsubishi Internal Combustion Engine Co., which he played an instrumental role in founding. He left Mitsubishi in 1922 to set up a machinery manufacturing firm of his own.

12 He joined Mitsubishi as a translator in 1875 after having studied

English and political economy at Fukuzawa Yukichi's Keio Gijuku. He was a director of Mitsubishi Goshi Kaisha as well as of NYK, when he assumed the managership of the Nagasaki Shipyard in 1897. He led the shipyard through the ordeal of building *Hitachi*. Although not an engineer, he had an excellent knowledge of current developments in shipbuilding technology and had a passion for promoting the industry in Japan. All of his sons became engineers, two of whom, Shoda Tatsuya and Kagami Kohei, worked at Nagasaki.

13 An 1891 mechanical engineering graduate of Tokyo Polytechnic (then Craftsmans School), he became manager of the shipyard in 1917 as well as a director of MZKK. He became the chairman of the board of directors in 1925.

14 As an official of Okayama *han*, he had once been sent to Britain to study naval engineering. He was an engineer of the Nagasaki yard under Kobusho when it was sold to Mitsubishi. He stayed on to become assistant manager. He became the first manager of the Kobe Shipyard in 1905.

15 A 1907 naval architect graduate of Tokyo Imperial University, he specialized in submarine design and building from 1917 at the Kobe Shipyard, and was eventually given an award by IJN for his achievements.

16 A 1909 mechanical engineering graduate of Tokyo Polytechnic, he worked at the Kobe Shipyard until 1926 when he was transferred to Nagasaki to become chief of the machinery factory.

17 This mission was sent from Kobe which was making Weir pumps.

18 Recruited in 1910, he spent most of his career at Nagasaki as an engineer in the foundry shop. He became a co-inventor of an alloy, NM bronze, which was adopted for propellers as well as turbine blades for a while. He later became assistant manager of the shipyard.

19 A 1908 mechanical engineering graduate of Tokyo Imperial University; after his return from London, he worked with diesel engines at the Kobe Shipyard.

20 A Weir auxiliary machinery licence may also have been requested by IJN for the construction of *Kirishima*. Weir granted a licence to Mitsubishi with permission from IJN. (Weir papers DC96/1/4, University of Glasgow archives.)

CHAPTER 4

1 Like Mitsubishi, Furukawa was a financial concern whose main industrial interest was in mining. Its Asio copper mine became the focus of the first environmental issue in Japan when the mine polluted the Watarase River to the extent that an entire village had to be evacuated. Some interpret Furukawa's donation to the universities as an attempt to soften public opinion towards the firm (Hiroshige 1973).

2 Also, some private *semmon gakko* had mechanical engineering courses that provided lectures in marine engineering. Many of

these institutions became universities under the 1918 Daigaku Rei (University Ordinance).

3 For example, Matsubayashi Yogoro, born in 1860, was a traditional shipwright. He learned the launching technique from a British employee as a worker at the Nagasaki yard in Kobusho days. He stayed on and became a *koshi* (see note 5) specializing in launching operations (Matsubayashi *Kaiso 1*).

4 A sample personal history indicates that a foreman in 1907 was originally recruited at the age of fifteen in 1880 and apprenticed to a master draughtsman upon entry (Mitsubishi Nagasaki Zosensho Shokkoka 1928).

5 Foremen at the yard were called *kogashira* since Kobusho days, later renamed *kocho*. Lower classes of foremen called *kumicho* and *gocho* were instituted in 1895. Also some selected *kocho* became *koshi*, who were considered as members of staff rather than workers (Mitsubishi Nagasaki Zosensho Shokkoka 1928).

6 Such as premium bonus system, premium time system, increase time system and piece work system (Mitsubishi Nagasaki Zosensho Shokkoka 1928).

7 The founding of MKG at this relatively early stage was due greatly to Shoda Heigoro's (then the manager of the shipyard) eagerness to promote industrial education. A conversation between Shoda and Shiota Taisuke shortly after the latter's return from Europe is indicative of Shoda's desire to found a school for the long-term benefit of the shipyard (Shiota 1938, Yadori 1932).

8 These technical subjects were mainly reserved for the *shugyosei* training period. The full-time education period at MKG stressed general secondary education.

9 Such as Jamieson's *A Textbook on Steam and Steam Engines*, Campbell-Holm's *Practical Shipbuilding* and Atwood's *Theoretical Naval Architecture* (Mitsubishi Goshi Kaisha Shomubu Chosaka 1914). These were standard textbooks in secondary and higher technical education in Britain.

10 This problem was discussed in the same conversation between Shoda and Shiota (see note 7). Also memoirs of workers often recount the difficulties they experienced in understanding blueprints and specifications.

11 The *shugyosei* training programme first instituted in 1899 originally aimed at replacing the *minaraiko* scheme; however, the firm eventually adopted the two programmes side by side. *Shugyosei* candidates by 1904 were defined as 'graduates of MKG or those possessing equivalent scholastic ability', and by 1910 only the graduates of MKG were recruited as *shugyosei* (*Nenpo* 1904, 1910).

12 The training period both for *shugyosei* and *minaraiko* was shortened to four years in 1917 (*Shashi Shiryo*).

13 They, of course, were workers then technicians before becoming engineers. Some immediately became technicians. The time that it took to become an engineer tended to lengthen for later graduates of MKG. For graduates up to 1914, the average was eight

to ten years, while it took twelve to fourteen years for later graduates.

14 This point was also made by Mr N. Kitaoka, a 1923 MKG graduate, in the interview with the author.

15 This was calculated from data included in 1924 *Nenpo*, which was the only record of the kind found in Mitsubishi records.

16 Calculated from the staff list published each year from 1917. A list of MKG graduates up to 1922 is included in Mitsubishi Kogyo Kyoikukai 1922.

17 Estimation at a later date is difficult due to a large number of dismissals in 1931–32 which probably included some MSG graduates.

18 In order to cover the lack of statistics, the educational background of the engineers whose names appear in the text is given in footnotes.

19 He was among the first naval students sent to study at Royal Naval College at Greenwich in the 1870s. He was a senior engineer officer in IJN when he was recruited to the Nagasaki Shipyard as chief engineer in 1893.

20 He was the director of Sasebo Naval Yard when he was recruited as a technical adviser to MZKK in 1927.

21 A 1925 marine engineering graduate of Tokyo Imperial University, he spent most of his career designing and building turbines.

22 A 1903 applied chemistry graduate of Osaka Polytechnic, he was working for the government mint as a chemical engineer in charge of analysing metal alloys (Yano 1966).

23 A 1905 naval architecture graduate of Tokyo Imperial University, he spent his career as an engineer specializing in research on resistance and stability in the Experimental Tank. He invented the Motora-type stabilizer. He became the manager of the shipyard in 1931, then the president of Mitsubishi Heavy Industries in 1934.

24 A 1913 mechanical engineering graduate of Tokyo Imperial University, he later specialized in building aircraft engines.

25 A 1910 mechanical engineering graduate of Tokyo Imperial University, he was with IJN as an engineer for two years before going to Nagasaki in 1913. He specialized in diesel engine building at Kobe.

26 A 1922 applied physics graduate of Kyushu Imperial University, he was recruited to Jikkenba in 1925 during his postgraduate studies. He spent his career in Jikkenba and later became its director.

27 As the youngest son of Shoda Heigoro, he had studied in Britain before joining the Nagasaki Shipyard in 1926.

CHAPTER 5

1 The use of this patent became available as a result of wartime industrial property law.

2 An early graduate of Kobu Daigakko (Imperial College of Engineering) and later a bureaucrat as well as an entrepreneur.

3 These were the following:

— Shigen Shingikai (Resources Research Council) organized in 1927 which made the following recommendations on research policy:
1 Improving communication and cooperation between research institutes;
2 Encouraging industrial application of research achievements;
3 Listing nationally important research topics;
4 Protecting researchers, increasing research grants;
5 Creating a government body to coordinate research bodies.

— Kokusan Shinko Iinkai (Committee for Promotion of Domestic Production) which in 1926 recommended the improvement of government and private research institutes as part of its general policy recommendation of import substitution and promotion of heavy and chemical industries.

— Shoko Shingikai (Research Council on Commerce and Industries) which also made a recommendation to promote communication and cooperation among government and private research institutes as part of measures for industrial rationalization in 1929 (Tsushosangyosho 1979).

4 Some topics taken up were:
— Economic problems of Manchuria, Mongolia and China
— Movements of Pacific Islands
— Science of natural catastrophe
— Geographical methods of locating mines
— Plant fibre materials
— Aeronautic fuel
— Wireless communication equipment
— Cosmic rays, atomic science
— Steel for specialized use
— Solution to scarce resources
— Anti-corrosive materials
— Organic synthesis
— Electric welding   (Hiroshige 1973: 125–6)

5 Hiroshige (1973) points out that some notable post-second world war scientific and engineering achievements were originally started as Gakushin-sponsored projects, e.g. atomic physics, which produced two Nobel prize winners, and electric welding.

6 There were a few like the Mitsubishi Shipbuilding Company's Nagasaki Laboratory which was relatively well equipped with staff and workers numbering considerably more than the average of about fifteen for private research institutes. Even so, Okuda Katsumi, recruited as a researcher from Kyushu Imperial University in 1925, recounts his surprise at seeing how poor the facilities were compared to the university (Okuda 1960).

7 Nakamura Michikata, a 1920 graduate of Tokyo Imperial University who specialized in electrical engineering.

8 Asado Jun, a 1918 chemistry graduate of Tokyo Imperial University. He was transferred to Nagasaki Arms Manufacturing in 1923, and the work he did in his career there included the invention of a new aluminium bronze alloy for which he became noted (Yano 1966).

9 A 1916 metallurgy graduate of Kyushu Imperial University.

10 A 1919 graduate of Waseda University who specialized in mechanical engineering.

11 See note 19, chapter 4, for biographical information. He was sent to Europe on several missions from 1896, and it is not clear when or how he learned of the Experimental Tank from Archibald Denny.

12 A 1901 naval architecture graduate of Tokyo Imperial University, he was sent to study tank operations in 1905–6. He left the shipyard because of illness after his return to Nagasaki. He had taken up a teaching post at Yokohama Polytechnic when he was re-recruited in 1910 to work at the tank. He left the tank in 1917 to take up a post in hull design.

13 An 1899 naval architecture graduate of Tokyo Imperial University, he was sent to Denny when Kawahara fell ill and left the shipyard in 1907. He left the tank for hull design when Kawahara was re-recruited. He became the manager of the yard in 1920, then a director of MZKK in 1925, and the chairman of the board of directors of Mitsubishi Heavy Industries in 1934.

14 In the records of the Denny firm, it is indicated that the firm charged the Nagasaki Shipyard a sum of £525 as a 'fee for training Japanese representatives in tank work and for ordering and supervision, the despatch of tools and equipment, also supplying plans and specification of tank' (Denny archives UGD 3/1/16 journals 1896–1911: 375).

15 A resistance dynamometer is used to measure the resistance of the model ship in the Experimental Tank while a propeller dynamometer measures that of the model propeller. These two are the most important tests that are performed in the Experimental Tank.

16 Iwasaki's original idea was to found one research institute to cover the research needs of all Mitsubishi's industrial enterprises; however, in the end two were founded. The other one was set up in the mining firm (*Shashi*).

17 His visit was limited to the USA because of the war. Two researchers, Iguchi Haruhisa and Kakinuma Usaku, were sent on another similar mission to Europe and America in 1920. Records indicate that the Mitsubishi Shipbuilding Company continued to make substantial investments in machines and facilities for MSCRI until 1923 (*Shashi Shiryo*).

18 Kobe had been manufacturing refrigerators since it obtained a licence for it from the Pulsometer firm in Britain in 1913 (Mitsubishi Jukogyo Kabushiki Kaisha 1956).

19 A total of ¥1,450,000 was put into this fund between 1924 and 1927. This account disappears after 1932. The fund seems to have been used up by then (*Shashi Shiryo*).

20 For example, Fukao Junji recounts his dissatisfaction with this policy and says that for some time he did inventive activities only outside working hours (Fukao 1979).

21 At Denny's an award scheme was introduced in 1871. It was to give money awards to a wide range of inventions and improvements in

the form of new machines or tools, new methods of work execution, prevention of accidents, avoiding waste and cutting costs of production (Denny 1932). Mitsubishi requested A. R. Brown of Glasgow to survey award schemes in operation in major British shipyards. The Denny scheme was the one for which details were sent by Brown to Mitsubishi (*Shashi*).

22 There are also a few other articles found in *Shashi* and *Shashi Shiryo*. Also, in the memoirs, there are quite a few instances of awards received for inventions and improvements cited (*Kaiso* and *Kaikyuroku*).

23 This committee was set up on the initiative of the manager of the Kobe Shipyard, Haramiishi Mototeru. He was so devoted to research on electric welding that even after retirement he set up a laboratory at his residence to continue research in the field.

24 The firm-level committee seems to have been dissolved after two meetings until it was revived in 1935. Nagasaki yard in the meantime had an intra-yard committee (Yano 1966, Ichibangase in *Kaiso* 2).

25 For example, under the Electric Welding Committee there were subcommittees on the welding of boiler drums, welding of hulls and automatic welding.

26 The meetings may have continued after 1925, but there are no records.

27 One of them, Kanamori Masao (a 1935 metallurgy graduate of Kyushu Imperial University and, until recently, the chairman of the board of directors of Mitsubishi Heavy Industries Ltd), said very emphatically that his decision to come to Nagasaki was a result of Sasaki's influence (Dr Kanamori in the interview with the author).

CHAPTER 6

1 IJN imported turbine manufacturing technology by becoming a sublicensee of the Kawasaki Shipbuilding Company which purchased a licence for the Curtis turbine in 1907.

2 *Kogaku Kaishi* (journal of the Society of Engineers) published an abstract of the article in *Engineering* of R. H. Thurston's lecture on the steam turbine given in August 1900, as well as that of C. A. Parsons' lecture on it given in January 1901 at the meeting of the Institute of Naval Architects and Marine Engineers of Scotland originally published in *Steamship* (*Kogaku Kaishi 230*, May 1901).

3 Esaki Ichiro was an 1895 mechanical engineering graduate of Tokyo Imperial University. He was sent to Parsons again on two occasions in the early 1910s for further studies. He later became assistant manager of the Nagasaki Shipyard. Araki Eisaburo worked as a foreman in the machinery building department specializing in turbines until retirement.

4 These were S. Pringle and W. Armstrong. Turbines for the naval vessel *Mogami* were likewise built at Parsons. Another Parsons' engineer, R. Atkinson, was recruited for their installation (see Figure 3.1).

5 Secrecy was a normal practice at the time. Esaki Ichiro had studied turbine design at Parsons. He taught it only to Shoda Tatsuya, Shoda Heigoro's eldest son, a 1904 mechanical engineering graduate of Tokyo Imperial University, who worked in the machinery design department at Nagasaki until 1922 when he was transferred to the head office and became the director of MSCRI the following year.

6 Although Yokoyama was sent on a mission to Vickers in Barrow-in-Furness in 1912–13, because of his status as naval inspector for *Kongo*, he was not allowed to visit the Parsons factory. The books that Yokoyama read to learn turbine design were those by Martin, Stodola and Goudie. He says he mastered it when he did check calculations for the turbines of the warship *Hyuga* (Yokayama 1955).

7 This obviously was a 'bug'. According to Yokoyama, in the hobbing process, the pitch naturally slips off the specified angle. The workers, not knowing this, adjusted the gear wheel several times during hobbing to correct this, which had caused the problem (Yokoyama 1955).

8 The Parsons contract had been renewed in 1919 (the 1904 contract was for fifteen years) for a further term of seven years. The final termination was in May 1926 (Kanazawa in *Kaikyuroku 1*). The warship *Tosa* was destroyed in accordance with the Washington arms reduction agreement. The turbines were kept at the Kure Naval Yard but never used.

9 Forty-three out of 684 Jikkenba reports between 1920 and 1927 were on turbine blade materials. Also, a number of reports on research on turbines by Nagasaki staff have been published by the Information Department of Mitsubishi Goshi Kaisha (*Shiryo Iho*).

10 A theoretical chemistry graduate of Tokyo Imperial University, later professor at the Metal Institute of Tohoku Imperial University.

11 See chapter 5.

12 They were Inagaki Tetsuro, who was at Vickers in Barrow-in-Furness, and Seki Minoru, stationed at Parsons in Newcastle. Their impression of this turbine was not favourable, in contrast to Yokoyama who, from the information obtained from the Vickers' representative in Japan, found it as good as, if not better than, Zölly's.

13 These were Yoshida Kotaro, Muto Yoshiichi, Koezuka Yoshiro and Oki (first name not known). At Escher Wyss they were instructed by Quiby and Spiess who were students of Stodola, the foremost authority at the time on turbines.

14 At this time, an engineer and two foremen were sent to Parsons' Heaton Works. One of the foremen, Nagai Shonosuke, impressed by the blade processing machine, sketched it from memory and had it built upon his return to Nagasaki (see chapter 3). The other foreman, Takahashi Kantaro, was an MKG graduate.

15 A 1915 mechanical engineering graduate of Tokyo Imperial University, he was one of the engineers who studied the Zölly turbine at Escher Wyss (see note 13).

16 Resistance welding uses heat resulting from the electric resistance

arising at the contact surface when an electric current is passed through two metal pieces put together. The heat melts the metals at the contact surface and they are welded. Arc welding uses the heat of the arc which arises between the electrodes and the metal to be welded.

17 Carbon arc welding and gas welding had started at Nagasaki before this. The former was brought by (unknown) foreign engineers who came to work at the Nagasaki yard in the first decade of the century; the latter was learned from IJN (Kakita 1961).

18 A 1910 mechanical engineering (marine engineering) graduate of Tokyo Imperial University. As a key engineer in machinery building, he was sent to Vickers in Barrow-in-Furness (1919–22) to study marine engineering, especially turbines, and later to Sulzer in Switzerland for diesels.

19 Mimura also does not seem to have been much impressed by the extent of technological advance at the time of his mission to America (Mimura in *Kaikyuroku* 2).

20 He wrote seven reports on the subject up to 1935.

21 Five Jikkenba reports written in 1921–31 on the welding of cast iron are found: two on stainless steel (1928, 1930); one each on aluminium alloy (1930) and gun metal (1931).

22 Sasaki introduced a summary translation of M. A. Horner's *Spot and Arc Welding* which describes the training scheme of the American Emergency Fleet Corporation (Sasaki 1922).

23 Ito Tatekichi, the boiler shop engineer, has put together his lecture notes in a Jikkenba report. The contents consist of a detailed explanation of electric welding and the basics of electrical engineering (Ito 1922).

24 Although consumption of electrodes before 1926 is not known, there is little doubt that it was very small. According to an estimate of electrode production at the shipyard around 1924, it was no more than a ton a month (Yosetsu Gojunenshi Hensan Iinkai 1962).

25 This became a sub-committee of the firm-level electric welding research committee in 1935.

26 There are three Jikkenba reports written in 1934, 1936 and 1938 on these topics.

27 According to Kanamori Masao, IJN probably pushed Sasaki Shintaro to develop automatic welding technology at Nagasaki (Dr Kanamori in the interview with the author).

28 He started his career as a Jikkenba engineer in 1935 and spent a number of years doing research on electric welding.

29 Details of Ito's repeated visits to Europe before and during the war are given in Ito 1919. Since this is not an official report of his mission, he does not say which diesel engine maker he found to be most appropriate, but he seems to have been most impressed by the German M.A.N.. Mitsubishi may have wanted to negotiate with this firm, but this was suspended by the war.

30 The correspondence concerning this negotiation is found in Vickers Archives R289 Naval Department, Mitsubishi Agreements 23A198.

Another reason for the suspension of this negotiation is probably the fact that the negotiation was originally mediated by the Japanese naval inspector in London who was convicted in the notorious naval bribery case in 1914.

31 According to Funakoshi Kajishiro, an engineering admiral, who at the time of Vickers' contract was stationed in London, following the Anglo-Japanese alliance of 1902, Britain wanted Japan to help it in the submarine warfare with Germany (Funakoshi in *Kaikyuroku 2*). In 1923 Funakoshi became the chief director of Mitsubishi International Combustion Engine Company, and in 1926 a director of MZKK.

32 An IJN engineering admiral who became the chairman of the board of directors of MZKK in 1918. See chapter 4.

33 The actual number of workers sent cannot be found in the records of the firm. At this time another group was sent to the Hispano Suiza firm in France from which a licence for aircrafts had been purchased.

34 A 1911 mechanical engineering graduate of Tokyo Imperial University, and the inventor of the MS diesel engine.

35 A veteran foreman in the machinery factory who had been working at Nagasaki since 1880.

36 A 1906 MKG graduate who was at this time working as Ito Kumezo's assistant.

37 The Internal Combustion Engine Department of the Kobe Shipyard became the Kobe factory of Mitsubishi Nainenki Kaisha (Mitsubishi Internal Combustion Engine Company) founded in 1920. Manufacturing of aircrafts, automobiles, diesel generators and submarine diesels were transferred to this firm. However, when this company became Mitsubishi Aircraft Company in 1928, the Kobe factory was re-integrated with the Kobe Shipyard.

38 By the 1930s turbines' fuel efficiency was 1lb/IHP/hr whereas diesels' was 0.35lb/IHP/hr (Guthrie 1971).

39 A 1919 mechanical engineering graduate of Tokyo Imperial University. He had worked at the Kobe factory of Mitsubishi Internal Combustion Engine Company designing Vickers' diesels until 1924 when he was transferred to Nagasaki specifically to work with Sulzer's engines.

40 According to a marine engineering historian 'a good compressor was at best a trouble maker, a poor compressor was a nightmare' (Guthrie 1971).

41 As the youngest son of Shoda Heigoro, Kagami studied in Britain before joining the Nagasaki Shipyard in 1926.

42 A 1929 mechanical engineering graduate of Tokyo Imperial University, Fujita cut short his training period to work on this research soon after he joined the Nagasaki Shipyard. The author interviewed him while he was an adviser to the Technical Headquarters of Mitsubishi Heavy Industries.

43 These initials were originally intended to denote 'marine single-acting'; however, because they were often taken for Mitsubishi-Sulzer, it was resolved to indicate 'Mitsubishi-Shimizu' after the inventor.

44 A 1924 mechanical engineering graduate of Kyoto Imperial University.

45 The Nagasaki Shipyard purchased a licence to build the newly developed Sulzer double acting engine in 1931 because double acting engines could produce more output. However, they had a more complex structure than single acting engines, and the Sulzer-type engines built at Nagasaki were subject to frequent breakdowns.

46 There are six Jikkenba reports on these topics between 1934 and 1937.

47 This section was first created in 1924 to do Sulzer's engines. In 1927, this was renamed reciprocating engine section and had sub-sections for the diesel engine and steam reciprocating engine. About twenty members of the section, which totalled about thirty-five, were involved with MS by 1930, of which five worked with Sulzer. The steam reciprocating engine section had about ten members (Fujita 1985).

48 Suzuki Yataro, who worked as an assistant to Shimizu, recounts how Hamada Hyo, the director of MZKK who chaired ICERC, discussed for hours with Shimizu when the firm was about to launch the MS project, to find out whether Shimizu really felt confident about the feasibility of the new engine (Yano 1966).

BIBLIOGRAPHY

REFERENCES ON THE MITSUBISHI FIRM

Archives and unpublished materials

Fujita H. (1985), 'Notes on the development of the diesel engine at Nagasaki Shipyard' (manuscript).

Ito T. (1922), 'Denki Yosetsu Kaitei' (Lectures on electric welding), *Jikkenba Hokoku* 136.

Jikkenba (1923), 'Denki Yosetsuko no Yosei no Keika Hokoku' (Report on the training of electric welders), *Jikkenba Hokoku* 209.

Kakita T. (1961), 'Nagasaki Zosensho Yosetsu Gojunenshi' (Fifty-year history of welding at Nagasaki Shipyard).

Kato T. (1899), 'Mission report to Europe' (manuscript).

Kawai K. (1940), 'MS Kikan no Kaiko' (MS engine in retrospect).

Kubo Y. (1972), *Jikkenba Hokoku Mokuji* (*List of laboratory reports*).

Letters re. J. S. Clark, Mitsubishi Research Institute.

Mitsubishi–Brown letters, Mitsubishi Research Institute.

Mitsubishi Goshi Kaisha Shiryoka, *Shiryo Iho* (*Reports*) (referred to as *Shiryo Iho* in text).

Mitsubishi Goshi Kaisha Shiryoka, *Shiryoka Nenpo* (*Annual Report of the Information Department*) (referred to as *Shiryoka Nenpo* in text).

Mitsubishi Goshi Kaisha Shomubu Chosaka (1914), *Rodosha Toriatsu-kaikata ni kansuru Chosa Hokokusho* (*Survey report on the management of labourers*).

Mitsubishi Jukogyo Kabushiki Kaisha (1960a), *Shashi Shiryo* (*Materials on the history of the firm*) *1916–1948* (referred to as *Shashi Shiryo* in text).

Mitsubishi Jukogyo Kabushiki Kaisha (1960b), *Shashi Shiryo Kaikyuroku* (*Materials on the history of the firm – Recollections*) 1 & 2 (referred to as *Kaikyuroku* in text).

Mitsubishi Kogyo Kyoikukai (ed.) (1922), *Mitsubishi Kogyo Gakko Ichirano* (*An inspection of Mitsubishi Industrial School*), Nagasaki.

Mitsubishi Nagasaki Zosensho, *Nenpo* (*Annual report*), *1898–1925*. (referred to as *Nenpo* in text).

Mitsubishi Nagasaki Zosensho Kinrobu (1978), *Mitsubishi Nagasaki*

Zosensho Gakko Kyoiku Seido Enkaku Gaiyo (*Outline of the development of education at Mitsubishi Nagasaki Shipyard*).

Mitsubishi Nagasaki Zosensho Shokkoka (1928), *Nagasaki Zosensho Romushi* (*History of labour management at Nagasaki Shipyard*).

Mitsubishi Zosen Kabushiki Kaisha, *Meibo* (*Staff list*).

Nagasaki Shipyard (1919), *Bijou* – *Review of Reviews 3*.

Sasaki S. (1921), 'Kaizen seraretaru Kohan Denki Yosetsuho' (Improved electric welding method of steel plates), *Jikkenba Hokoku 59*.

Sasaki S. (1922), 'Beikoku ni Jisshi serareshi Denki Yosetsuko Yosei Kyoan' (A training programme for electric welders in use in the USA), *Jikkenba Hokoku 90*.

Sasaki S. (1925), 'Turbine Yokuzai toshiteno N.M. Seido' (N.M. bronze as turbine blade material), *Shiryo Iho 29*.

Sasaki S. (1931), 'Mitsubishi Nagasaki Zosensho ni okeru Denki Yosetsu no Hattatsushi' (A history of the development of electric welding at Mitsubishi Nagasaki Shipyard), *Jikkenba Hokoku 1078*.

Shiota T. (1938), *Shiota Taisuke Jishoden* (*Shiota Taisuke, an autobiography*).

Yano T. (1966), *Nagasaki Kenkyushoshi Shiryo* (*Materials on the history of Nagasaki Research Institute*).

Yokoyama K. (1913), 'Mission report to Vickers Shipyard in Barrow-in-Furness' (manuscript).

Yokoyama K. (1955), 'Joki turbine' (Steam turbine) (manuscript).

Yokoyama K. (1958), 'Yonjuneumae ni okeru Nagasaki Zosensho no Joki turbine no Jokyo o Katarumono' (Steam turbines at Nagasaki Shipyard forty years ago) (manuscript).

Published materials

Fukao J. (1979), *Fukao Junji Gijutsu Kaiso Nanajunen* (*Seventy years of recollections on technology*), Tokyo.

Iwasaki Denki Hensankai (1971), *Iwasaki Yanosuke den* (*Biography of Iwasaki Yanosuke*), Tokyo.

Matsushita I. (1960), 'Senkei Shikenjo Jidai no Omoide' (Memoirs of the days at the Experimental Tank) in Mitsubishi Zosen Kabushiki Kaisha, *Mitsubishi Zosen no Kenkyu Kikan* (*Research departments of Mitsubishi Shipyard*), Nagasaki.

Mitsubishi Jukogyo Nagasaki Zosensho (1974), *Kaiso no Hyakunen 1–3* (*A hundred years of retrospect*), Nagasaki, (referred to as *Kaiso* in text).

Mitsubishi Jukogyo Kabushiki Kaisha (ed.) (1956), *Mitsubishi Jukogyo Kabushiki Kaishashi* (*History of Mitsubishi Heavy Industries Ltd*), Tokyo.

Mitsubishi Nagasaki Zosensho (1928), *Mitsubishi Nagasaki Zosenshoshi* (*History of Mitsubishi Nagasaki Shipyard*), Nagasaki.

Mitsubishi Nagasaki Zosensho (1957), *Sogyo Hyakunen no Nagasaki Zosensho* (*Hundred year history of Nagasaki Shipyard*), Nagasaki.

Mitsubishi Shashi Kankokai (ed.) (1972), *Mitsubishi Shashi 1–40* (*1870–1952*), Tokyo (referred to as *Shashi*).

Nishinippon Jukogyo Kabushiki Kaisha (ed.) (1951), *Mitsubishi Nagasaki*

Zosenshoshi – zokuhen (*History of Mitsubishi Nagasaki Shipyard – sequel*), Nagasaki.

Okuda K. (1960), 'Jikkenba Jidai no Omoide' (Memoirs of the laboratory days) in Mitsubishi Zosen Kabushuki Kaisha, *Mitsubishi Zosen no Kenkyu Kikan* (*Research departments of Mitsubishi Shipyard*), Nagasaki.

OTHER REFERENCES

Archives

Archives of Wm Denny & Bros Co. (University of Glasgow).

Archives of Vickers Ltd (University of Cambridge).

Archives of G. & J. Weir Co. (University of Glasgow).

General

Abramovitz, M. (1956), 'Resource and Output Trends in the United States Since 1870', *American Economics Association Papers* 46 (2), May.

Alchian, A. (1963), 'Reliability of Progress Curves in Airframe Production', *Econometrica*, October.

Ando Y. (ed.) (1975), *Kindai Nippon Keizaishi Yoran* (*Handbook of economic history of modern Japan*), Tokyo, Tokyo Daigaku Shuppankai.

Arisawa H. (ed.) (1959), *Gendai Nippon Sangyo Koza* (*Discourse on industry in contemporary Japan*), Vol. I: Kindai Sangyo no Hatten (Development of Modern Industries), Tokyo, Iwanami Shoten.

Arrow, K. (1962), 'The Economic Implications of Learning by Doing', *Review of Economic Studies* 29, June.

Atkinson, A. B. and Stiglitz, J. E. (1969), 'A New View of Technological Change', *Economic Journal* 79, September.

Bank of Japan (1935), *Economic Statistics of Japan*, Tokyo.

Bank of Japan (1966), *Hundred Year Statistics of the Japanese Economy*, Tokyo.

Bell, R. M. (1982), '"Learning" and the Accumulation of Industrial Technological Capacity in Developing Countries', paper prepared for the *International Workshop in Facilitating Indigenous Technological Capability*, Centre for African Studies, Edinburgh University, May.

Bell, R. M., Scott-Kemis, D. and Satyarakwit, W. (1982), 'Limited Learning in Infant Industry, a Case Study' in F. Stewart and J. James (eds), *The Economics of New Technology in Developing Countries*, London, Frances Pinter.

Blumenthal, T. (1976), 'The Japanese Shipbuilding Industry' in H. Patrick (ed.), *Japanese Industrialization and its Social Consequences*, Berkeley, University of California Press.

Bush, L. (1969), *The Life and Times of Illustrious Captain Brown*, Tokyo, Voyagers Press.

Cooper, C. (1973), 'Science, Technology and Production in the Underdeveloped Countries: An Introduction' in C. Cooper (ed.), *Science Technology and Development: The Political Economy of Technical Advance in Underdeveloped Countries*, London, Frank Cass.

179

Cooper, C. M. and Sercovitch, F. (1971), *The Channels and Mechanisms for the Transfer of Technology from Developed to Developing Countries*, UNCTAD, TD/B/AC.11/5.

Crane, D. (1977), 'Technological innovation in developing countries: A Review of the literature', *Research Policy* 6.

Dahlman, C. J. and Fonseca, F. V. (1978), *From Technological Dependence to Technological Development: The Case of the USIMINAS Steel Plant in Brazil*, IDB/ECLA Research Programme on Science and Technology, Buenos Aires.

David, P. (1975), *Technical Choice, Innovation and Economic Growth*, Cambridge, Cambridge University Press.

Denny Bros Ltd. (1932), *Denny – Dumbarton 1844–1932*, Dumbarton.

Dore, R. P. (1965), *Education in Tokugawa Japan*, London, Routledge & Kegan Paul.

Dore, R. (1973), *British Factory – Japanese Factory – The Origins of National Diversity in Industrial Relations*, Berkeley, University of California Press.

Dore, R. (1984), 'Technological Self-Reliance: Sturdy Ideal or Self-serving Rhetoric' in M. Fransman and K. King (eds), *Technological Capability in the Third World*, London, MacMillan.

Emi K. (1963), *Government Fiscal Activity and Economic Growth in Japan 1868–1960*, Tokyo, Kinokuniya Shoten.

Enos, J. L. (1962), 'Invention and Innovation in the Petroleum Refining Industry' in National Bureau of Economic Research, *The Rate and Direction of Inventive Activity*, Princeton, Princeton University Press.

Frank, A. G. (1967), *Capitalism and Underdevelopment in Latin America*, New York, Monthly Review Press.

Fransman, M. (1982), 'Learning under Free Trade: the Case of Hong Kong', *World Development* 10 (11).

Freeman, C. (1974), *The Economics of Industrial Innovation*, London, Penguin.

Freeman, C., Clarke, J. and Soete, L. (1982), *Unemployment and Technical Innovation*, London, Frances Pinter.

Freeman, C. (1987), *Technology Policy and Economic Performance – Lessons from Japan*, London, Pinter.

Gershenkron, A. (1952), 'Economic Backwardness in Historical Perspective' in B. F. Hoselitz (ed.), *The Progress of Underdeveloped Areas*, Chicago.

Gilfillan, S. (1935a), *Inventing the Ship*, Chicago, Follett.

Gilfillan, S. (1935b), *The Sociology of Invention*, Chicago, Follett.

Guthrie, J. (1971), *A History of Marine Engineering*, London.

Herrera, A. (1973), 'Social Determinants of Science in Latin America: Explicit Science Policy and Implicit Science Policy' in C. Cooper (ed.), *Science, Technology and Development: The Political Economy of Technical Advance in Underdeveloped Countries*, London, Frank Cass.

Hiroshige T. (1973), *Kagaku no Shakaishi* (*A social history of science*), Tokyo, Chuokoronsha.

Hollander, S. (1965), *The Sources of Increased Efficiency: A Study of Du Pont Rayon Plants*, Cambridge, Mass., MIT Press.

Hyodo T. (1971), *Nippon ni okeru Roshi Kankei no Tenkai* (*Development of industrial relations in Japan*), Tokyo, Tokyo Daigaku Shuppankai.

Ishizuki M. (1972), *Kindai Nippon no Kaigai Ryugakushi* (*Overseas studies in modern Japan*), Kyoto, Minerva Shobo.

Ito K. (1919), 'Senji ni okeru Oshu no Kogyo' (Industries in Europe during the war), *Kikai Gakkaishi* (*Journal of the Society of Mechanical Engineers*) 22 (75), June.

Japan, Ministry of Education (1963), *Japan's Growth and Education*, Tokyo.

Johnson, C. (1982), *MITI and the Japanese Miracle: The Growth of Industrial Policy: 1925–1975*, Stanford, Stanford University Press.

Jones, H. J. (1980), *Live Machines – Hired Foreigners and Meiji Japan*, Vancouver, University of British Columbia Press.

Kaneko E. (ed.) (1964), *Gendai Nippon Sangyo Hattatsushi* (*Industrial development in contemporary Japan*), Vol. IX: Zosen (Shipbuilding) Tokyo, Kodansha.

Katz, J. (1978), *Technological Change, Economic Development and Intra and Extra Regional Relations in Latin America*, IDB/ECLA Research Programme on Science and Technology, Buenos Aires.

Katz, J. and Ablin, E. (1978), *From Infant Industry to Technology Exports: The Argentine Experience in the International Sale of Industrial Plants and Engineering Works*, IDB/ECLA Research Programme on Science and Technology, Buenos Aires.

Katz, J., Gutkowski, M., Rodriguez, M. and Goity, G. (1977), *Productivity, Technology and Development*, IDB/ECLA Research Programme on Science and Technology, Buenos Aires.

Kogaku Kaishi (*Journal of the Society of Engineers*).

Kuznets, S. (1966), *Modern Economic Growth Rate: Structure and Spread*, London, Yale University Press.

Lall, S. (1980), 'Developing Countries as Exporters of Industrial Technology', *Research Policy* 9.

Lall, S. (1985), 'Trade in Technology by a Slowly Industrializing Country: India' in N. Rosenberg and C. Frischtak, *International Technology Transfer: Concepts, Measures and Comparisons*, New York, Praeger.

Levine, B. and Kawada, H. (1980), *Human Resources in Japanese Industrial Development*, Princeton, Princeton University Press.

Maeda M. (ed.) (1884), *Kogyo Iken Shoken* (*Opinion on the promotion of industries*) in *Meiji Zenki Zaisei Keizai Shiryo Shusei 18*.

Makino K. (1906), 'Nagasakishi Mitsubishi Zosenshoritsu Mitsubishi Kogyo Yobiko no Gaikyo' (The state of affairs at Mitsubishi industrial school at Nagasaki), *Kyoiku Koho* 308, June.

Masumoto U. (1926), *Roshi Kaihoron* (*On liberation of labour–management relations*), Tokyo.

Maxwell, P. (1977), *Learning and Technical Change in the Steel Plant of Ascindar S.A. in Rosario, Argentina*, IDB/ECLA Research Programme on Science and Technology, Buenos Aires.

Minami R. (1976), *Doryoku Kakumei to Gijutsu Shinpo* (*Power, revolution and technological progress*), Tokyo, Toyo Keizai Shinposha.

Minami R. (1981), *Nippon no Keizai Hatten* (*Economic Development of Japan*), Tokyo, Toyo Keizai Shinposha.

Minami R. and Kiyokawa Y. (eds) (1987), *Nihon no Kogyoka to Gijutsu Hatten* (*Industrialization in Japan and technological development*), Tokyo, Toyo Keizai Shinposha.

Morishima M. (1982), *Why Has Japan Succeeded? – Western Technology and the Japanese Ethos*, Cambridge, Cambridge University Press.

Motora N. (1916), 'An Analysis of Model Screw Propeller Experiments', *Zosen Kyokai Kaiho* 19, September.

Motora N. (1927), 'Dokeisen Renko baai Kozekusen no ukuru Eikyo ni tsuite' (Effect the follower ship receives when being pulled by another ship), *Zosen Kyokai Kaiho* 41, October.

Nakamura T. (1983), *Economic Growth in Pre-War Japan* (Translation of *Senzenki Nihon Keizai Seicho no Bunseki*, Tokyo 1971, by Robert A. Feldman), New Haven.

Nakanishi Y. (1982), *Nippon Kindai ka no Kisokatei – Nagasaki Zosensho to sono Roshi Kankei: 1855–1900* (*Basic processes in modernization of Japan – Nagasaki Shipyard and its Industrial Relations 1855–1900*), Tokyo, Tokyo Daigaku Shuppankai.

Nelson, R. and Winter, S. (1977), 'In Search of a Useful Theory of Innovation', *Research Policy* 6 (1), January.

Nelson, R. (1978), *Innovation and Economic Development: Theoretical Retrospect and Prospect*, IDB/ECLA Research Programme on Science and Technology, Buenos Aires.

Nelson, R. (1981), 'Research on Productivity Growth and Productiviy Differences: Dead Ends and New Departures', *The Journal of Economic Literature* 19 (3), September.

Nelson, R. (1986), 'Institutions supporting Technical Advance in Industry', *American Economic Review* 76 (2), May.

Nelson, R. and Winter, S. G. (1982), *An Evolutionary Theory of Economic Change*, Cambridge, Mass., Belknap Press.

Nippon Kagakushi Gakkai (ed.) (1966), *Nippon Kagaku Gijutsushi Taikei* (*History of science and technology in Japan*) 18, Kikai Gijutsu (Mechanical Engineering), Tokyo, Daiichi Hoki Shuppan Kabushiki Kaisha.

Nippon Steel Corporation (1973), *History of Steel in Japan*, Tokyo.

Nippon Zosen Gakkai (1977), *Showa Zosenshi* (*History of shipbuilding in Showa period*), Tokyo.

Nishinarita A. (1978), 'Nichiro Sensogo ni okeru Zaibatsu Zosen Kigyono Keiei Kozo to Roshi Kankei' (Managerial structure and industrial relations of *zaibatsu* shipbuilding enterprises after the Russo–Japanese War), *Ryukoku Daigaku Keizai Keiei Ronshu* 18 (1), June.

Odaka K. (1984), *Rodo Shijo Bunseki* (*Analysis of the labour market*), Tokyo, Iwanami Shoten.

Ohkawa K. (1957), *The Growth Rate of the Japanese Economy since 1878*, Tokyo, Kinokuniya Shoten.

Ohkawa K. and Rosovsky, H. (1965), 'A Century of Japanese Economic Growth' in William W. Lockwood (ed.), *The State and Economic Enterprise in Japan*, Princeton, Princeton University Press.

Ohkawa K. and Shinohara M. (1979), *Patterns of Japanese Economic*

Development – A Quantitative Appraisal, New Haven, Yale University Press.

Oshima K. (1973), 'Research and Development and Economic Growth in Japan' in B. R. Williams (ed.), *Science and Technology in Economic Growth*, New York, Wiley.

Oriental Economist (1934), 'Foreign Trade of Japan', Tokyo.

Ozawa T. (1974), *Japan's Technological Challenge to the West 1950–1974*, Cambridge, Mass., MIT Press.

Ozawa T. (1985), 'Macroeconomic Factors Affecting Japan's Technology Inflows and Outflows: the Post-War Experience' in N. Rosenberg and C. Frischtak, *International Technology Transfer: Concepts, Measures and Comparisons*, New York, Praeger.

Pavitt, K. (1979), 'Technical Innovation and Industrial Development, 1. The New Causality', *Futures*, December.

Pavitt, K. (1980), 'Technical Innovation and Industrial Development, 2. The Dangers of Divergence', *Futures*, February.

Pavitt, K. (1985), 'Technology Transfer among the Industrially Advanced Countries: An Overview' in N. Rosenberg and C. Frischtak, *International Technology Transfer: Concepts, Measures and Comparisons*, New York, Praeger.

Peck, M. J. and Tamura, S. (1976), 'Technology' in H. Patrick and H. Rosovsky (eds), *Asia's New Giant*, Washington, Brookings Institution.

Peck, M. J. and Goto, A. (1981), 'Technology and Economic Growth: The Case of Japan', *Research Policy* 10.

Rosenberg, N. (1976), *Perspectives on Technology*, Cambridge, Cambridge University Press.

Rosenberg, N. (1982), *Inside the Black Box – Technology and Economics*, Cambridge, Cambridge University Press.

Rosenberg, N. and Frischtak, C. (1985), *International Technology Transfer: Concepts, Measures and Comparisons*, New York, Praeger.

Rosovsky, H. (1972), 'What are the "lessons" of Japanese economic history?' in A. J. Youngson (ed.), *Economic Development in the Long Run*, New York, St. Martins Press.

Sangyo Kunren Hakusho Henshu Jinkai, *Sangyo Kunren Hyakunenshi (Hundred-year history of industrial training)*, Tokyo, Nippon Sangyo Kunren Kyokai.

Sasaki S. (1953), 'Nippon Yosetsu Gijutsu Hattatsushi' (Development of welding technology in Japan) in Okada M. (ed.), *Gendai no Yosetsu (Modern welding)*, Tokyo, Nikkan Kogyo Shinbunsha.

Seisan Gijutsu Kyokai (1970), *Kyu Kaigun Gijutsu Shiryo (Materials on the technology of the old navy)*, Tokyo.

Seoul National University (1980), 'The Absorption and Diffusion of Imported Technology in Korea', mimeo, Institute of Economic Research.

Shiba K. (1920), 'Zosen ni Oyo Seru Denki Yosetsu' (Application of electric welding to shipbuilding), *Zosen Kyokai Kaiho (Journal of the Society of Naval Architects)*, 26, April.

Shimizu K. and Kawai K. (1934), 'Mitsubishi MS gata Diesel Kikan ni tsuite' (On Mitsubishi MS type diesel engine), *Zosen Kyokai Kaiho* 53, April.

Smith, T. C. (1955), *Political Change and Industrial Development in Japan: Government Enterprise, 1868–1880*, Stanford, Stanford University Press.

Solow, R. (1957), 'Technical Change and the Aggregate Production Function', *Review of Economics and Statistics*, August.

Stewart, F. (1973), 'Choice of Techniques in Developing Countries' in C. Cooper (ed.), *Science, Technology and Development. The Political Economy of Technical Advance in Underdeveloped Countries*, London, Frank Cass.

Sumiya Mikio (ed.) (1971), *Nippon Shokugyo Kunren Hattenshi* (Development of Vocational Training in Japan), Tokyo, Nippon Rodo Kyokai.

Takahashi K. (1969), *The Rise and Development of Japan's Modern Economy*, Tokyo, Jiji Tsushinsha.

Teratani T. (1979), *Nippon Kindai Zosenshi Josetsu* (*Introduction to the history of shipbuilding in modern Japan*), Tokyo, Gannando.

Tokkyocho (ed.) (1955), *Tokkyo Seido Nanajunenshi* (*Seventy-year history of the patent system*), Tokyo.

Tokyo Kogyo Shikensho (1951), *Tokyo Kogyo Shikensho Gojunenshi* (*Fifty-year history of Tokyo Industrial Research Institute*), Tokyo.

Tsushosangyosho (1979), *Shoko Seisakushi 13 Kogyo Gijutsu* (*History of policies on commerce and industry, 13, Industrial technology*), Tokyo.

Umetani N. (1965), *Oyatoi Gaikokujin* (*Foreign employees*), Tokyo.

Usher, A. (1954), *A History of Mechanical Inventions*, Cambridge, Mass., Harvard University Press.

Vaitsos, C. V. (1974), *Intercountry Income Distribution and Transnational Enterprises*, Oxford, Clarendon Press.

Vogel, E. F. (1979), *Japan as Number One*, Tokyo, Tuttle.

Watanabe M. (1977), *Kindai Nippon Kaigai Ryugakuseishi* (*Students sent overseas in modern Japan*), Tokyo, Kodansha.

Westphal, L. E. (1981), 'Empirical Justification for Infant Industry Protection', World Bank Staff Working Paper No. 445, Washington.

Westphal, L. E., Rhee, Y. W. and Pursell, G. (1984), 'Sources of Technological Capability in South Korea' in M. Fransman and K. King (eds), *Technological Capability in the Third World*, London, MacMillan.

Yadori S. (1932), *Shoda Heigoro*, Tokyo, Taikyosha.

Yamashita M. (1979), 'Meiji Taishoki Mitsubishi Zosensho no Genka Keisan' (Cost accounting at Mitsubishi Shipyard in Meiji and Taisho eras), *Kaikei* 116 (3), September.

Yamashita Y. (1984), *Kaiun to Zosengyo* (*Shipping and shipbuilding industry*), Tokyo, Nihon Keizai Shinbunsha.

Yamauchi I. (1986), 'Long Range R&D', in C. Freeman (ed.), *Design, Innovation and Long Cycles in Economic Development*, London, Frances Pinter.

Yosetu Gojunenshi Hensan Iinkai (1962), *Yosetsu Gojunenshi* (*Fifty-year history of welding*), Tokyo.

Zosen Kyokai (ed.) (1973a), *Nippon Kinsei Zosenshi – Meiji Jidai* (*History of shipbuilding in modern Japan – Meiji Era*), Tokyo, Hara Shobo.

Zosen Kyokai (ed.) (1973b), *Nippon Kinsei Zosenshi – Taisho Jidai* (*History of shipbuilding in Modern Japan – Taisho Era*), Tokyo, Hara Shobo.

INDEX

agriculture: 20, 22, 25;
    research in, 85, 92
Akiba Yoshie, 137
Anyo (ship), 117
Araki Eisaburo, 114
Argentina (ship), 143

bakufu (shogunate), 17–18, 19, 28,
    35, 43, 45
Bijou-Review of Reviews, 60
boiler-drums, 130–1
books, 46, 60
Boyd shipbuilding firm, 36, 50
Brown, A. R., & MacFarlane Co.
    Ltd, 50–1, 113

Calder, J. F., 50
chemical industries: 24, 26;
    research in, 85–6, 94–5
Chikugogawa (ship), 38
Chiyo (liner), 114
Chiyoda-gata (gunboat), 28, 35
Clark, J. S., 49, 50, 51
competition: 13–14; in shipping,
    35
cost accounting, 41, 54
cotton industry, 23, 26

dependence, technological, 2–3
diesel engines: 31, 32, 33, 41, 42,
    133–45; and overseas missions,
    53, 133–4, 135, 137; research on,
    99, 108, 138–44; and shipping
    companies, 59, 136–7, 138

economic system/performance:
    11, 14, 19–20, 21, 22–5, 46–7;
    and technology, 3–4, 7; under
    Tokugawa regime, 17–18
education: 62–7, 147–8; *see also*
    training
efficiency, 41
electric welding: 31, 34, 41,
    123–32, 144–5; automatic, 131–2;
    importing of, 59, 124; research
    on, 99–100, 107, 110, 125,
    131–2; training in, 82, 128
Electric Welding Research
    Committee, 107
electricity generation: history of
    22, 24; research in, 94–5; studies
    of, 11; turbines for, 117, 118,
    120, 122–3
employment, *see* labour force
engineering: research in, 95–6;
    training in, 65–7, 73–4, 77–82,
    147–8; *see also individual fields*
Esaki Ichiro, 114, 117, 133
Experimental Tank, 93, 100–1

first world war: 24, 27, 31, 36, 56,
    124–5; and research, 86–7, 89,
    94
foreign capital, 46–7
foreigners, employment of: 20,
    43–4, 46; at Nagasaki Shipyard,
    47–51, 61, 96
free trade, 6
'free-riding', 9–10

Fuji Kensuke, 106
Fujita Hideo, 15, 139
Fukao Junji, 54, 60, 106

Gakushin, 91–2, 132
gogaku, 62, 63
government: 18–27, 149–50, 151; and economy, 19–20, 21, 22–5, 46–7; and education, 63–7; and foreign employees, 20, 43–4; and overseas missions, 45–6; and protectionism, 6, 151; and research, 12, 85–96; and shipbuilding, 26–7, 28–34, 35, 146, 148, 149–50, 151; under Tokugawa regime, 17–18, 27–8, 43, 45, 62–3; *see also individual departments*
grants, research, 90, 92
Hakone (cargo vessel), 117
Hamada Hyo, 54, 78, 107, 138
han, 17, 18, 28, 45
hanko, 62
Hitachi (liner), 38, 40–1, 49, 51, 53, 55, 113
Hokkai (ship), 143
Honda Kotaro, 110
Honda Tomozo, 106
Hori Yasuemon, 105–6

Ichibangase Kiyoshi, 99, 127
Ichikawa Shigesaburo, 57
Iguchi Haruhisa, 103
Iidaka metal, 102, 103, 120
IJN (Japanese Navy), *see* navy
Imperial College of Engineering, 44, 64, 66
imports, *see* technology imports
impulse turbine, 113, 121–3
Inagaki Tetsuro, 124, 137
Internal Combustion Engine Research Committee (ICERC), 108, 138–42
internal training missions, 79–82
invention: policy towards, 104–6; *see also* research and development
iron (industry): 23, 26–7, 29; in shipbuilding, 30–1

Ito Kumezo, 53–4, 59, 124, 133–4, 135
Iwasaki Koyata, 102
Iwasaki Yataro, 21, 35

Japan Industrial Bank, 47
Jikkenba: 96–100, 104, 111, 145; and diesel engines, 99, 142–3; and electric welding, 99–100, 124, 125, 127–8, 131, 132; and turbines, 99, 117, 119–20
journals and periodicals, 46, 60, 110, 131

Kagami Kohei, 79, 139
Kamigo Denji, 50
Kanamori Masao, 15, 132
Kato Tomomichi, 53
Kato Tomoo, 15
Kawahara Goro, 101
Kawai Kiyoshi, 140
Kawai Shuntaro, 78
Kawasaki Shipbuilding company, 13, 30, 33, 34, 89, 134
Kirishima (cruiser), 38, 51, 120
Kiso (ship), 107
Kitaoka Nobuo, 15
Kiuno Jozo, 79, 135
knowledge, technological, 6–7
Kobe Shipyard, 135–6
Kobu Daigakko (Imperial College of Engineering), 44, 64, 66
Kobusho (Ministry of Engineering and Public Works), 20, 28, 44, 49, 64
kokugaku, 17, 62
Kogyo Shikensho, 85–6
Kongo (cruiser), 33, 51, 53
Koryu (ship), 140, 141
Koshu Gakko, 65
Kosuga (steamer), 35
Kumon Noboru, 143
Kuno Itsuo, 121
Kyoto Imperial University, 66
Kyushu Imperial University, 66, 79, 82, 110, 132

labour force: 36; foreigners in, 20, 43–4, 46, 47–51, 61, 96;

management of, 9, 10, 105–6; mobility of 68–9; in research, 97, 105–6; training of, *see* training; in welding, 129
La Plata (liner), 137
latecomer hypothesis, 10
'learning-by-doing', 4–5, 8
licensing agreements: 47, 56, 57–60, 61; for diesel engines, 134–5, 136, 137; for electric welding, 59, 124; and overseas missions, 52, 59–60, 61; for turbines, 58–9, 113–14, 121–2
literacy rate, 62

machine tools, 24, 27
machinery (industry): 13, 23–4, 27, 148, 149; imports of, 46, 55–7, 61; and shipbuilding industry, 24, 29–30, 31, 148, 149–50, 151; (research, 100, 102)
management: 9, 10; of research 104–11
marine engineering, study of, 66–7, 77–8, 147–8
Maruta Hidemi, 78, 100
Mase Tokuzo, 79
Matsumae (ferry boat), 118, 120
Matsumoto Koji, 54, 135
Meiji government, *see* government
Mimura Tetsuo, 106, 124, 127
minaraiko, 68, 70, 76–7, 83
Ministry of Agriculture and Commerce (Noshomusho), 25–7, 46, 85, 90
Ministry of Education, 45, 64–5, 90
Ministry of Engineering and Public Works (Kobusho), 20, 28, 44, 49, 64
Ministry of Finance, 64
Ministry of Internal Affairs (Naimusho), 20, 64
Ministry of International Trade and Industry (MITI), 10
Misumi (cruiser), 126
Mitsubishi Kogyo Gakko (MKG), 41, 70–4, 82, 83, 149

Mitsubishi Nagasaki Shipyard, history of, 12–14, 19, 21, 28–9, 30, 33, 34–42
Mitsubishi Shipbuilding Company: 42; and research, 41–2, 96–111
Mitsubishi Shipbuilding Research Institute (MSCRI), 42, 102–4, 120–1, 145, 149
Mitsubishi Shokko Gakko (MSG), 74–7, 149
Mitsubishi Technical Education Foundation, 75
Mitsubishi Technological Research Meetings, 108–9
Mizutani Rokuro, 54
model testing, 31, 32, 54, 100–1
Mogami (ship), 114
Montevideo (liner), 137
Morris, A., 50, 101
Motora Nobutaro, 79, 101
MS diesel engine, 138–43, 147

Nagai Shonosuke, 55
Nagasaki Arms Manufacturing Company, 89
Nagasaki Iron Works, 19, 28, 46
Nagasaki Naval School, 28, 35, 43
Naimusho (Ministry of Internal Affairs), 20, 64
Nakamura Sadao, 135
Nankai (cargo vessel), 141
naval architecture, 65–6, 67, 72, 77–8, 110, 147–8
Naval Technical Research Institute, 93–4
navy (IJN): 12–13, 31, 33–4, 38, 148, 150; creation of, 18, 45; and diesel engines, 33, 59, 134; and education/training, 66, 67, 78, 79; and electric welding, 99–100, 125–6, 127, 128; and research, 89, 93–4, 99–100; and technology imports, 57, 59; and turbines, 118, 119–20, 122
Nikko (ship), 50
Nippon Gakujutsu Shinkokai (Gakushin), 91–2, 132
Nippon Kaiji Kyokai, 128

Nippon Kogaku Kogyo, 89
Nippon Petroleum Company, 126, 131
Nippon Yusen Kaisha (NYK), 30, 32, 35, 136–7, 138
NM (nickel-manganese) bronze, 98, 120
Noguchi Ken-ichi, 15
Nomura Shogo, 110
Noro Kageyoshi, 23
Noshomusho (Ministry of Agriculture and Commerce), 25–7, 46, 85, 90

Ogata Masaya, 57, 98
Okano Sanshichiro, 117
Okinawa Electric Company, 117, 118, 120, 122
Okuda Katsumi, 79, 99, 139, 142–3
Ominato Zosen Totei Gakko, 65
Osaka Iron Works, 30
Osaka Polytechnic, 66–7
Osaka Shosen Kaisha (OSK), 30, 32, 136, 137, 138
overseas missions: 44–6; from Nagasaki shipyard, 33, 51–5, 57, 59–60, 61, 144, 153–61; (and diesel engines, 53, 133–4, 135, 137; and electric welding, 124–5; and turbines, 53, 55, 113–14, 121, 122)

patents, 90, 105
periodicals, 46, 60, 110, 131
polytechnics, 65, 66–7, 147–8
Productivity Research Council, 26, 27
professional societies, 46, 53, 60–1, 110, 132
protectionism, 6, 151

railways: 20, 22; turbines for, 118, 120, 123
rangaku, 17, 19, 28, 62
Reed, J. G., 49, 50
research and development (R&D): 5, 8, 9; in Mitsubishi Shipbuilding Company, 41–2, 96–111, 145, 147; (on diesel engines, 99, 108, 138–44; on electric welding, 99–100, 107, 110, 125, 127–8, 131–2; management of, 104–11; on turbines, 99, 103, 107, 119–21); at national level, 10, 12, 85–96, 110–11
Rikagaku Kenkyusho (Riken), 87, 89, 103

Sakura (ship), 56, 114
San Louis (cargo vessel), 138, 140
Santos (liner), 137
Sasaki Shintaro, 98, 99–100, 110, 120, 125, 127, 128, 132, 145
Sawakaze (destroyer), 117, 118, 119
second world war, 11
semmon gakko 65, 66–7, 147–8
Seo Saburo, 78, 123
Shiba Chuzaburo, 109, 114
Shiba Koshiro, 101, 127
Shimizu Kikuhei, 135, 138–9, 143–4, 145
Shiota Taisuke, 47, 49, 53, 75, 78
shipbuilding industry: and government, 26–7, 28–34, 35, 146, 148, 149–50, 151; history and development of, 12–13, 27–34, 148; and machinery production, 24, 29–30, 31, 148, 149–50, 151; studies of, 12
shipping industry: 21, 22, 26–7, 30, 35–6; and diesel engines, 59, 136–7, 138
Shoda Heigoro, 54, 113
shogunate, see bakufu shugyosei, 70–4, 76–7, 83
Society of Engineering Sciences, 60
Society of Mechanical Engineers, 27, 53, 60, 110, 135
Society of Naval Architects, 110, 127
South Manchurian Railroad, 118, 120
stabilizers, 101
standards, 90
steam turbines, see turbines
steel (industry): 23, 26–7, 55–6; in

shipbuilding, 30–2, 38, 40–1, 56; (electric welding, 126, 127; research, 96; turbines, 120)
submarines, 33, 59, 134–6
Sulzer diesel engine, 134, 136–8
Suma (ship), 78
Suwa (ferry boat), 125
Suyehiro Kyoji, 102, 120
Suzuki Eitaro, 79, 96

Tadokoro Motoki, 49
Takaba Ichitaro, 99
Takaira Fumio, 143
Takamine Jokichi, 87
Takeda Hideo, 78, 135
Tama (ship), 107
Tanaka Shigesaburo, 135
technological learning, concept of, 4–9
technological research committees, 106–8
technology imports: at Nagasaki shipyard, 47–61, 144; (of diesel engines, 134–8; of electric welding, 59, 124; of turbines, 56–7, 58–9, 113–14, 121–2); at national level, 43–7, 151
Tenyo (liner), 38, 41, 56, 114, 120
terakoya, 62, 63
textiles industry, 23, 26
Tohoku Imperial University, 66, 87, 110
Tokugawa regime, 17–18, 27–8, 43, 45, 62–3
Tokyo Gas Company, 135
Tokyo Imperial University, 66, 78, 139
torpedo boats, 57, 59
Tosa (warship), 38, 119
Toyo Kisen Kaisha (TKK), 30, 114

training: 5, 9; at Nagasaki shipyard, 41, 67–84, 147–8; (in electric welding, 82, 128); at national level, 11, 12, 19, 20, 34, 62–7
transfer of technology, perspectives on, 1–9
Tsugaru (ferry boat), 118, 120
turbines: 31, 41, 42, 112–23, 144–5; imports of, 56–7, 58–9, 113–14, 121–2; and overseas missions, 53, 55, 113–14, 121, 122; research on, 99, 103, 107, 119–21
turbo-generators, 117, 118, 120, 122–3

UE diesel engines, 144
universities: 63, 64, 66, 147–8; and research, 87–9, 109–10, 132

Vickers, 33, 51, 53, 54, 55, 133–6

welding, *see* electric welding
Welding Society of Japan, 110, 132
Wingel, F., 50

Yamaguchi Prefectural Railroad, 123
Yamamoto Shichiro, 105
Yawata Steel Mill: 23, 26, 55–6, 87; generator for, 122
Yokohama, Mitsubishi Engine Works in, 47, 50
Yokosuka naval yard, 28, 33, 34, 36, 43, 71
Yokoyama Kozo, 53, 55, 60, 116–18, 120, 122, 145

Zölly turbine, 58–9, 121–3